A STRATEGY FOR THE ECU

A STRATEGY FOR THE ECU

A report prepared by Ernst & Young Management Consultants
with
the National Institute of Economic and Social Research
for
the Association for the Monetary Union of Europe

ASSOCIATION FOR THE MONETARY UNION OF EUROPE

Ernst & Young

National Institute of Economic and Social Research

KOGAN PAGE

A Strategy for the Ecu will also be available in French, Italian, German and Swedish.

First published in 1990 by
Kogan Page Ltd,
120 Pentonville Rd, London N1 9JN

Typeset by Spectrum Typesetting, London.

Printed and bound in Great Britain by Richard Clay Ltd, Bungay, Suffolk.

British Library Cataloguing in Publication Data

A CIP catalogue record for this book is available from the British Library.

ISBN 0-7494-0261-X

NETWORK

Euro-Business Publishing Network

Contents

Appendices

Foreword

The political debate on EMU has now reached its point of no return. History is accelerating, and so is the need for European economic, monetary and political union. It is therefore of great importance to feed the minds of the politicians with the expectations and the needs of the market. Several studies have already shown that European firms would greatly benefit – for strong economic and financial motives – from a single currency, especially in the context of the Internal Market.

In the final state of Economic and Monetary Union, a single currency is the only clearly sustainable and efficient solution. What is at stake now is the Ecu's role in the transition period. A common currency which possesses competitive characteristics and the advantages of political neutrality already exists: the Ecu. Its international financial role is growing rapidly, but its transaction use remains limited. Its potential for an increasing role in the transition period has already been recognized by many operators and has been advocated by the Commission. But it has still to be developed.

The merit of the work, accomplished by Ernst & Young and the National Institute of Economic and Social Research on behalf of the Association for the Monetary Union of Europe, is not only to have addressed the precise difficulties which firms are facing on their way towards the completion of the Internal Market and the creation of monetary union, but also to have placed these problems in a macroeconomic context.

As clearly stressed in this report, 'problems of transition and political sensitivities mean that the best candidate for [such] a single currency is the Ecu... The place of the Ecu must not be usurped by another currency, whatever the short-term temptation may be to let that happen'.

But, as shown by the survey, the removal of the administrative obstacles to the use of the Ecu, which will take place in Stage I of EMU, will not alone be sufficient to stimulate rapid and self-sustained increase in the use of the Ecu. What operators rightly wish to secure before entering into Ecu operations and transactions is a credible announcement that the Ecu will be the single currency of Europe.

The Commission, for its part, has provided such an announcement in a report to the informal economic and financial council held at Ashford

Castle on March 31. This report presents the essential features of economic and monetary union, among which is

'...A SINGLE CURRENCY, THE ECU, TO EXPLOIT TO THE FULL THE POTENTIAL BENEFIT OF THE SINGLE MARKET AND MONETARY UNION...'

Given that the Commission will pursue its efforts in order to remove existing obstacles to the use of the Ecu, it is now up to the operators, including governments and Central Banks, and to associations such as the Association for the Monetary Union of Europe to catch the ball and carry on the game.

Jacques Delors
April 1990

Preface

Monetary union in Europe is seen by many as a vital step towards achieving total European unity after the completion of the single European market in 1992. If member countries within the Community are to reap the benefits of the free movement of goods, services, capital and people, unnecessary transaction costs, hedging costs and higher interest rates from the existence of multiple currencies also need to be eliminated. So how can the goal of Economic and Monetary Union (EMU) be achieved and what role can the Ecu play as the proposed single currency?

Our book presents the results of a study to answer this question. The study was commissioned by the Association for the Monetary Union of Europe. It has been prepared by Ernst & Young Management Consultants who had overall responsibility for the study, and the National Institute of Economic and Social Research (NIESR), who focused on the macro-economic analysis.

The issues which the study addresses are: what are the current obstacles to the wider use of the Ecu and how might they be removed? What is needed to alter the behaviour of firms so as to promote the wider use of the Ecu? Based on a comprehensive survey of companies and financial institutions throughout the EC, and prepared in collaboration with leading macroeconomic institutes and European monetary experts, this report provides practical analysis of:

- the advantages of a single European currency
- the need for a credible announcement that the Ecu should be this currency
- current obstacles to the greater use of the Ecu
- strategies for overcoming obstacles to the use of the Ecu
- the macroeconomic implications for policy making
- the costs and benefits as perceived by banks and other organizations

and suggests detailed recommendations to the private and public sectors within the EC.

It became very clear early on in the study that these issues could not be tackled in isolation from the wider context set by the proposals for the development of Economic and Monetary Union in Europe (EMU). Consequently, the study, especially the macroeconomic chapters, contains analysis of the possible development and timing of EMU.

The study teams at Ernst & Young and NIESR received valuable advice and contributions from a variety of European experts and institutions. The names of those concerned are noted in appendices to this book. However, responsibility for the analysis and conclusions rests with Ernst & Young and NIESR.

Clearly, the questions addressed in this book need to be set in the wider context of the political and institutional development of Europe. But consideration of the issues, arguments and points of view involved lie outside the scope of the study reported here.

Ernst & Young
NIESR
March 1990

The Authors

Ernst & Young is a leading international firm providing business and financial advice to a large number of private and public sector organizations. We currently have 1,100 partners and 23,500 staff in Europe, providing Ernst & Young with local representation in every Community Member State and in the European Free Trade Association. Worldwide Ernst & Young has over 70,000 partners and professional staff based in over 120 countries.

The **National Institute of Economic and Social Research** (NIESR) is the UK's oldest independent economic research institute. It undertakes studies into a variety of economic issues including those associated with international economic relations. It is funded by research grants and contributions from a wide variety of firms. It undertakes studies for other bodies, as in the present instance, strictly on condition that its independence is preserved and that its results are fully published.

The **Association for the Monetary Union of Europe** (AUME) was created in October 1987 by European manufacturers who have settled on the objectives of strengthening the European Monetary System, promoting the use of the Ecu, and encouraging the establishment of European Central Bank. In April 1990, over 200 companies are active members of the Association. They globally employ more than 5,000,000 people, while a very large number of small and medium-sized companies participate in the activities of AUME through membership of professional organizations, eg Italian Confindustria, Federation of Greek Industries, French Chambers of Commerce, etc.

The Association acts in close cooperation with the Committee for the Monetary Union of Europe which is chaired by former President V. Giscard d'Estaing and former Chancellor H. Schmidt.

Summary

The single European market will not realize its full potential as long as multiple currencies remain. For corporate users, the common currency is an advantage but a single currency is clearly superior, but transaction costs and idle balances would be lower and the need for hedging would be removed.

The survey of firms undertaken by Ernst & Young shows that the vast majority anticipate greater cost savings and larger benefits from a single currency than a common currency.

A good European currency needs to be politically neutral and effective as money. The Ecu has the advantage of political neutrality but, despite its significance in financial transactions, its current limited operations use makes it less attractive as a means of payment than existing currencies.

Removal of administrative obstacles, as advocated in the Delors Report, while necessary, is not sufficient to stimulate self sustaining, rapid growth in the Ecu's market share.

The private sector is most unlikely to act as the principal initiator of the Ecu's development as Europe's principal means of payment, because most firms see little competitive benefit to offset the costs involved unless others do the same.

To generate critical mass for the Ecu, a catalyst is needed, in the form of credible political action. Responses from firms show that this requires a credible announcement, if the necessary political will exists, that the Ecu will be the single currency of Europe. This announcement needs to include the concrete steps to be taken and a clear timetable for its adoption.

The macroeconomic analysis in this study suggests the necessary degree of economic convergence which could permit Economic and Monetary Union, with the Ecu as the single currency, by 1997, assuming all countries join the Exchange Rate Mechanism and that appropriate transitional arrangements exist for certain countries in the meantime.

Appropriate institutional, especially central bank, arrangements will be needed.

The recommended strategy – a credible political announcement – directly attacks the most serious obstacles to the use of the Ecu: inertia, the lack of end uses, and the risk that an existing currency will develop as the common currency without the political neutrality needed in a single currency.

The strategy also involves the adoption of several legislative and regulatory changes by the authorities, according to a clear timetable, in order to admit the wider use of the Ecu in such areas as accounting and taxation.

It also recommends a series of actions on the part of the private sector, again according to a clear timetable in the run up to 1997, to develop the use of the Ecu. A credible announcement will induce firms to initiate the necessary investments in systems, training, business and financial operations in good time so that a mutually reinforcing process will develop in the use of the Ecu.

March 1990

Summary timetable of recommendations

	Public sector institutions (Community and/or National)	*Private sector institutions*
1990/91	• Credible announcement made that Ecu will become the single European currency	• Bank customers should be given clear and concise information regarding the Ecu • Banks should avoid discriminatory transaction costs assigned to the Ecu
1991	• European agreement of overall strategy and Treaty amended • Community institutional arrangements should be established to manage the adoption of the Ecu • Proposals made for the removal of the administrative barriers	• Banks should ensure they offer their full range of services in Ecu as well as their normal currency • Each company should study the cost/benefit of a single European currency • Companies should ensure employee knowledge of the Ecu is improved

1991 (cont)	• A European-wide campaign of information should be co-ordinated • National information campaigns should be organized • Collector Ecu coins should be minted • Postage stamps should be denominated in Ecu as well as national currency	• Each bank should undertake a full cost/benefit study regarding the adoption of the Ecu • Banks should ensure that their views are communicated to political and institutional decision makers
1992	• The Ecu used for European-wide receipts, expenditures and lending • System of central bank co-operation co-ordinates current national government issues of Ecu bonds and increases the number of short-term issues • Contributions in the forms of grants and loan facilities to international organizations should be in Ecu • National procurement should be denominated in Ecu and national currency • Ecu life insurance policies should be designed and marketed	• The Ecu should be given the necessary legal backing for inter-firm contracts at a European level • Companies should be allowed by their stock exchanges to report in Ecu as well as their national currency • Companies to make increasing use of Ecu-denominated commercial paper • In order to establish a competitive advantage for the Ecu, banks should offer the shortest processing time interval for Ecu-products

1993	• Companies incorporated under the European Statute should be allowed to pay tax in Ecu • Companies in all countries should be allowed to issue share capital in Ecu	• The travel industry should adopt the Ecu for pricing as fast as possible • Deposit accounts in Ecu should be opened by companies • Companies should increasingly issue share capital in Ecu denomination
1994	• Discriminatory legislation against the Ecu should be removed • An annual tax free European-wide lottery in Ecu should be established • Reports and accounts should include Ecu denominations	• Companies should issue Ecu bonds • The quotation of raw materials and commodities traded in European markets should be expressed exclusively in Ecu
1995	• Companies should be allowed to calculate and pay their taxes in Ecu	• Large companies should adopt the Ecu as much as possible for invoicing and import–export financing • Reports and accounts should include Ecu denominations

1996

- The Ecu should become legal tender
- A 'Year of the Ecu' should be announced the year prior to the full adoption of the Ecu as the single currency
- A European-wide competition should be run for the design of a common 20 Ecu note
- Legal tender Ecu coins and notes should be issued
- National institutions mint Ecu notes and coins using their current national designs
- During the 'Year of the Ecu', prices should be quoted in Ecu wherever practical
- Accounting devices like taxometers, computer software coin and card operated automats to be prepared for the change of currency

---

1997

- The Ecu should become the single currency

March 1990

Part I
The Ecu Strategy

1: The Ecu as a European Currency

The achievement of the single European market in 1992 will change the rules and structures for doing business in Europe. It will allow not only for the free flow of goods and services but also of people and capital. However, the persistence of national currencies in each country impedes the full development of all potential benefits that can be reaped from such a large market; the uncertainty about exchange rate variations can necessitate expensive short-term hedging costs and deter long-term rate investment. The unequal weight of small and large countries in the Community favours the international role of currencies with greater liquidity and therefore establishes a competitive advantage for these with respect to their status and interest rates.

Not surprisingly, the single European market has given rise to renewed interest in, and demands for, a European currency. A survey of European business leaders undertaken in 1989 by the Association for the Monetary Union of Europe has shown that 83 per cent of them were in favour of a common currency. In recent years the private Ecu has increasingly taken the role of such a currency. It has grown significantly as a financial instrument, but to a much lesser degree as a means of payment in Europe. In the following chapters a strategy will be proposed that would turn the Ecu into a fully-fledged European currency, replacing all present national currencies if the necessary political will exists. In this first chapter we will look at the potential advantages of a common and a single European currency and appraise the qualities of the Ecu against the requirements of a good European currency.

1.1 Potential advantages of a common or single European currency

The aim of the single European market for 1992 is the creation of a unified and competitive market intended to stimulate growth by removing internal barriers to the efficient allocation of resources. However, as long as this market is characterized by a multi-currency system, it will necessarily be suboptimal. Furthermore, the lack of consistent legal enforceability can deter investors.

Firms will gain if they can eliminate the costs of currency management, financial hedging and uncertainty. Firms and whole sectors will gain from a common currency by having better and clearer information on prices and costs.

It is difficult to evaluate these costs and benefits. A recent study by the European Commission has estimated that the economies to be made, strictly in terms of reductions in costs of multi-currency handling, are of the order of Ecu15 billion on intra-EC transactions. Further opportunity costs of the present multiple-currency systems of Europe will include the loss of benefit from investments which are *not* undertaken in the present multi-currency system because of long-term exchange rate insecurity.

One could argue that a *common* currency, such as the present basket Ecu could fulfil most of these requirements. However, the necessity to operate in a larger economic environment where wages and non-traded goods and services would still be paid in local national currencies, prevents reaping the full benefits of a single currency system. What are the differences?

A European currency, whichever form it takes, would present the following potential advantages to the private sector.

- It would be a *common unit of account*. Companies with operations in more than one member state would record all accounting in one currency thus simplifying administrative procedures and gaining in efficiency and transparency.
- It would be a *common store of value*. It would reduce long-term uncertainty. It is also more risk-efficient for European and non-European firms to use a common interest rate for their investment and financing operations rather than a number of different rates.
- It would be a *common means of payment*. A European currency would enable companies to dispense with exchange rate costs and risks when dealing with non-domestic clients or suppliers in Europe, thus increasing efficiency.

A *single* European currency replacing all national currencies presents greater potential advantages than a *common* European currency for the following reasons (see Chapter Five):

- Transaction costs and the 'idle' money balances are lower; and

- The need to hedge against possible exchange rate changes is avoided with a single currency.

The first of these groups of potential advantages relates to efficiency, mainly with respect to the means of payment and unit of account uses of the European currency; the second group concerns predictability and stability and mainly relates to the store of value function of a European currency in the context of monetary union. (These wider macro-economic costs and benefits of a monetary union ('MU') with a single currency are further explored in Chapter Five.)

In order to realize the potential benefits of a European currency, and in particular the larger benefits associated with a single currency, significant transition costs and redistribution effects need to be addressed. The balance of cost and benefit for individual organizations will influence their attitudes towards the changes and governments may thus wish to consider who should bear these once-and-for-all costs.

There are one-off costs of moving to a single currency to firms and banks in converting their procedures, to owners of coin and note operated machines, to governments in reprinting and minting and to the public at large in adopting a new system. However, the lifetime of banknotes is in any case limited and some coins may be able to continue in circulation, with an equivalent value, over quite a prolonged period, (i.e. by redefining their value, so that a coin of £1, FFr1 or DM1 may serve as a Ecu1 coin). Costs falling on the private sector include those resulting from changes to systems, cash changing and money dispensers, retraining personnel, long-term contracts and re-labelling. For companies involved in international trade, there will be a balance between their reduced transaction costs and their conversion costs, while for companies which are not trading, there may be few benefits to offset the costs. Financial intermediaries also face significant transition costs.

1.2 Appraisal of the Ecu against the requirements of a genuine European currency

The Ecu is one candidate for the European currency of the future, though not the only candidate. The requirements of a good European currency are that it should have political neutrality in order to ensure that it is generally acceptable – a prerequisite of a good currency (see Chapter Eleven), and that it should be effective as money, which requires confidence and trust and hence central bank backing. Effectiveness as money implies being a good store of value, means of payment and unit of account.

Political neutrality

The continuing political debate has varied both in intensity and in content across member states and over the course of the year.

West Germany has repeatedly stressed the imperative that the future European currency, which could be the Ecu, should be a strong one, backed by an independent European central bank committed to price stability. The prospect of early MU with East Germany has not reduced the country's commitment to European economic and monetary union ('EMU'), although how soon this will be politically feasible is in question.

The French have a long-standing commitment to the Ecu as a future currency of Europe. Whilst this commitment has been tempered by bursts of enthusiasm for the French franc, the Ecu is seen by the French government as the only practical alternative to the *de facto* Deutschmark zone.

In the UK, the debate has been couched in terms of the loss of political sovereignty that MU entails. This concern focused firstly on whether and when the UK should enter the exchange rate mechanism of the European Monetary System ('EMS'), and latterly on the institutional nature of the Delors approach. The UK appears to have relatively little trouble with the concept of a common currency for Europe provided it is based on a market-driven approach and emerges from competition among existing currencies. However, the currency competition approach does not attract much support elsewhere in Europe on the grounds that it does not eliminate the uncertainties of a multi-currency system.

In southern Europe, there has been considerable debate on the domestic repercussions of MU. In Spain this debate is manifested in a concern that the structural adjustments it implies are too great for a young and fast growing economy. In Italy monetary union seems to be welcomed as a more viable alternative for controlling her large budget deficit than reliance on domestic monetary policy after the removal of capital controls.

The overwhelming picture which emerged from the advice and comments we received was that whereas certain existing currencies were widely used in Europe, notably the US dollar and the Deutschmark, any existing currency was likely to be politically unacceptable as the *single* currency of Europe.

Effectiveness as money

The Ecu has benefits as a store of value in comparison with most other European currencies. Its rapid and spontaneous growth in financial markets in the early-1980's is indicative of this. The Ecu's basket properties offer risk advantages due to its relative predictability/stability in comparison with all but the strongest individual currencies. It should be noted, however, that the Ecu has had temporary attractions in certain countries due to positive discrimination in its favour. Against these benefits as a store of value, there are additional uncertainties in the Ecu which are not present in other European currencies. The open basket creates a certain perceived 'basic risk' when tendering for long-term contracts or committing funds for long-term investment. However, its 'open basket' nature gives the Ecu its character as a European common currency and as an investment currency. The lack of consistent legal enforceability can also deter investors.

Against its imperfection as a unit of account there are some circumstantial advantages. To the extent that the cost and revenue structure of a company more closely reflects that of the Ecu than any other currency, using the Ecu in management accounting can result in improved decisions. However, this advantage may not be realized unless the company can also report its results to shareholders in Ecu.

The *current* limited use of the basket Ecu as a means of payment presents a disadvantage with respect to transactions which cannot be completely offset by administrative cost advantages. However, against its imperfections as a unit of account, it should be noted that the Ecu has transaction cost advantages for multilateral trade flows, assisting companies operationally in terms of cost transparency and transfer pricing.

The more widely a given means of payment is used, the more effective it becomes for all concerned. In other words, money is a 'public good'. But this quality means that while it is in *everyone's* interests to see this potential is realized, the benefits to *individual firms* may not justify the costs involved in promoting the Ecu and investing in new systems on a scale sufficient to promote a 'critical mass' and to ensure self-sustaining, rapid growth in its market share. As is well known from the theory of public goods and market failure, such a situation can require public action, involving public sector institutions and action based on political decisions: naturally such decisions will involve judgements about the costs and benefits of alternative courses of action/inaction and their timing.

The Ecu has the disadvantage of lacking a privileged domain, backed by history and law. All companies we spoke to stated that the single most encouraging factor which would make them use the Ecu as a means of payment would be if many others used it. However, very few are willing to make the first move within the private sector to the extent that the majority of others would be encouraged. In the course of the interviews many firms stated that *clear commitment by member states to the use of the Ecu as a future currency for Europe, with European central bank backing, would be the most important incentive for them to take the Ecu seriously.* Such a commitment would act as a catalyst to the wider private use of the Ecu.

We conclude that the Ecu's current competitive advantage is its political neutrality. Its current competitive disadvantage lies in its shortcomings as an effective means of payment. A strategy should lever the current advantage and start to rectify the disadvantage. Such a strategy involves both public and private sector dimensions.

2: The Importance of a Credible Announcement

The development of the private Ecu in financial operations over recent years was linked to its 'store of value' function. In an economic environment of exchange rate uncertainty the use of the currency basket Ecu provided greater security for the preservation of real value. With the success of the European Monetary System in stabilizing exchange rates between currencies participating in the exchange rate mechanism, this incentive to use the Ecu diminishes in importance. On the other hand, the potential transaction function of the Ecu as a unit of account and means of payment becomes more relevant. Our study started with the hypothesis that the elimination of 'administrative obstacles', as advocated in the Delors Report, would strengthen the transaction function of the Ecu. *The most important result emerging from the study is that the removal of these 'obstacles', while necessary, would be far from sufficient to generate rapid and self-sustaining growth in the private use of the Ecu.*

Our study provided overwhelming evidence in support of the hypothesis that the private sector is unlikely to act as an initiator in increasing or encouraging greatly increased use of the Ecu. A catalyst, provided by credible official action, is needed. A fundamental reason is that use of the Ecu at present provides no significant competitive advantage. Firms and banks are essentially interested in their own market position and profit and will not embark upon a course of action involving, initially, considerable expense and effort if there is no perceived advantage to themselves in doing so. It was emphasized by many firms in our survey that, as long as the Ecu is not seen as a credible future European currency, which would require the full commitment of EC institutions, national governments and central banks, firms see little point in planning now for wider use of the Ecu at some indeterminate future date.

The private sector would first need to be assured that the Ecu would be a permanent feature within the single European market before investing in systems to accommodate it and, furthermore, would look to their competitors, suppliers, customers and trade associations before acting. Of the firms in the survey, 85 per cent said greater use of the Ecu by customers would encourage them to use it themselves; 75 per cent said widespread applications by competitors would likewise induce greater use. These responses were much higher than the effects claimed for the removal of various legal and administrative obstacles.

The degree of permanency which the Ecu will enjoy within the European Community is a political question and requires a political solution. At present a significant body of opinion within the European private sector regards the Ecu as a political tool, not a credible natural choice as an efficient European currency: consequent caution with regard to the Ecu is a significant obstacle to its use.

In these circumstances spontaneous initiatives by the private sector alone leading to a significant expansion in the use of the Ecu are unlikely to occur. Official stimulus is needed. The removal of administrative obstacles, while necessary, is not sufficient to provide the necessary stimulus.

An analysis of firms' perceptions about three scenarios: the single market ('1992') with the present regime of flexible, adjustable exchange rates; the Ecu as a common, 13th, currency with fixed exchange rates; and the Ecu as a single currency, shows that the single currency scenario has a much more positive impact on firms' behaviour (Figure 1) and that it will generate much greater cost savings (see Chapter Four).

We recommend, provided the political will exists, that there should be a credible announcement that the Ecu will be the single currency of Europe. Unless there is such an announcement, our respondents emphasized that the private sector will not be prepared to incur the considerable costs involved in changing their accounting and information systems, business and financial operations, and in staff training. On the other hand, with a credible announcement that the Ecu will be the single currency of Europe, the necessary learning process and investment can be expected to take place during the transition period and the use of the Ecu should expand; also the risk that an existing currency, without the political potential to be the *single* currency, will become the common currency may be averted.

Political will

As mentioned, such an announcement is dependent on the existence of the necessary political will. We recognize that attempting to go too fast could make the target – of greatly increasing the use of the Ecu – less rather than more likely. It is beyond the competence and scope of this report to evaluate or comment upon the various, very seriously held, political viewpoints involved. But *if the political will were there*, the macroeconomic analysis by NIESR suggests that by the late 1990s the Ecu could be the single currency of Europe. This assumes that, in the meantime, flexible transitional arrangements are put in place for certain countries such as Italy, the UK and more recent members of the EC.

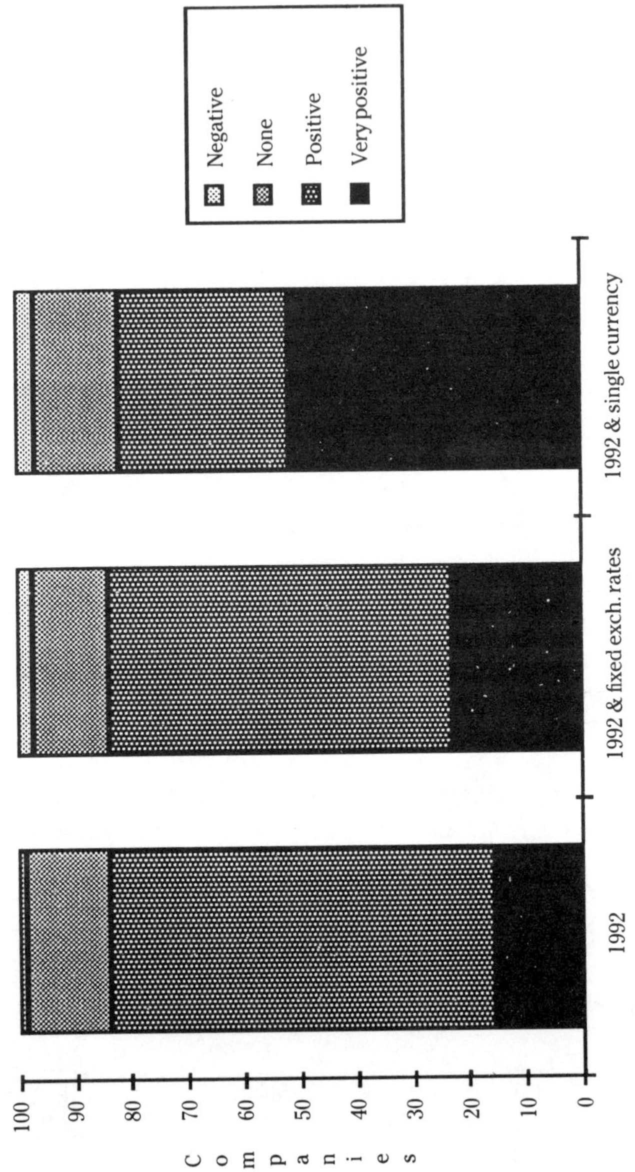

Figure 1: Impact of different scenarios on companies

A credible announcement should include:

- *A declaration that, over time, the Ecu will become the single European currency;*
- *The concrete steps which will be taken; and*
- *A specific timetable, which should be as short as possible.*

The most effective way of stimulating the use of the Ecu would be for such an announcement to be made at the end of the Inter-Governmental Conference although the announcement of the intention to adopt the Ecu as the single currency could be made by the European Council in advance of that Conference, given the necessary political agreement.

Timetable

A number of industrialists impressed upon us that unless a clear timetable is set down they will be unlikely to take any announcement seriously. They also said that if the timetable is very long they will see no need to take any concrete steps until near the end of the proposed process, and only if the proposed target date looks credible.

If such an announcement could be made within the next 12 months then, on the basis of the NIESR analysis, the end point (for the Ecu to become fully legal tender within the Community as its single currency) could be 1997. The timetable could be: 1991–announcement made; 1991/92–agreement on overall strategy and Treaty amended; and 1997–completion by the end of the year.

This timetable follows the 1992 programme which had the announcement in the 1985 White Paper, agreement in 1986 with the Single European Act and the completion targeted for 1992. The timetable assumes that EC economies achieve the necessary degree of convergence and that all currencies join the ERM.

Community institutional arrangements should be established to manage the adoption of the Ecu.

Once an announcement is made that the Ecu will become the single European currency, Community institutional arrangements will be needed to monitor and co-ordinate the actions and recommendations below. This specifically requires that European central banking arrangements are set up. These arrangements could be structured along the lines of Eurofed (The Federation of Central Banks) proposed by the European Commission. Such arrangements would be for the Inter-Governmental Conference to determine. It is beyond the scope of this report to examine the important political issues which surround the debate on the appropriate arrangements.

In order for the Ecu to develop, EC central banks would need to confirm their intention to lend full support to the development of the role of the Ecu as Europe's single currency. The central bank governors would need to be closely involved in planning the concrete steps including the institutional arrangements required.

Impact of an announcement

The responses from firms indicate that the impact of a credible announcement on the private sector would be to provide greater incentives to develop the use of the Ecu and the necessary supporting infrastructure.

Within the private sector firms would need to review the threats and opportunities emanating from the development of the Ecu as the single currency of Europe. If they are convinced by the announcement that the Ecu will become the currency of Europe within a realistic but relatively short timetable they can be expected to consider the implications for their own competitive position and strategies. This will require them to consider the impact of the development of the Ecu on their customers, their suppliers, their competitors and their own operations and systems. Given that their commercial customers envisage greater use of the Ecu, companies will need to examine such things as:

- Their price lists and invoicing arrangements, including the development of pan-European Ecu-denominated price lists;
- Arrangements for paying their own creditors in Ecu;
- Their treasury and financial systems and operations – including hardware, software and staff training; and
- Location decisions in Europe in so far as they are influenced by the objective of minimizing exchange risks (for example, current high-inflation or peripheral regions might become more attractive locations).

A wide range of financial services firms – banking, insurance, investment services – will need to examine the extent to which they can extend the range of Ecu-denominated products; banks in particular will need to undertake very careful analyses of the necessary changes to their systems.

Banks and treasury departments of large corporates will need to assess the threat which the development of the Ecu will pose to the profitability of their currency operations, and the opportunities it might create with respect to countries outside the EC. Also, they will need to consider how to respond. All quoted companies will need to examine the case for publishing their accounts in Ecu in advance of the agreed date.

In short, all EC companies will need to examine the implications of the development of the European Community as a single currency area for their transactions with customers and clients in the rest of the world. The emergence of the EC as a single currency area will make the Ecu a major world currency. European monetary authorities will need to develop the use of the Ecu in their foreign exchange operations and this is likely to be reflected by similarly increased use of the Ecu by authorities in the rest of the world. Public bodies and the private sector in non-European countries which have substantial dealings with Europe, for example the ACP countries, will need to review the extent to which they use the Ecu for their dealings with the Community. Community institutions and firms should take the initiative in the development of the Ecu in this regard.

A mutually reinforcing process

In the manner described above, a credible announcement concerning the development of the Ecu can be expected to stimulate major shifts in behaviour in the private sector within the EC and in dealings with the rest of the world. In their turn, these developments should reinforce and might even accelerate the political process of adopting the Ecu as the single currency for Europe.

3: A Strategy For Removing The Obstacles

3.1 Overview

The previous chapter stressed the importance of a credible announcement. This underpins our strategy. We now turn in detail to the strategy itself and how to overcome the obstacles.

The obstacles which our study has identified can be classified as:

- Psychological obstacles relating to market inertia and pockets of ignorance;
- Problems relating to the status of the Ecu including its legal status and its position *vis-à-vis* strong and weak currencies in the EMS; and
- Obstacles relating to the limitations of the Ecu market – lack of end uses, and lack of liquidity and availability.

Analysis of responses from companies suggests that the priority for effort to remove the obstacles should be in the following order, notwithstanding important inter-relations between them:

- Inertia;
- Lack of end uses;
- Legal status;
- Liquidity and availability;
- Strong and weak currencies;
- Pockets of ignorance.

The obstacles to the further private use of the Ecu are considered in detail on a macroeconomic level in Chapter Five and on a microeconomic level in Chapter Six. Here we consider each of these obstacles and provide recommendations for action to remove them. The timings of the various actions are coincidental with the timings we proposed earlier in Chapter Two. By way of introduction, an overview of the strategy is outlined in this section.

The obstacles can be positioned with regard to the following considerations; the extent to which it is difficult to remove the obstacles; and the extent to which increased private usage of the Ecu would occur if they were removed. When plotted in relation to each other, two possible strategies emerge:

1. An indirect strategy aimed at removing administrative obstacles. This strategy is easier to pursue but will do less to stimulate the use of the Ecu.
2. A direct strategy aimed at current inertia and the lack of end uses. This strategy is intended as the catalyst to stimulate much greater private sector use, by providing the political and central bank support which firms need. It is harder to pursue but will have a greater impact on the use of the Ecu.

Figure 2 illustrates these points.

Indirect strategy

The indirect approach typifies the move to European integration prior to the Single European Act. Before the Act there was an implicit will to integrate but no direct and formal programme had been drawn up. Moves towards integration had concentrated on technical issues but a statement of purpose was lacking. Thus the single market lacked an overall credibility. The 1992 programme changed that perception.

The same can be said with regard to the increased private use of the Ecu. While addressing pockets of ignorance and technical obstacles such as lack of liquidity and legal status, the removal of such obstacles will have a marginal effect. *Without a statement of purpose and a planned strategy with deadlines such moves will lack an overall credibility.*

Direct strategy

The direct approach typifies the move towards European integration after the Single European Act. Once the Act had been signed the momentum towards integration took off. The removal of obstacles to the free flow of capital, labour and goods became credible and more effective.

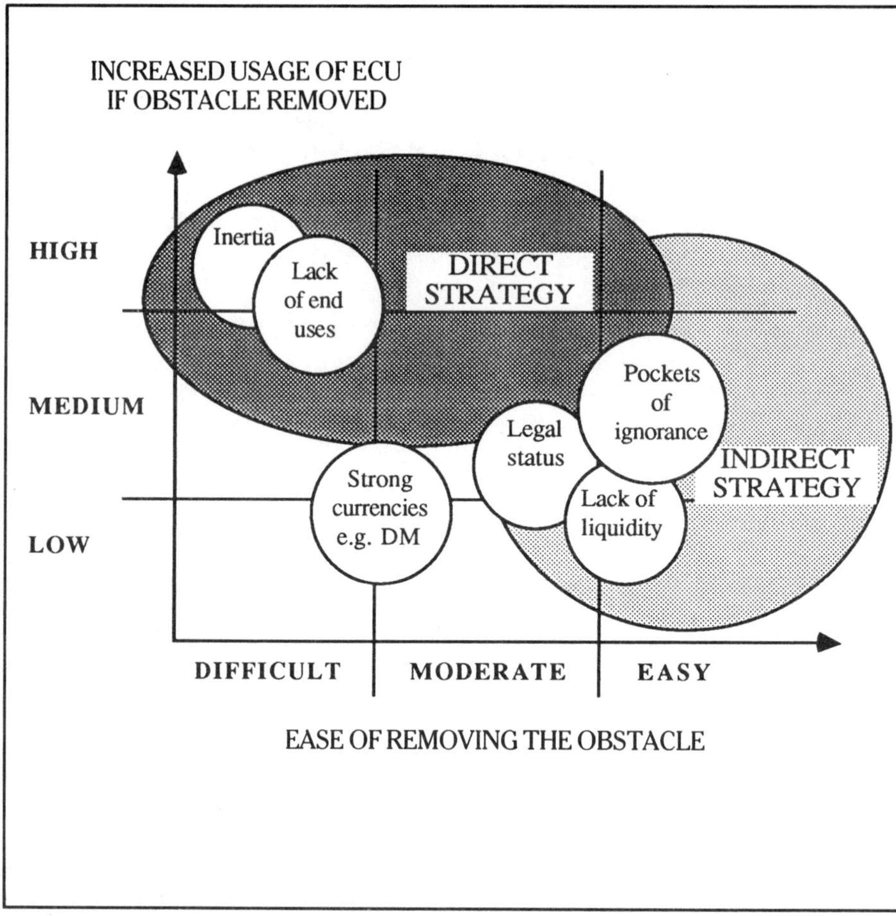

Figure 2: Strategies for removing obstacles.

The direct strategy is preferred and the timing is right.
Although harder to initiate, the direct strategy is the one which promises success. Without an announcement to the effect that the Ecu will become the single European currency, the move towards monetary union will repeat the fate of the ineffectual approach towards the single market prior to the Single European Act.

The 'obstacle' which is not a factor in the above considerations is the present strength of the Deutschmark. In the past it was hoped that the economies of Europe would converge to an average sufficiently close to the strongest so as to facilitate the establishment of monetary union.

As argued in Chapter Two, in an environment of greater exchange rate stability the attractions of the Ecu as a unit of account diminish, especially in relation to a currency offering a high probability of exchange rate gains – notably the Deutschmark in recent times. In practice the Ecu has to compete with the Deutschmark, which is managed by a strong central bank, has been the strongest EC currency, and which has attractions for transaction purposes associated with the large scale of the German economy.

The Deutschmark is a powerful anchor in the EMS and this role should not be discarded. However, the scene has changed and there now exists an important opportunity to adopt the direct approach. To the extent that use of the Deutschmark as a common currency in Europe and as a reserve currency elsewhere grows, the conduct of monetary policy in Germany will become more difficult. In the circumstances it might be in the interests of Germany to be part of a more collective approach to monetary affairs, provided that Germany is assured that monetary stability remains the objective and will be achievable within such a collective framework. The rapid pace of development in eastern Europe has induced many in Germany to emphasize the need for such a collective EC approach. Furthermore, the precise outcome and consequences of monetary union between the FRG and the GDR are not absolutely clear. The alternative is that although the private use of the Deutschmark may grow, for political reasons (on the part of Germany as well as fellow member states of the EC), it is unlikely to become the single currency of Europe and the full benefits of monetary union will not be achieved.

None of this reasoning is intended to deny the existence and strength of the political obstacles to monetary union. It is simply that 'currently' circumstances exist in which Germany may find a collective approach more attractive than hitherto.

We now turn to consideration of the individual obstacles as well as detailed recommendations concerning what should be done and when. The recommendations below are addressed to official institutions and also the private sector.

3.2 Obstacle of inertia

The obstacle of inertia and the recommendations to overcome it were dealt with in Chapter Two in relation to the importance of a credible announcement that the Ecu will be the single currency of Europe. We consider it to be the prime obstacle and the recommendations which address it underpin those which follow.

3.3 Obstacle of lack of end uses

Overview

The lack of end uses for the Ecu currently presents a barrier to its wider use beyond central bank, EC institution and financial market circles. Although its use has spread to the treasuries of some large multinational organizations, there is little incentive for either small or medium enterprises ('SMEs') or the person in the street to follow suit. Hence, present use is almost exclusively confined to international transactions. Established global trade practice shows a preference for using the US dollar (international/raw materials trade) and the Deutschmark (intra-EC) in cross-border trading. It will be difficult for the Ecu to break through currency market barriers and establish a niche for itself as a preferred international trading currency.

Companies in a number of countries, such as Spain and Portugal, expressed the view that they had hardly any need to use the Ecu because they rarely conducted international business, and if they did it was usually with just another (EC) country and in this instance a straightforward two-currency transaction was preferred. A recent study of 50 firms in Belgium (*De Pecunia*, February 1990) showed that there is a real advantage in using the Ecu for exchange risk management. Companies are unlikely to take advantage of this as either they are ignorant of the technique (see 'Obstacle of pockets of ignorance' (3.7) below) or the cost of change is perceived to be too great.

Recommendations

Official institutions

1991: Proposals for removal of administrative barriers. The Commission should initiate the tabling of proposals for the removal of all administrative obstacles which inhibit or discriminate against the use of the Ecu throughout the Community.

1992: The Ecu should be used for European-wide receipts, expenditures and lending. Collection of customs tariffs by national authorities and payments to the Commission, VAT and special contributions (such as aid to the Third World and eastern Europe) should be made in Ecu. Similarly, expenditures at a European level, such as the CAP and social and regional programmes, should also be made in Ecu. This move can be made with the Ecu in its current basket form and would greatly assist the creation of an 'Ecu habitat' both within Europe and with regard to perceptions outside Europe. The levy of customs tariffs throughout Europe would both be feasible and credible, and would not only make the Ecu available for expenditure within Europe but would, at an international level, make importers become used to using the Ecu for transactions. Likewise, payments in Ecu from the Structural Funds and under the CAP at national level within countries would have a major impact on the attitude of companies. They would see not only a demonstrable political will through the European-wide announcement, but also concrete pragmatic action by European institutions which is taken seriously by the international trading community.

1992: The system of central bank co-operation should carry out the following steps:

1. *Co-ordinate the current national government treasury bill programmes and the national treasuries should co-ordinate the issues of Ecu bonds.* Interviews with banks suggest a current obstacle to the use of Ecu bonds is the lack of benchmark issues. This problem could be managed by such a close liaison through co-ordinating issue dates, maturities and coupons. The Association of International Bond Dealers (AIBD) and the European Investment Bank (EIB) might also be able to play a role.
2. *Increase the number of short-term issues.* Banks indicate that the market lacks liquidity due to the shortage of short-term Ecu bonds. A programmed and co-ordinated issues calendar would, to a large degree, address this problem.

1992: Contributions in the form of grants and loan facilities to international organizations should be in Ecu. Budgetary contributions, the provision of grant assistance and loan facilities to extra-EC international organizations made by member states should be in Ecu. Such bodies include the UN organizations, IMF, IBRD, OECD and NATO. This would encourage the use of the Ecu in the rest of the world and by institutions and firms within developing countries which receive assistance from non-EC multilateral aid agencies.

1992: National procurement should be denominated in Ecu and national currency. Government procurement (especially where procurement crosses national boundaries) should be denominated in Ecu as well as national currency, whether or not the invitations to tender are of the type which need to be notified in the EC Official Journal. Awareness of the Ecu will be increased and the Ecu will be given more credibility than it currently has. Secondly, with national procurement tenders priced in Ecu, the demand for Ecu denomination will be increased and this will act as a stimulus for the private sector to invest time and effort in exploring how best they can use the Ecu.

1993: Companies incorporated under the European Statute should be allowed to pay tax in Ecu. The proposed European Company Statute would enable 'European' companies to be taxed on all their separate national operations under the tax regime of whichever country is their home base. The use of the Ecu would be promoted if such companies could be allowed to pay their taxes in Ecu.

1995: Companies should be allowed to calculate and pay their taxes in Ecu. Calculation and payment of tax in Ecu would give an improved, harmonized tax base to Europe (as opposed to harmonized tax rates). The current Commission proposals for a harmonized tax base (published in early 1988) do not fully take into account inflation and foreign exchange movements. This recommendation would be of particular benefit to those member countries which have higher inflation than the average because it would put pressure on them to either bring down their inflation or adopt the Ecu to a greater degree. This would benefit multinational enterprises trading with different member countries, which would not suffer tax disadvantages if based in a member country where inflation and interest rates were higher than the Community averages. Thus, while in the short term a national government might suffer some loss of income from corporation tax, during the process of monetary integration, it would be able to attract international investment and be able to compete on a more even footing with member countries which have lower inflation and lower interest rates.

Private Sector

1992: Ecu life insurance policies should be designed and marketed. In view of the long-term financial planning involved, this is a logical consequence of the credible announcement about the Ecu as a single currency.

1993: The travel industry and European joint ventures should, as far as possible, adopt the Ecu for pricing. Companies such as airlines are well placed to adopt an Ecu pricing policy within Europe. As the industry is largely US dollar based, this use of the Ecu by European airlines would encourage Ecu-US dollar relationships.

1994: Quotations for raw materials and commodities traded in European markets should be expressed exclusively in Ecu.

1995: Large companies should adopt the Ecu as much as possible for invoicing and import-export financing. Our research suggests that once a company adopts the Ecu for one purpose (either for invoicing or financing) then it finds it easier to appreciate the benefits the Ecu can sometimes give through other Ecu instruments as well. One of the greatest difficulties experienced is getting trading partners to accept the Ecu. This difficulty would be removed by the announcement, and thus companies will find it easier and worth their while to begin to adopt the Ecu, to a limited extent, in its current form. By quoting prices in Ecu, even if the settlement currency may turn out to be different, companies will ensure their sales and invoicing departments become knowledgeable and comfortable with the Ecu.

1996: Accounting devices like taxometers, computer software, coin and card operated automats should be prepared for the change of currency.

3.4 Obstacle of legal status

Overview

The fact that Ecu-denominated contracts are not usually legally enforceable detracts from their international status and impedes their competing equally with contracts in other currencies. (This is particularly an obstacle to Ecu-denominated bills of exchange.) Furthermore, as long as the Ecu prevails as an 'open basket currency', the composition of which may be altered on a five-yearly basis, it will be regarded as an unstable vehicle for long-term investments. Supporting our conclusion that the issue of legal status is widely felt to be important by the European private sector, was the repeated response that the existence of a European central bank would lend credibility to the Ecu and consequently encourage its use.

The legality of the Ecu is an obstacle which should be dealt with in a gradual way. A suggested approach is:

- Give the Ecu contractual backing;
- Gradually remove discriminatory legal impediments, including foreign currency laws;
- Make the Ecu legal tender on a European basis; and
- Give the Ecu legal-tender status on a national basis.

Recommendations

Official institutions

1992: The Ecu should be given the necessary legal backing for inter-company contracts at a European level. Unlike the 12 national currencies, which have their respective national laws to back them, the Ecu does not have a national law which recognizes it as legal tender. Thus, at a European level, laws should be adopted to make contractual Ecu obligations legally enforceable. Such legislation would also enable European consortia, involved in collaborations, to draw up their accounts in a common currency, thus removing some of the accounting chaos from which such collaborations frequently suffer.

1992: Companies should be allowed by their stock exchanges to report in Ecu as well as in their national currency. To facilitate the move to Ecu, stock exchange regulations should be adjusted to allow companies to report in Ecu if they so choose. During the transition to the single currency, many companies may choose to report in Ecu as well as their national currency. This is especially relevant for those top companies which will be involved in the programme to provide Ecu balance sheets on a European basis.

1993: Companies in all countries should be allowed to issue share capital in Ecu.

1994: Reports and accounts should include Ecu-denominated versions. During the transition from 12 currencies to the use of the Ecu as a single currency, companies should consider preparing their reports and accounts in Ecu as well as the currency they normally use. This will help shareholders and investment analysts begin to interpret the effect that a common currency will have.

1994: Discriminatory national legislation should be removed. In some countries the Ecu faces discriminatory legislation as a foreign currency. Foreign currency controls exist in countries such as Greece. While these controls are planned to be lifted, the Ecu should be given positive discrimination over other foreign currencies during the process of transition to a single currency. Thus restrictions on the Ecu should be lifted as soon as possible, and in advance of other restrictions which some countries apply to foreign currency.

1996: The Ecu should become legal tender, usable in retail operations.

1997: The Ecu should become the single currency, replacing national currencies. Ecu coins and bills would be issued by the European central banking authorities.

Private Sector

1992: Companies should make increasing use of Ecu-denominated commercial paper.

1993: Companies should increasingly issue share capital denominated in Ecu.

1995: Reports and accounts should include Ecu denomination.

3.5 Obstacle of liquidity and availability

Overview

The currently perceived lack of liquidity and availability of Ecu-denominated products was felt to be an obstacle by the majority of those private sector representatives consulted. In some respects, this obstacle may be regarded as the result of legal status of the Ecu and general inertia and is therefore not only of less importance, but is also likely to be remedied by removal of those obstacles discussed earlier in this chapter.

Recommendations

Private Sector

1990: Banks should give their customers clear and concise information regarding the Ecu. Many companies complained that they were unable to get information from their banks regarding the Ecu. Bank employees, especially outside head office treasury departments, often have little knowledge of the Ecu. Banks responded that this is due to lack of demand. To ensure they keep their customers fully informed, banks should give training to staff at all levels of the bank who have a direct interface with their clients, and also have educational and publicity material prepared. The current advantages of the Ecu (in areas such as same day values, volatility and risk) should be communicated as soon as possible to ensure that customers can begin to appreciate some of the benefits which the Ecu can give prior to its full adoption as a single currency.

1990: Banks should avoid assigning discriminatory transaction costs to the Ecu. There is a perception that the Ecu is a expensive currency to use as banks often charge higher transaction costs than for major currencies. Banks told us that any higher charges for Ecu operations simply reflect their low frequency or volume. In any event, banks should ensure that the price they charge to the customer for Ecu transactions is fair and competitive. If necessary, a lowering of price should be considered in order to gain greater share of an expanding market.

1991: Banks should ensure that they offer their full range of legally available services in Ecu as well as their normal currency. In order to prepare for the adoption of the Ecu, as well as to meet increasing demand from their customers, banks should study and implement how they can offer their products in Ecu. This to a limited extent has been done by some banks already – for example, Italian and French banks offering Ecu mortgages in the UK. The adoption of the Ecu will allow banks to compete on a wider scale than they currently enjoy.

1992: In order to establish a competitive advantage for the Ecu, banks should offer the shortest possible processing time for Ecu-products.

1994: Companies should issue Ecu bonds. Companies should develop their use of the Ecu further by issuing Ecu bonds.

3.6 Strong and weak currencies

Overview

Our survey revealed a difference in perceived obstacles as well as benefits regarding use of Ecu, between those countries with a strong and those with a weaker currency. Generally speaking, those countries with a weaker currency, such as Spain or Greece, were more favourably disposed towards increased use of the Ecu and perceived greater benefits as a result of this. In view of its international prestige and tradition, the US dollar has a preponderant position as foreign currency in some countries, especially in the smaller ones.

Due to its stability and strength, many European countries consulted in our survey expressed the view that they preferred to use the Deutschmark for international transactions, as opposed to the Ecu, while German companies and banks saw no reason to transact in any currency weaker than their own. One result of this financial asymmetry within Europe, coupled with the geographical centrality of the Federal Republic, has been that many EC currencies shadow Deutschmark movements on the international money markets. Furthermore, the strength of the Deutschmark has placed West German companies and banks in an advantageous bargaining situation, so much so that they may insist upon the settlement of international transactions in their own currency.

The reason is that from the point of view of a hard currency (Deutschmark or DM-linked currency), the Ecu appears to be more volatile due to the fluctuations of UK sterling and the wider band of oscillation for some other currencies. The lower rate of inflation in hard currency countries gives rise to medium- or long-term currency devaluations in countries with higher inflation within the EMS. Alternatively, stabilization is obtained by high interest rates for weak currencies and this affects Ecu interest rates unfavourably for strong currency borrowers.

Recommendations

The nature and timing of recommendations regarding this obstacle were set out in Chapter Two and are further discussed in Chapters Five and Seven. Suffice it to say here that the timing is now critical for overcoming this obstacle. If the recommendations which we have detailed in this report are not accompanied by the necessary economic convergence within Europe, and carried out within the timescale specified, it is unlikely that this obstacle will be removed.

Furthermore, the full participation of all Ecu-component currencies in the ERM and the application of increasingly smaller bands of oscillation in the EMS would reduce the fluctuations of the Ecu with respect to the stronger currencies.

3.7 Obstacle of pockets of ignorance

Overview

It was made clear from our survey that increased use of the Ecu was further hindered by the lack of knowledge and awareness within the private sector. Pockets of ignorance may be identified at three levels: on a pan-European basis, they appear to be concentrated in more recent EC member states such as Portugal and Greece; on a national basis one may differentiate between banks, which generally appear to have a higher level of awareness, and companies; and, finally, one may make a distinction between large multinationals and small- and medium-sized firms, where the latter are generally less aware.

Ignorance not only prevails in the form of a lack of awareness of the Ecu among corporate and banking decision-makers, but also among their staff, who would require training. This problem is particularly acute in countries such as Greece, Portugal and Spain. In these countries the issue is compounded by the fact that SMEs constitute a large proportion of their economies. Thus, ironically, many of those in a position where they are most likely to benefit from use of the Ecu appear to be unaware of what it is and what it has to offer. However, many SMEs indicated that under the present system their foreign currency transactions are rather limited and so is their need for knowledge about the Ecu. This would of course change once a credible announcement has indicated the necessity to be prepared for the single currency.

Recommendations

Community institutions

1991: A European information campaign should be organized. Our interviews revealed that ignorance of the Ecu and of the benefits of a European currency is widespread. The European Commission is uniquely placed to co-ordinate an information campaign throughout Europe. Such a campaign should include not only published material but also seminars which could be staged with national federations of industry and media announcements. Initially these should be aimed at companies and banks. The campaign would need its own unique strategy, but should increase in pace up to the year before the full adoption of the Ecu (in whatever form is decided), and should then be followed by a detailed 'Year of the Ecu' (see below).

1991: The information campaign should be co-ordinated. Analysis of responses to our survey shows that each member state has a different level of knowledge of the Ecu. As a first step, national governments should organize a campaign about the specific advantages that the Ecu can currently bring to their own country. Such a campaign could include the adoption of information policies which, for example, could include national TV and radio reporting of Ecu movements as well as those of the dollar. As the date of the adoption of the Ecu approaches, the level of information should be increased both in quantity and in exposure to the target audience.

1991: Collector Ecu coins should be minted. Following the example of Belgium, special Ecu coins should be minted and given legal tender status. More than anything else, these are likely to attract collector investment interest, but they will also demonstrate the support of national governments for the adoption of the Ecu.

1991: Postage stamps should be denominated in Ecu as well as national currency. Public awareness of the Ecu could be increased by printing, from time to time, Ecu prices alongside national currency prices on postage stamps. Post offices are also a good outlet for educational literature. Such a move has precedents in France and Italy where postage stamps have carried Ecu equivalent prices.

1994: An annual tax-free European-wide lottery in Ecu should be established. In order to get wider public awareness of the Ecu in all countries, a European-wide lottery should be established with the prizes denominated in Ecu.

1996: A 'Year of the Ecu' should be announced the year prior to the full adoption of the Ecu as the single currency. While the information campaign will initially be aimed at companies and banks, the general public will increasingly need to be involved. Thus, the year before the adoption of the Ecu, a detailed and intensive campaign should be organized. Grouping the various actions under a single banner of 'The Year of the Ecu' would be an effective way of both providing a common vehicle of publicity and ensuring consistency of information.

1996: A European-wide competition should be run for the design of a Ecu20 note. Although we recommend that notes and coins initially retain their national design and characteristics, there is scope for having a common design. As part of the publicity campaign, a European-wide competition to design one of the more common notes (likely to be Ecu20) should be run.

1996: Legal tender Ecu coins and notes should be minted. The possibility of minting the Ecu centrally is fraught with problems. What size should the coins be? Who should shoulder the cost of replacing slot machines? Whose King/Queen/president/leader etc. should be on the notes? National institutions could produce the Ecu coins and notes using their current national designs. Over time these would circulate across Europe. Early on the in 21st century, a common approach using central production and design could be introduced.

Private Sector

1991: Each company should study the cost/benefit profile of a single European currency. As a first step towards implementation of the use of the Ecu, companies should carry out a detailed study to identify what the benefits and costs would be for them, taking into account the new threats and opportunities which are likely to arise as a result of the increasing use of the Ecu and the introduction of the Ecu as Europe's single currency. In so doing, a greater appreciation of the need for implementation should be achieved.

1991: Companies should ensure that employee knowledge of the Ecu is improved. Internal publicity regarding the Ecu and the implication of its adoption as a single European currency should be organized by companies to ensure a smooth transition. This will be especially important for treasury functions.

1991: Banks should undertake a full cost/benefit study of the adoption of the Ecu. In order to highlight the issues involved in adopting the Ecu, and to plan for implementation, banks should assess the costs and benefits that the use of the Ecu as the single currency will produce. For instance, while arbitrage opportunities will diminish, the greater stability in the internal market should create new opportunities for banks, especially in long-term investment. On the other hand, complex issues will be created for information systems (hardware and software), which warrant careful analysis and may require major changes.

1991: Banks should ensure that their views are communicated to political and institutional decision makers. Banks will play a key role in the adoption of the Ecu as a single European currency. To this end they should ensure that their views and recommendations are known at all levels of decision making. The Ecu Banking Association could play a central role in ensuring that a formal body with national representation is set up as a conduit of information and as a counterpart to the European central banking authorities.

1996: During the 'Year of the Ecu', Ecu prices should be quoted wherever practical. In order to facilitate a general adoption of the Ecu within each member state, national governments should adopt a pricing policy which encourages companies to quote Ecu prices wherever practical.

4: Perceived Cost Implications

4.1 Perceived savings and costs of common and single currencies

As part of the survey of private use of the Ecu we asked companies and banks to assess the differences in impact of two scenarios: (1) the Ecu as a thirteenth currency; and (2) the Ecu as a single European currency. From the responses, the first overall impression is that companies tended to see more benefits in the second scenario while banks were more ambivalent.

General attitude

Figures 3 and 4 illustrate the general attitude of companies towards a European currency as it would affect different aspects of their business strategy. There are three messages that can be drawn from these graphs:

1. Over 50 per cent of companies feel that a European currency would have a positive effect on their export, sourcing, marketing and distribution strategies. On the other hand the impact on R&D and production is felt to be less important;

2. There are no perceived negative aspects on any part of corporate strategy, with impact deemed to be either positive or non-existent; and

3. There is a definite preference for scenario two, as is shown by the higher number of companies which feel there would be a very positive impact.

These findings can be compared to the responses made by banks to the question on whether the lack of European currency hinders the development of certain activities or not (Figures 5 and 6). Of the banks that responded, on this issue it is clear that there is no perceived difference between the two options. It is also evident that a majority of the banks felt that the lack of a European currency had not been an obstacle to any aspect of their strategy.

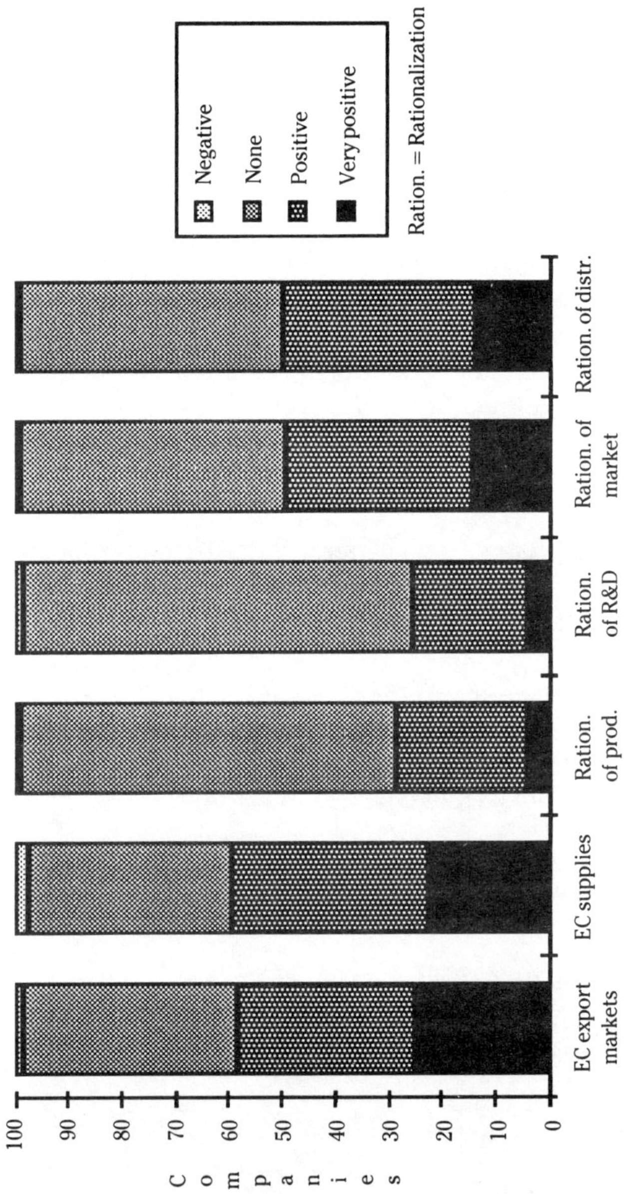

Figure 3: Effect of scenario one on different aspects of business strategy

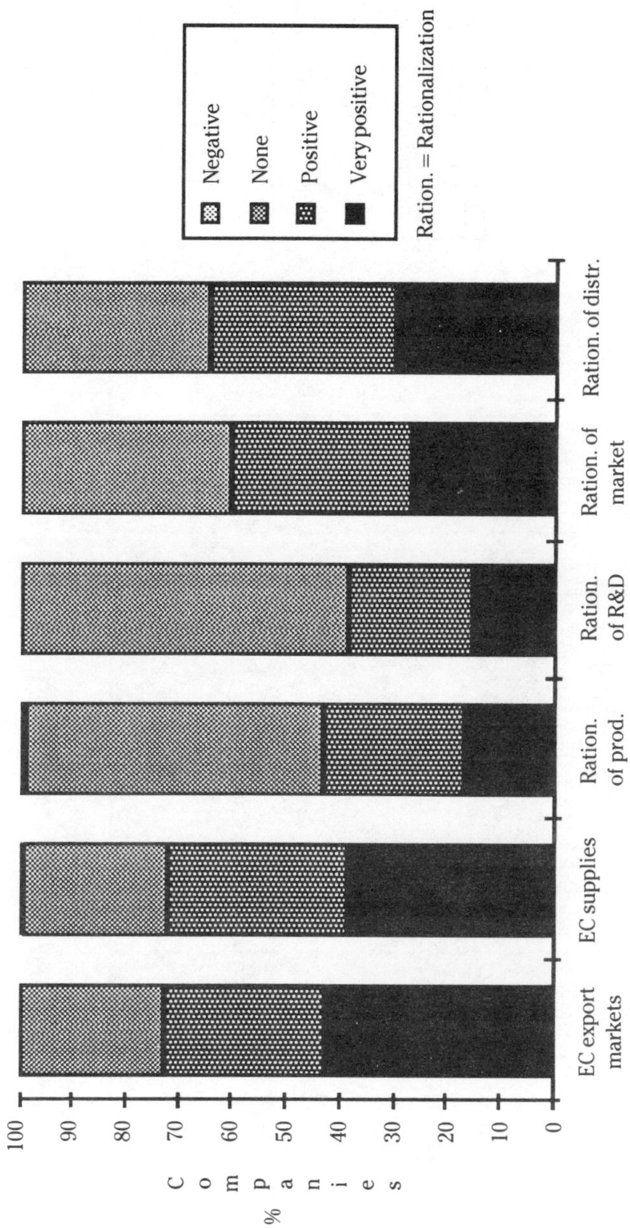

Figure 4: Effect of scenario two on different aspects of business strategy

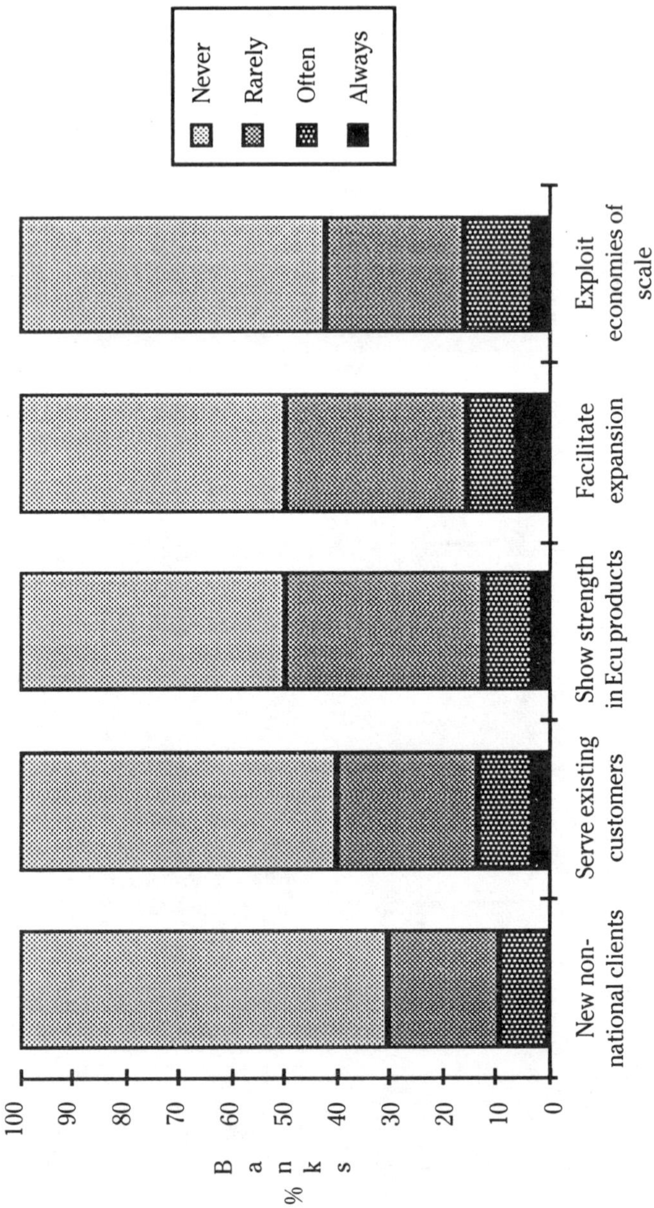

Figure 5: Obstacle to banking activities – scenario one

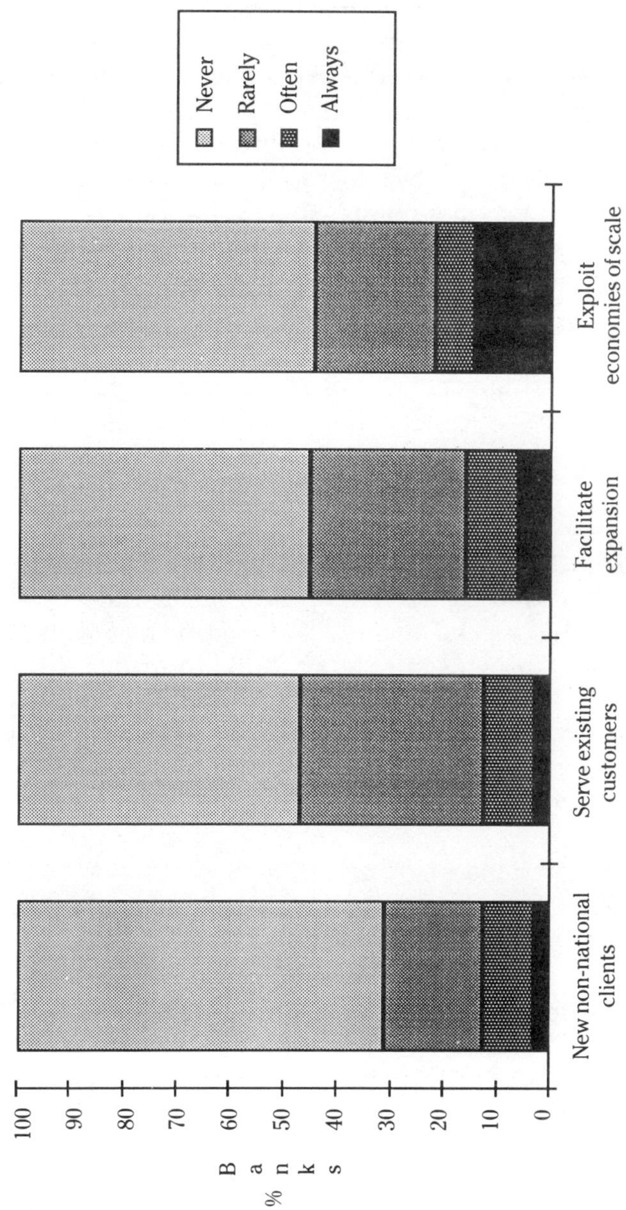

Figure 6: Obstacle to banking activities – scenario two

Financial costs or savings

In Figure 7 we examine the impact of both scenarios on financial costs (e.g. foreign exchange and interest rates). These costs or savings should be compared to the perceived costs or savings as expressed by the banks that were surveyed. The argument was made by some respondents that a single European currency would have a neutral effect on costs as reduced interest and foreign exchange costs in a company would be entirely off-set by a loss of income in the banking sector. The charts illustrate two key points: 30 per cent of respondents felt that a common European currency would entail savings of 0.5 per cent of turnover or more; and 55 per cent felt that a single currency would produce such savings.

In order to obtain a more detailed picture of the costs of operating in several European currencies, close examination of eight companies was undertaken. Costs were broken down into internal administrative costs (especially systems and staff) and financial costs (bank charges).

Non-financial costs or savings

In Figure 8 we have illustrated to what extent companies feel that their non-financial costs (e.g. administration, advertising, production, sales, distribution etc.) will be affected by the implementation of a European currency. Three conclusions can be drawn from these two charts:

1. Whatever the option, a majority of companies feel that there will be no effect on their non-financial costs, with a significant minority feeling that there will be savings in these areas;

2. There is a marginal preference for scenario two, with more companies feeling that the savings induced by having a single currency would be substantial; and

3. Portugal seems to be a case apart. It is the only country where the general feeling is that there will be higher costs rather than savings. The Portuguese are also ambivalent as to which scenario they prefer.

Companies trading with clients overseas claimed that the costs of operating in multiple currencies in Europe were small or close to zero because of their sophisticated systems or because they operate in US dollars or Deutschmarks. But other companies, operating mainly in Europe, reported costs in the region of 1–2 per cent of their EC turnover.

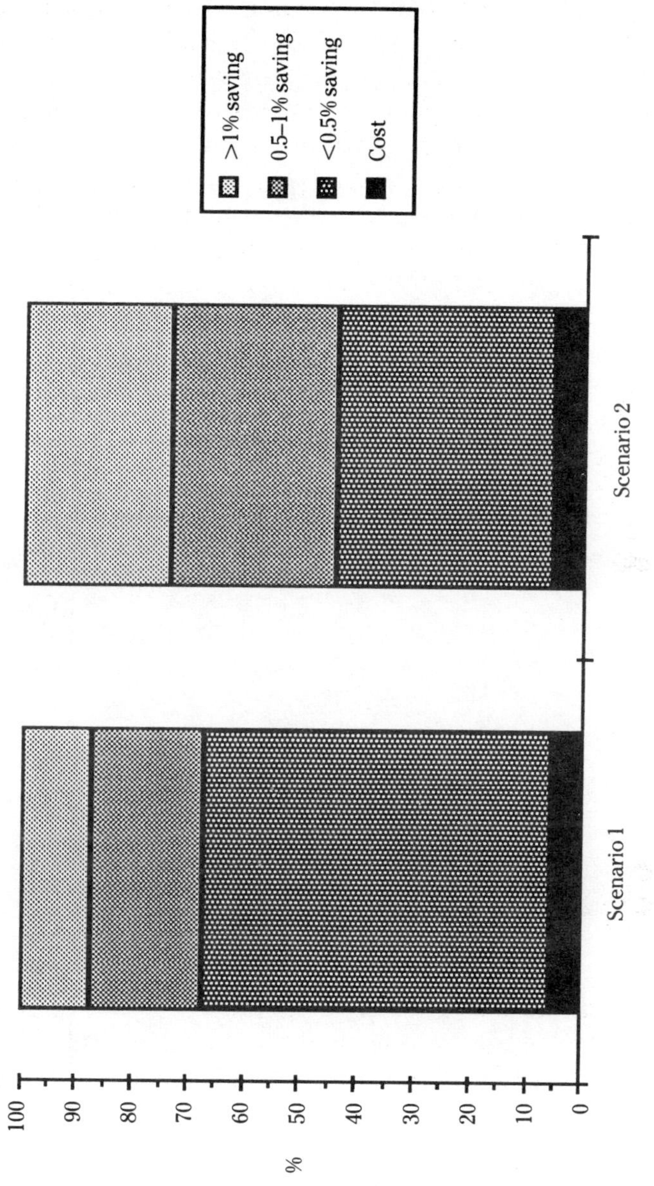

Figure 7: Financial costs or savings

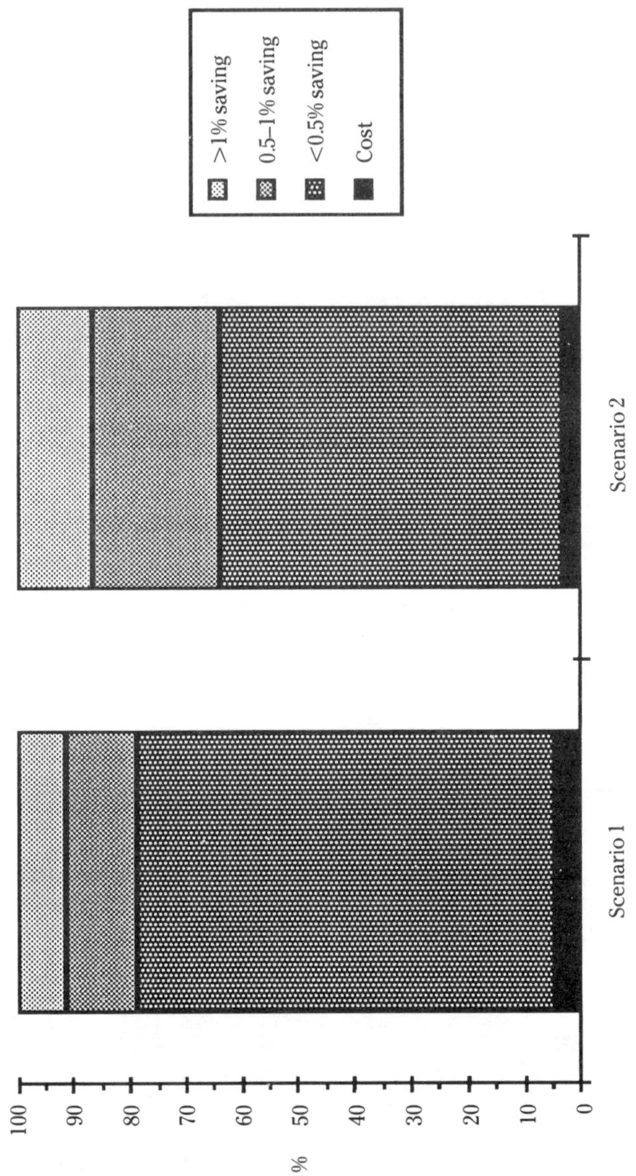

Figure 8: Non-financial costs or savings

On the banking side (see Figures 9 and 10) the situation is quite different:

- Overall, the banks split into three approximately equal groups. One group feels there will be increased income from the adoption of a European currency, a second group feels there will be no effects and a third group expects that there will be reduced income.
- The differences between options one and two are quite strong. The banks feel much more threatened by a single currency than by a thirteenth. Over half the respondents felt they would lose income if the second scenario was to be implemented, although there was a definite feeling that the first scenario would result in increased income opportunities in most banking products.

Taking account of banking attitudes and companies' attitudes on this issue it would seem that a European currency would have a redistributive effect on income between banks and companies. It is difficult to say whether this would result in global gain, loss or in a neutral result. However, consideration of resource efficiency would tend to support the idea that the net result for European economies would be to generate a gain in the longer term, once the effects of redistribution have worked through.

4.2 Transition costs

Inevitably, even if there is the necessary political will to implement a common European currency as fast as possible, there will be transition costs linked to changing systems, retraining personnel, long-term contracts, re-labelling, possible uncertainties, etc.

Over 55 per cent of the companies that responded to our survey felt that these costs would be negligible as opposed to less than 35 per cent which felt that they would be significant or very significant. When a more detailed analysis of the responses is made, three major areas stand out as being the most likely to generate transition costs: adapting to new client needs; changing accounting systems; and adapting systems for suppliers.

We found that there was no link between perceived transition costs and respondents' general attitudes towards the value of moving to a common or single currency for Europe. Thus Italian or Belgian

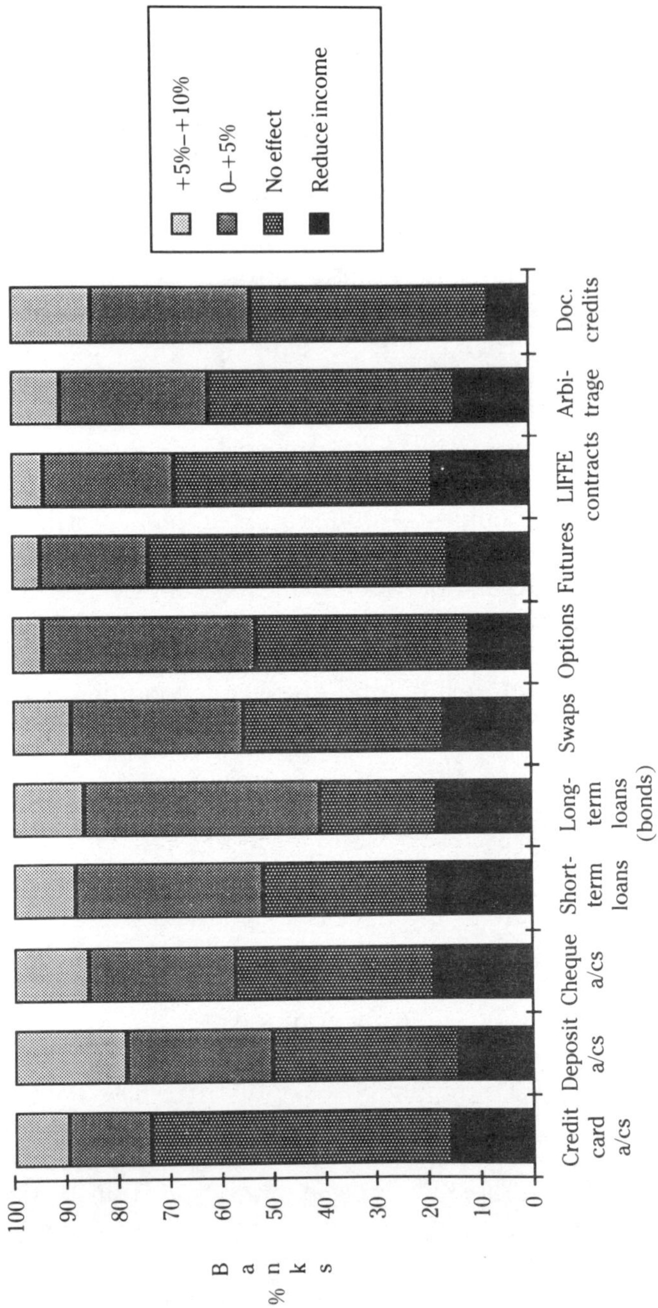

Figure 9: Reduced or increased income – scenario one

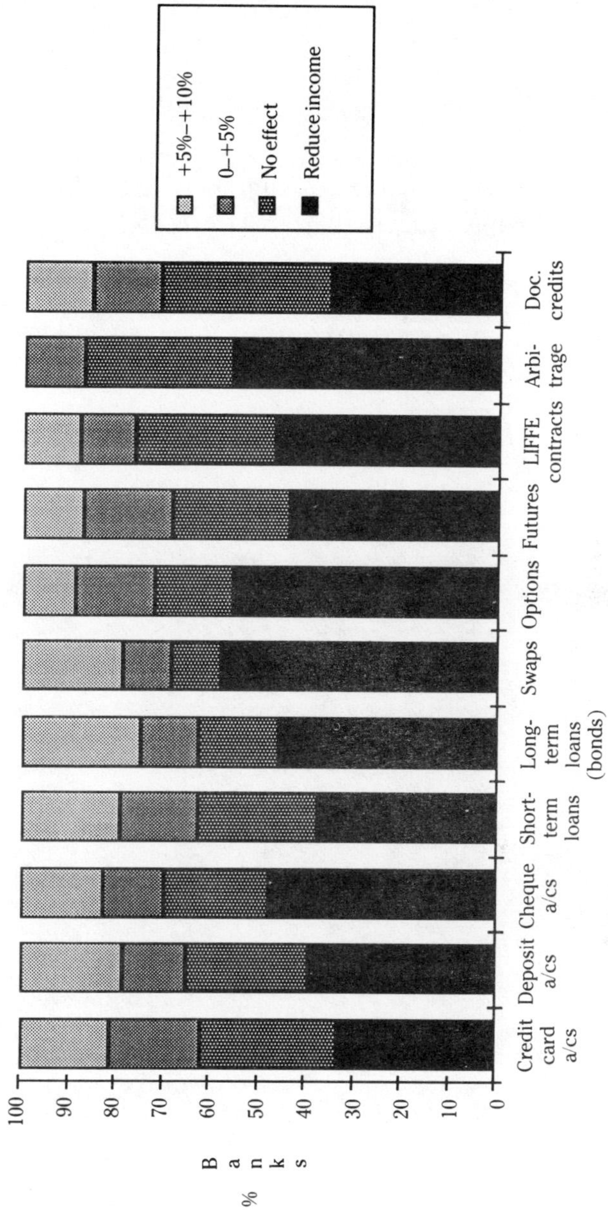

Figure 10: Reduced or increased income – scenario two

companies, where a majority felt that these costs would be significant, also had a very positive attitude to the concept of a European currency.

4.3 Conclusion

The main conclusion we draw from the survey results is that, in general, companies seem to feel that they would benefit to a greater extent from a single European currency than from a thirteenth.

5: Macroeconomic Aspects of the Ecu Strategy

Report by NIESR

The Delors Committee agreed 'that there should be no discrimination against the private use of the Ecu and that existing administrative obstacles should be removed'. Work is being done to follow up that recommendation. The report by Ernst & Young notes that the administrative obstacles are not considered to be a major problem by most businesses. As anyone familiar with the continuing debate over the use of the Ecu will know, the obstacles are not purely administrative. The future of the private use of the Ecu cannot be considered in isolation from the future of the Ecu as the single currency of the Community, once the process of economic and monetary union is completed.

The purpose of this report is to provide the necessary macroeconomic background to an assessment of the macroeconomic arguments for a wider use of the Ecu, and to consider what the implications might be at a macroeconomic level of a spontaneous movement to adopt the Ecu as a common European currency, even in advance of the political process of economic and monetary union ('EMU').

We begin by describing briefly the advantages of a common currency, and more particularly of a single currency, within Europe. We then ask whether these advantages might come about by a spontaneous evolution. This leads us into a short discussion of the possible results of 'currency competition' in advance of further progress towards EMU. With that scenario we contrast one in which the steps towards EMU are announced well in advance, making clear what the future role of the Ecu is intended to be. We give our reasons for preferring this second scenario to the first.

The next section of the report considers how wider use of the Ecu might be encouraged over the next year or two. We discuss, but only briefly, the possibility of converting the Ecu from a 'currency basket' into an independent currency in its own right. We examine, in more detail, the scope for using the Ecu much more extensively in foreign exchange market intervention – and more generally its role in the development of a common monetary policy within the Community. This is where we see the most immediate advantages from the wider use of the Ecu, because it could reduce some of the problems arising from currency competition and from the wider external use of the domestic currencies of member states.

Our final section is concerned with longer-term issues, corresponding to stages two and three of the Delors Report. It is important to have in mind at least a sketch of the whole of the path ahead in order to decide what the first steps should be. On the one hand there are arguments for making progress towards EMU as rapidly as possible; on the other there are very real dangers involved in forcing the pace. We assume that a timetable for EMU is drawn up, with the process to be completed towards the end of this decade.

At the end of the report some recommendations are made as to the action which could be taken now to remove the 'macroeconomic obstacles' to the wider use of the Ecu.

5.1 The advantages of a common currency

The Delors Report says (paragraph 46): 'Although a monetary union does not necessarily require a single currency, it would be a desirable feature of a monetary union. The Committee was of the opinion that the Ecu has the potential to be developed into such a common currency.'

It is important to distinguish on the one hand a 'common currency' used throughout Europe alongside domestic currencies. The text of the Delors Report is not 100 per cent clear on this point, but it probably envisages the Ecu becoming the single currency of Europe after EMU is complete. It is even less clear what role (if any) they see for the Ecu as a common currency in the period of transition.

The advantages of a *single currency* are well-known. Even within a monetary union there would be costs associated with the existence of more than one currency:

1. There are transaction costs involved in switching from one currency to another even if exchange rates are fixed. There may also be a need to hold larger 'idle' money balances in total, if balances are needed in a variety of currencies. Apart from that, there is the inconvenience of keeping accounts in several currencies, or more generally of making calculations whenever business is being transacted across national boundaries.

2. Until there is a single currency there will always be an incentive to hedge against the possibility of exchange rate changes, however 'irrevocable' the commitment of governments to hold to existing parities. Movements in foreign exchange markets, even within a monetary union, could be so large and so rapid as to overcome official attempts to offset them. Thus a single currency would give the private sector greater confidence that monetary union will be maintained, and so facilitate the economic integration of Europe.

Against these advantages of a single currency must be set the initial cost of the changeover. This would involve recalculating the value, in terms of Ecu, of literally millions of existing contracts. It would involve calling in and reissuing all the existing notes and coins in circulation. This once-and-for-all cost is necessary in order to achieve the permanent cost savings resulting from a single currency.

The advantages of a *common 'thirteenth' currency* prior to monetary union are not so great, but they are of the same kind. In France, for example, it might be possible to work with only two currencies, the franc and the Ecu, saving the need for transactions or calculations in Deutschmarks, sterling and so on. This would be of benefit to all firms and others involved in international business within Europe. On the other hand the thirteenth currency could actually make life more difficult for those engaged in purely domestic business, who at present are never involved in the use of foreign currency at all.

Taking our cue from the Delors Report, we assume that, eventually, Europe will have the Ecu as its single currency. The questions we address in this study concern the route by which that destination might be reached. Some routes would involve the Ecu as a thirteenth common currency, but others would not.

5.2 Spontaneous evolution and the need for a clear announcement

It would be wrong to assume that the use of currencies in Europe will be unchanged if nothing is done to encourage the use of the Ecu. Capital controls are being lifted, financial markets are becoming more integrated, and trade flows within Europe are growing. In these circumstances the advantages of using a common currency are such that a tendency in that direction could develop spontaneously at any time. We cannot say when this might happen or on what scale (we appreciate that opinions differ), but the possibility of large-scale movements is one that must be taken very seriously. The result would be a kind of 'currency competition' – that is to say a process by which the use of some currencies grew at the expense of the others.

The process is reminiscent of a chemical reaction, which requires only the presence of a catalyst for the speed to be increased a hundredfold. In this case the process of 'standardization' on a particular currency could be triggered by the enterprise of financial institutions. An international bank which operated only in Ecu could reduce its transaction charges quite considerably if, but only if, it could generate enough business and balance its transactions so as to avoid large-scale purchases or sales of individual currencies.

There is nothing to guarantee that the 'currency competition' would be won by the Ecu, however. On the contrary, a wider use would probably develop for those European currencies which are already most used internationally – that is, the Deutschmark, French franc and sterling. Success in the competition would depend on several factors. The size of its home country gives a currency an initial advantage, as does existing international use. 'Strong' currencies would be attractive to lenders, and 'weak' currencies to borrowers, due to the differences in their rates of interest. Even so the competition would favour currencies that were regarded as relatively 'safe', that is currencies whose value, in terms of purchasing power, was most predictable and in general the low-inflation currencies like the Deutschmark, not the high-inflation currencies like the lira or sterling. The Ecu, as a basket currency, must necessarily reflect the average strength of its constituent parts.

The Deutschmark already has a wider international use than other European currencies. The unification of East and West Germany, and the opening up of the rest of eastern Europe to trade and capital flows could powerfully reinforce the position of the Deutschmark. It is already used as a reserve currency outside Europe – a use which might have developed further had the Bundesbank not discouraged it. In this case the advantages of size, of existing use, and of stability come together. The most likely alternative to the Ecu as the common currency of Europe must surely be the Deutschmark.

It is doubtful whether the Bundesbank would welcome such an outcome since it would make the conduct of monetary policy in Germany more difficult. It would, however, be to the advantage of commercial banks and other financial institutions in Germany. It could be that the development of their international business would speed up the integration of Europe as a Deutschmark-zone.

It is difficult to see, however, that the Deutschmark could ever become the single European currency. The political objections to such a development would surely be acute. Thus the Deutschmark-route involves separating off international and domestic transactions. The 'common' currency is not the single currency even at the end of the day. Thus the full advantages of monetary union are never realized.

If this scenario is unacceptable, for political or economic reasons, there would be advantage in announcing straight away that, once monetary union is achieved, the Ecu will be the single currency of Europe. Assuming that the announcement is believed, everyone will know that in due course all the national currencies will disappear. The force of the announcement would be much increased if a timetable for monetary union was attached to it.

At present there is a great deal of uncertainty as to the likelihood of EMU, the nature of its operation, and the date of its implementation. (This is reflected in the different rates of interest paid on long-term bonds denominated in different currencies.) It may be unrealistic to expect this uncertainly to be resolved immediately, and a detailed programme to be announced straight away. Nevertheless we would strongly argue for a clear statement as soon as possible that EMU will involve a single currency which is continuous with the existing Ecu. At the same time a target date would be announced for the completion of EMU – a date which is not too distant in order to influence private sector dealings as soon as it is made known. (The credibility of the announcement might be reflected in an immediate adjustment of long-term interest rates.)

In these circumstances banks all over Europe (or elsewhere) would have an incentive to develop their business in Ecu, as this would give them a competitive advantage during the transition to a single currency. Conversely, there would be a disincentive to conversion to some other international standard. It would hardly be worth making the change from doing business in, say, sterling to doing business in the Deutschmark or the US dollar, if a general move to the Ecu was expected soon.

Thus the early announcement of a commitment to a single currency could, in itself, speed up the process, acting as the catalyst that is necessary to the reaction. This would facilitate the process of monetary union, and shut off the 'digression' of the wider international use of the Deutschmark or other national currencies.

5.3 The use of the Ecu in the early stages of EMU

Some of the proposals for developing the use of the Ecu have assumed that it can be converted from a 'currency basket' to a 'true currency' with its own exchange rate independent of all other currencies. After some consideration we decided that this was not an alternative to be discussed at length in this study. The Delors Committee felt that 'this strategy was not to be recommended' and it is evident that it now lacks political support. Moreover, it would be impossible to implement until effective European central banking institutions had been set up. It is not therefore an alternative to be considered for the immediate future.

The Ecu as a currency basket must have its risk and return characteristics determined by those of its constituent parts. As such its characteristics of risk and return can generally, in principle, be bettered by choosing a different combination of the same national currencies more appropriate to the circumstances of the individual holder. The advantages of the Ecu as a store of value arise because it is a readily available portfolio of currencies which may approximate to an optimum portfolio for a large number of holders. Even so, we judge that the Ecu cannot win the currency competition simply on the basis of its merits as a store of value. It can only do so if its transaction costs are lower, because it is widely used, than the costs of dealing in all the currencies that make up the basket.

In a quite different context, however, the fact that the Ecu is a currency basket could be its main attraction. We are thinking now of its wider use (in appropriate circumstances) as an intervention currency in foreign exchange markets. If, for example, the lira is under downward pressure against all European currencies, the Italian central bank must sell foreign currency to support it. If only Deutschmarks were sold, the intervention might pull the Deutschmark out of line with other EMS currencies. If the Banca d'Italia deals in the Ecu instead of the Deutschmark, then the balance of supply and demand as between other EMS currencies is much less disturbed. Similarly, if only one EMS currency is strong and all the others are broadly in line with one another, then the central bank with the strong currency could buy Ecu rather than any individual currency.

The issue is not confined to transactions among European currencies. In just the same way the use of the Deutschmark in world markets often threatens the stability of the EMS, (although less so as co-operation between central banks has developed). This is true of commercial or speculative transactions in Deutschmarks and also of transactions by central banks, including the Federal Reserve Bank of America. Moreover, when negotiations take place between the central banks of European countries, America and Japan, they could centre on the Ecu value of the dollar or the yen, not on the value of these currencies relative to the Deutschmark, the French franc or sterling. The more the international use of the Ecu develops (and the less the international use of the Deutschmark develops), the easier it will be to preserve the stability of the EMS.

It would be quite wrong to imagine that the private sector use of the Ecu, even in the next few years, should be confined to the EC countries themselves. On the contrary, the convenience of dealing in one European currency rather than twelve may be especially evident to traders in (say) Latin America, and increasingly now in eastern Europe. On a related point, much of commodity trade, worldwide and even in Europe, is denominated in dollars. It is possible that the Ecu would be a more convenient denomination to use at least for those commodities for which Europe is the main market. All these are developments which might be encouraged by the clear identification of the Ecu as the future single currency of Europe.

We have argued that unless some encouragement is given to the use of the Ecu, the next few years could see a wider international use of the Deutschmark, and also perhaps of sterling, the French franc and so on. This could make the conduct of monetary policy in each country more difficult. The Bank of England, for example, will need to worry more and more about the quantity of sterling held abroad and also about the quantity of foreign currency held in Britain. (The former is especially relevant to the control of interest rates and exchange rates, the latter to the control of monetary growth and domestic demand.)

The situation is in fact most difficult for the monetary authorities in the country whose currency 'wins' the competition. The Bundesbank, for example, would find it increasingly difficult to control the rate of interest on the Deutschmark, if its use became very widespread outside Germany. One way of looking at the wider use of the Ecu is to see it as an expansion of all its constituent currencies at the same pace. Thus the burden of greater capital mobility is spread more evenly around the central banks of Europe. It was suggested to us that wider use of the Ecu might for this reason be necessary in order to avoid unacceptable instability with the EMS in the next few years.

The fact that the Ecu is a currency basket makes it a useful focus for policy co-ordination. The central banks could, straightaway, set objectives for the Ecu interest rate or the Ecu price level (that is for an index of consumer prices in Europe using the weighting that defines the Ecu), which they would work together to achieve. The only way of achieving the objectives, by definition, would be by adjustment of the monetary policies of member states. The worth of the Ecu reflects both the collective decisions of the emergent European monetary authority and their implementation by individual central banks. These collective aims would be adopted in addition to, not instead of, the existing targets for price stability in each member state individually.

The Ecu, as a currency basket, is affected by the behaviour of all its constituent currencies. If even one currency becomes very weak, the Ecu must necessarily become at least a little weak relative to the others. It is necessary therefore to the successful development of the Ecu that convergence and policy co-ordination take place throughout the Community.

The case for using the Ecu as a focus for policy co-ordination stands in its own right, independently of the private sector Ecu market and its development. But, of course, the two uses of the Ecu would reinforce one another, and work together towards the closer integration of European financial markets. If central banks were trading actively in the Ecu, the commercial banks would have the incentive to develop their own Ecu business.

To start with, the supply and demand for Ecu could be a long way out of line. If that happens, of course, the value of the Ecu relative to its constituent currencies and its relative rate of interest cannot change by definition. The banks must be active in 'bundling' or 'unbundling' the constituents of the Ecu to suit the needs of their customers. The more active the markets in Ecu, the less need for these activities – and hence the lower the costs of transacting business in Ecu.

5.4 The implications for monetary control

The macroeconomic background to any discussion of the wider use of the Ecu in the private sector is a very real concern that this development could threaten price stability. Some of the administrative obstacles to the wider use of the Ecu are there because monetary authorities do not wish to encourage it. The underlying obstacle is their fear of its inflationary effect.

After EMU is complete the monetary policy of Europe will be determined by the European monetary authorities. The setting up of new central banking institutions is already under active discussion. The most likely outcome seems to be a federal system, enjoying a high degree of independence, and committed by its terms of reference to the maintenance of price stability. Once it is under the management of this system therefore, the Ecu, as the single currency of Europe, stands a good chance of being a 'strong' currency, at least as strong as the Deutschmark is now. The more open questions concern its characteristics in the period of transition.

As a basket currency, the Ecu reflects its constituent parts. The Ecu rate of inflation is the weighted average of the rates of inflation in the member states. As a matter of arithmetic, it is lower than the rate in the high-inflation countries and higher than that in the low-inflation countries. The only way to make the Ecu a 'strong' currency is to make its constituent parts stronger. Unless there is the political will to make this happen, it is difficult to see how EMU itself can ever take place.

This fundamental issue should not be confused with the very different question of the effect that wider use of the Ecu might have on inflation measured in terms of domestic currency. Is the Ecu really a sort of Trojan Horse? If Germans, for example, started using the Ecu more than they do now, would that in some way undermine the strength of the Deutschmark, or the ability of the Bundesbank to underwrite price stability in Germany? There is no reason why these fears need be justified. The Bundesbank would retain sole charge of the supply of the Deutschmark. If the German price level began to rise, the Bundesbank could raise interest rates on the Deutschmark and restrict its supply. If need be, until exchange rates are irrevocably fixed, the Deutschmark could be increased in value relative to other European currencies. In fact the wider use of the Ecu, as such, does nothing at all to undermine price stability anywhere in Europe.

It is well known that the lifting of international controls on capital movements makes the measurement of consistent series for monetary aggregates more difficult. The fact that French people can now hold sterling or US dollar deposits does shift the demand for 'money' in France. Similarly, the closer integration of financial markets within Europe, however it takes place, will make it more difficult to monitor monetary statistics in any member state. The wider international use of the Ecu, as against the wider international use of say the Deutschmark, the French franc or sterling, does not alter this unavoidable consequence of financial liberalization.

During the transition to EMU, more emphasis will have to be placed on direct measures of inflation or inflationary pressure, less on traditional monetary aggregates. This may suggest to European central bankers that they should err on the side of caution in setting interest rates and exchange rates. It does not mean that they need be content with anything less than price stability if that is their aim.

5.5 Macroeconomic convergence

The time-scale over which it is realistic to expect EMU to be achieved depends in part on political developments, the enthusiasm with which the goal is pursued and the support won for it in member states. But the time-scale must also reflect the degree of macroeconomic convergence between member states, and the progress towards price stability. The formation of EMU is itself, of course, a powerful force for convergence, but the 'glue' of monetary union will not be powerful enough to hold the component parts together if their inherent tendency to spring apart is still too strong. We need therefore to examine some alternative projections for macroeconomic conditions in Europe in the 1990s before hazarding a view as to what a realistic timetable for EMU might be.

The NIESR's *Economic Review*, published at the end of February 1990, includes projections to 1999 for France, West Germany, Italy, the UK and the Benelux countries. These forecasts take account of the dramatic political developments in eastern Europe during 1989 and at the beginning of this year, but inevitably the full consequences for Germany in particular remain very uncertain. We do not believe, however, that these uncertainties are themselves a reason for delaying the transition to EMU. Neither do they invalidate attempts to foresee the general course of events in the economies of the EC over the next ten years.

The forecasts show the growth of output in the world economy slowing over the next few years compared with the rapid growth of 1988 and 1989. Germany grows by about 3 per cent a year in 1990-92, slowing to 2.7 per cent a year in 1993-5 and 2.4 per cent a year in 1996-9. The outlook for growth in France is rather slower at about 2.5 per cent a year throughout the 1990s, whilst in Italy there may be some acceleration from about 2.5 per cent this year to 3 per cent a year later in the decade. The position of the United Kingdom is more difficult, as the need to reduce inflation and the external deficit is expected to limit the growth rate to just 1.5 per cent a year.

The outlook for inflation is crucial to the time-scale for EMU. In 1989 the rates of consumer price increase were about 3.5 per cent in Germany and in France, but 5 or 6 per cent in Italy and the UK. There is little prospect of convergence in underlying inflation rates in 1990. Looking ahead to 1991 the prospects for slower inflation in Italy are good, but progress is likely to be slower in the UK. Some have argued that inflation will be faster in West Germany as a result of unification with East Germany. This view may well underestimate the determination of the Bundesbank, and it is not adopted in the Institute's forecasts.

It is likely that some further exchange rate realignments will take place in the 1990s if the 'rules of the game' for the EMS remain as they have been in the 1980s. The interest rate differentials between member countries appear to be consistent with this expectation. In forecasting, the Institute has assumed that the franc depreciates on average by about 1 per cent a year and the lira by 2 or 3 per cent a year relative to the Deutschmark. The pound sterling is assumed to join the exchange rate mechanism around the end of 1990, but to realign within the system, keeping broadly in line with the lira.

Taking this forecast together with the known risk attached to it, we conclude that:

- There will be a progressive convergence of inflation rates and interest rates within the EC over the next ten years;
- Belgium, Luxembourg and The Netherlands (and perhaps Denmark) have already reached the point where monetary union with West Germany is feasible;
- That group could be joined by France within the next few years, although there may be a continuing small inflation rate differential;
- The problems for Italy are more severe and some further structural adjustment would be required as well as a tight monetary policy to achieve adequate convergence by the mid-1990s;
- The UK is a special case because it is not yet even a member of the ERM and because, even if it joined the ERM by the end of this year, convergence would still be relatively slow; and
- In the absence of further policy initiatives it would be difficult to achieve EMU for the whole EC even by the end of the decade.

5.6 Alternative strategies for macroeconomic convergence

There is a real danger that steps towards EMU may falter in the course of the 1990s if progress towards macroeconomic convergence is slow. In these circumstances, the European system of central banks could achieve no more than the existing EMCF, and the current initiative for EMU could wane, as did that which followed the Werner Report 20 years ago. We have briefly considered four alternative policy options.

Alternative A: Greater exchange rate flexibility
Concern has been expressed that the freeing of capital markets and the development of a single market in financial services will make the EMS in its present form unstable. One response would be to allow more exchange rate flexibility during an initial period, either by widening margins or by allowing larger and more frequent realignments. As a way of managing the existing EMS this idea could have some appeal, but as a step on the way to EMU it is unattractive. It would make the commitment to price stability weaker in those countries which allowed their currencies to depreciate. It would delay the process of macroeconomic convergence.

Alternative B: Currency competition
The Delors Committee proposals have been characterized as institutionally driven, rather than market driven. A quite different route to monetary union would rely on free mobility of capital and the natural forces of competition to create a spontaneous movement towards a common, or even a single, currency. This is the route described by the UK Treasury in its response to the Delors Report. As we have argued earlier, the most likely outcome of a purely market-driven approach would be the more widespread international use of existing currencies, especially the Deutschmark, but perhaps also the US dollar, the French franc and sterling. The Ecu is unlikely to win such a competition because it has no 'home base' on which to build. We would prefer a system which is led by institutional change, in a way which harnesses market forces to assist the transition. It is by no means clear that the proposals of the UK Treasury would ever result in monetary union, nor indeed that they were framed with that end in view.

Alternative C: Forcing the pace of change
The gains from a single currency arise after the period of transition is complete. It is tempting therefore to move straight to that point as quickly as the administrative changes can be made. A simulation study,

using the National Institute's model *GEM*, shows that the successful implementation of monetary union in 1991 would result in the convergence of inflation rates at an average of only 2.25 per cent, but it is doubtful whether the costs of this convergence are manageable in economic or political terms. To keep domestic demand under control as nominal interest rates come down, fiscal policy would have to be tightened sharply (by tax increases or public spending cuts) in France, Italy and the UK. The scale of imbalance on the current account of the balance of payments as international competitiveness deteriorates would be an additional worry, especially in the case of the UK. We conclude that forcing the pace in this way is too risky an alternative to recommend, if all the major countries of the EC are to participate. We therefore turn to the last of our four alternatives.

Alternative D: A two-speed Europe

A general problem of integration is that its implementation often depends on the pace of the slowest country. In the case of the 1992 single market programme, the areas where full harmonization is required have been kept to a minimum. In the past the monetary arrangements of the EC have not required uniformity of behaviour. Not every country joined the 'snake' and some countries 'took congé'; not all countries are members of the ERM. It would certainly be easier to accelerate the timetable for EMU if some countries decided that they did not want to be part of it, at least to begin with. The political implications for the countries that are left out are clearly profound, but outside the remit of this report. It is worth emphasizing, however, that in both Italy and the UK, the countries most likely to delay the starting date for EMU, industry and financial institutions are rightly concerned that exclusions could be a competitive handicap. We assume that a timetable is adopted that gives all member states a realistic chance of joining EMU from the start, although we cannot be certain that in the event all of them would avail themselves of the opportunity. We believe that such a timetable would have to date EMU in the latter half of the 1990s.

5.7 The time for EMU and a single currency

The expectation of future policy developments can have a powerful effect on private sector behaviour, even in the short term. We have argued for the maximum of public announcement of aims and objectives with respect to EMU. The 1992 process provides a useful precedent. After many years of frustration, a clear decision to set a timetable has brought about change well beyond the expectation of most realists five or ten years ago. The focus on the year 1992 itself was in this case the key to the change in expectations. A similar sort of commitment to EMU now would make it more likely to happen, and also make the transition easier, because the ground would be better prepared.

There is evidence that membership of the existing EMS has helped the process of convergence in inflation rates, notably in France and in Italy. Confidence in the stability of exchange rates has been reinforced by the relative infrequency and small size of realignments in the last five years. It may also have been helped by the active discussion of EMU and the widespread political support for that objective in most member states. Convergence will be further helped by the ease of capital mobility in Europe, and the more widespread use of the Ecu.

In considering the transition period prior to the final fixing of exchange rates, we shall assume a timetable rather similar to that leading up to the single market of 1992. This involved an announcement in 1985, enactment in 1986 and completion by the end of 1992. A similar timescale for EMU might mean announcement in 1990, and completion by the end of 1997.

Once monetary union is complete, the existence of 12 domestic currencies is an unnecessary complication, serving no useful purpose. We would suppose therefore that the move to a single currency takes place at the same time as, or very soon after, the final fixing of exchange rates. If the parties to the monetary union are in earnest there is no reason for delay.

5.8 The transition to a single currency

It remains to consider the role of the Ecu in the later stages of the transition to EMU. We are looking now at the situation in or about 1996; exchange rates are not yet irrevocably fixed and narrow margins still exist around the agreed parities; the arrangements for co-ordinating fiscal and monetary policy are in place and the new central banking system has been set up; the 'count-down' to a single currency has begun.

Even at this stage the Ecu is still a currency basket, its exchange rate and interest rate determined by those of its component parts. Moreover, the Ecu is still (strictly speaking) outside the process of monetary creation – there is no 'high powered' Ecu monetary base, and Ecu deposits are (strictly speaking) 'inside' rather than 'outside' money. In other words the Ecu even then is not a 'thirteenth currency'. All this may be true, but we would emphasize that by then the Ecu may, and should, be playing a very important part in financial affairs in Europe.

Prior to EMU, the advantage of the Ecu over existing national currencies is in the conduct of international business. By the mid-1990s we would expect the Ecu to have a large share of the market for securities, bonds and wholesale bank deposits and to have taken over from the Deutschmark, the French franc and sterling much of their usage outside their home territories (in Europe and throughout the world). Ordinary household transactions and the payment of nearly all wages, however, would still be in national currencies. Until monetary union is imminent we would not seek to foster the use of the Ecu for purely domestic transactions. A protracted period in which the Ecu was used in this way, alongside national currencies, would be inefficient as a transactional arrangement, and perhaps unpopular.

Some time in the mid-1990s the pace of change could be accelerated. There might be a stage towards the end of the transition to EMU when it would be appropriate to allow the settlement of all contractual obligations in all member countries in Ecu, as well as in domestic currency. This corresponds to the British concept of 'legal tender' and would involve giving the Ecu privileges that are not enjoyed by other foreign currencies. From that point, the private use of the Ecu in domestic transactions could expand very rapidly. It would mean that anyone receiving payment in Ecu could avoid the costs of currency conversion, which would clearly make the Ecu much more acceptable than it had been before.

The infant central banking system of Europe might also decide to print Ecu bank notes (in small and judicious quantities), say a year prior to completion of EMU. The purpose would be simply to make the replacement of national currencies by the Ecu rather less of an upheaval when it came. Having some Ecu notes (or even coins) in circulation would make the new units familiar to all members of the public.

Then the final step would be taken, we suggest in or about 1997. The monetary union would be formed and at the same time the single currency would be introduced. All domestic currency and all contracts made in domestic currencies would be converted into Ecu, at the ruling exchange rates prior to EMU. From that point on, of course, there would be an Ecu money supply, and each country would have an Ecu-denominated monetary base – all firmly under the control of the new banking system.

In one sense then, the Ecu after 1997 is a different creature from the

Ecu we know today. In another sense, however, it is very important to emphasize the continuity between the two. The existence of private sector Ecu markets makes it possible to anticipate today some of the advantages of a monetary union. Moreover, contracts can now be made in Ecu which should carry over, with no alteration, into the units which will be universal in Europe, we assume, by the end of the decade. It would be possible, no doubt, to manage the transition to EMU without any private use of the Ecu at all before the event. However, the Ecu is already widely used, and it would seem perverse not to exploit its potential.

5.9 Conclusions

We have reviewed some alternative macroeconomic scenarios within which the private use of the Ecu might develop over the next five to ten years. It seems to us that the movement to EMU must be a gradual one, with political and economic considerations, not financial arrangements, dictating its pace. Nevertheless it is very important not to let financial arrangements set off spontaneously in a direction inappropriate to the objective of a single currency in Europe within this decade. In particular, the place of the Ecu must not be usurped by another currency, whatever the short-term temptations may be to let that happen. Moreover, we see a good case for immediately using the special character of the Ecu as a 'currency basket' as a medium for conducting foreign exchange intervention and as a means of setting co-ordinated objectives for monetary policy.

From this discussion we draw four main conclusions:

1. It is important to announce at the outset of the agreed progress to EMU that the Ecu is going to be the single currency that will be used at the end of the day.
2. The market should be familiarized with the use of the Ecu in the period of transition to EMU and the wider international use of the currencies of member states in any other form should be discouraged.
3. The use of the Ecu for 'retail' financial business within member states is not appropriate until the final stage of the transition. It is at that stage that it should be made universally acceptable under law in payment of any contract.

4. As soon as possible the time scale of the transition to EMU should be announced. We suggest that the process could be complete by about 1997. The message of the announcement would be reinforced if it was combined with some concrete steps to remove obstacles to the use of the Ecu. The Community institutions should also give a lead to the private use of the Ecu, by employing it more widely in their own transactions.

Part II
Foundations of the Ecu Strategy

6: Country Analyses of the Microeconomic Obstacles to the Private Use of the Ecu

6.1 Introduction

In this section we discuss the microeconomic obstacles to private sector use of the Ecu within each EC member state. The obstacles discussed are a reflection of desk research conducted by our national offices in the respective countries, the results of face-to-face interviews and the analysis of postal questionnaires from companies and banks. Our findings are organized, first, in the form of a summary of regulatory obstacles in the private use of the Ecu:

- Legal tender;
- Company law;
- Stock exchange regulation;
- Financial services legislation;
- Accounting standards;
- Tax, customs and excise duties;
- Central bank and banking systems.

Secondly, there is a summary of private sector perceived obstacles to use of the Ecu:

- Inertia;
- Lack of end uses;
- Currency status;
- Liquidity and availability;
- Strong/weak economies;
- Pockets of ignorance;
- Internal administration;
- Other legal.

Sections 6.3 – 6.14 then consider, for each EC member state (in alphabetical order), regulatory obstacles and perceived obstacles.

The summary of regulatory obstacles is intended as an overview and is not intended to represent a detailed analysis of national legislation. The primary emphasis of this section is to provide an understanding of firms' perceptions, in order to provide the basis for determining what is needed to alter their behaviour.

6.2 General overview

Throughout the survey it has been apparent that the main obstacle to further use of the Ecu by any individual company is the present lack of acceptability and general commercial use. This analysis is evidenced in Figure 11. We conclude that until the Ecu has strong, credible backing from the European Commission and the governments of the member states, the private use of the Ecu will remain marginal.

As is shown in Figure 12, obstacles linked to the Ecu's legal status were felt to be particularly discouraging to its extended use. Thus, over two-thirds of companies felt that as long as the Ecu's legal status was that of a foreign currency, it was difficult, if not impossible, for them to use it for settlement of domestic transactions, issuing share capital or for assessing and paying taxes.

As for banking factors (such as banking fees, comparative interest rates and the availability of Ecu accounts) and internal factors (such as administrative costs, accounting systems and level of knowledge), these were felt to have little impact on the attractiveness of the Ecu.

Respondents' attitudes to external factors (such as legal acceptability of the Ecu for contracts, level of present use of the Ecu, and level of public awareness) was ambiguous (see Figure 13): the sample was split into three equally sized groups, one of which considered that it was an encouragement, one an inhibitor and one group which believed that external factors had no effect.

It is interesting to note that the technical complexities associated with using the Ecu (such as fees, bid-offer rate and interest rate volatility) were felt to have little effect on its use by a comfortable majority of respondents.

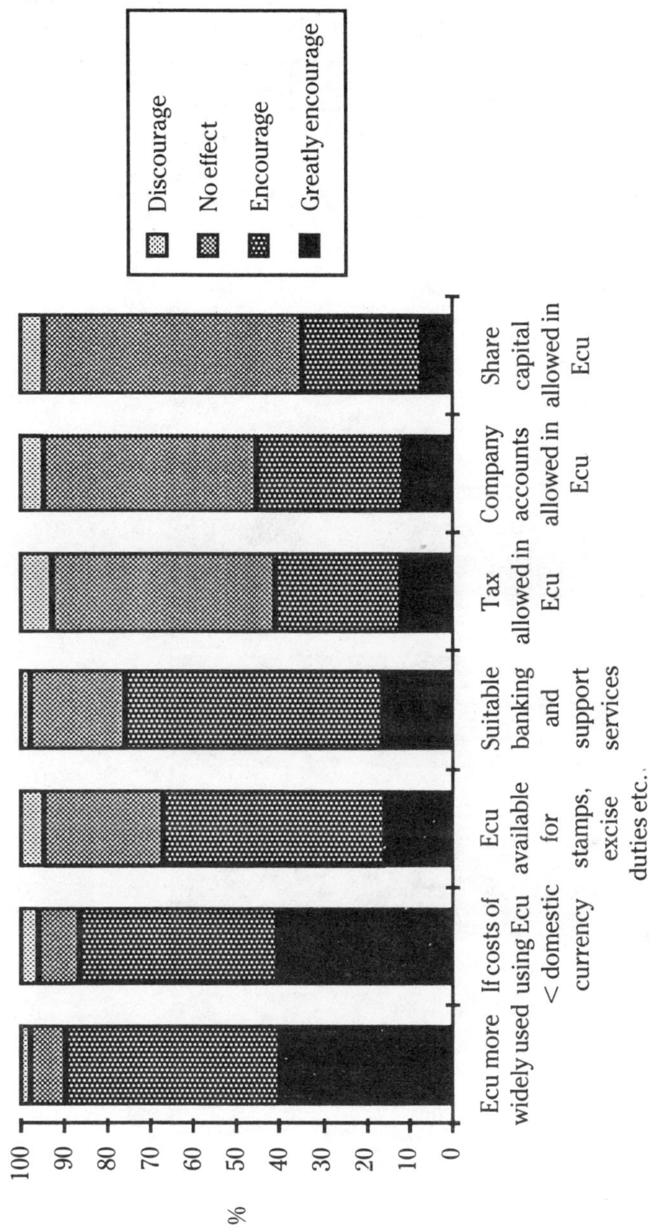

Figure 11: Which of the following categories would encourage your company to use the Ecu?

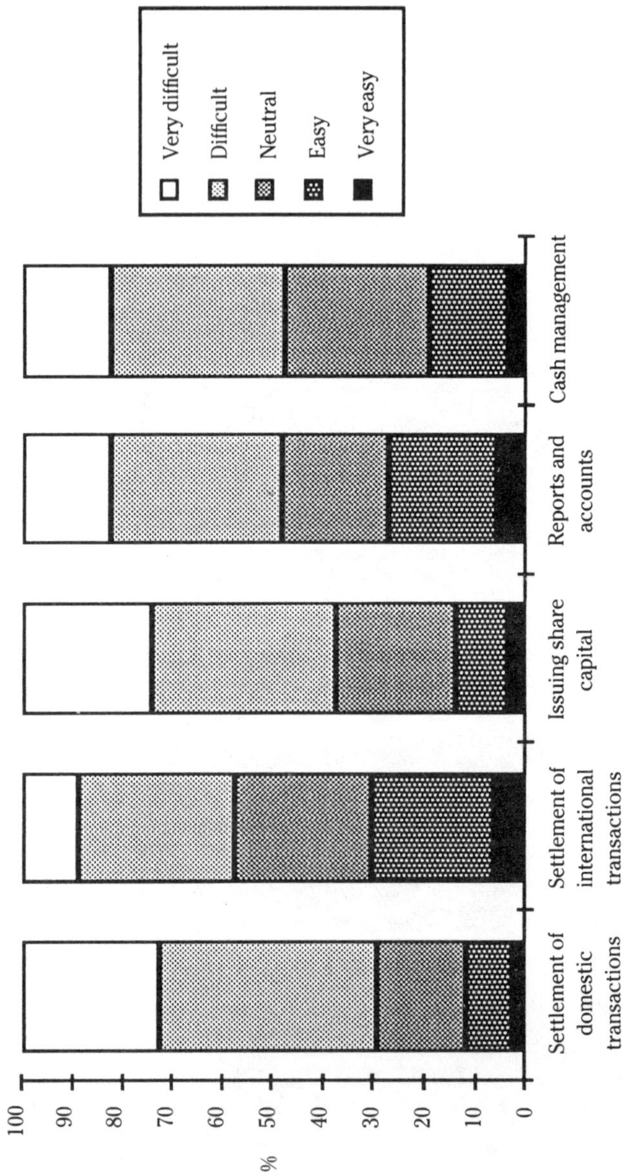

Figure 12: Considering the Ecu's present legal status, how easy is it for your company to use it for the following categories?

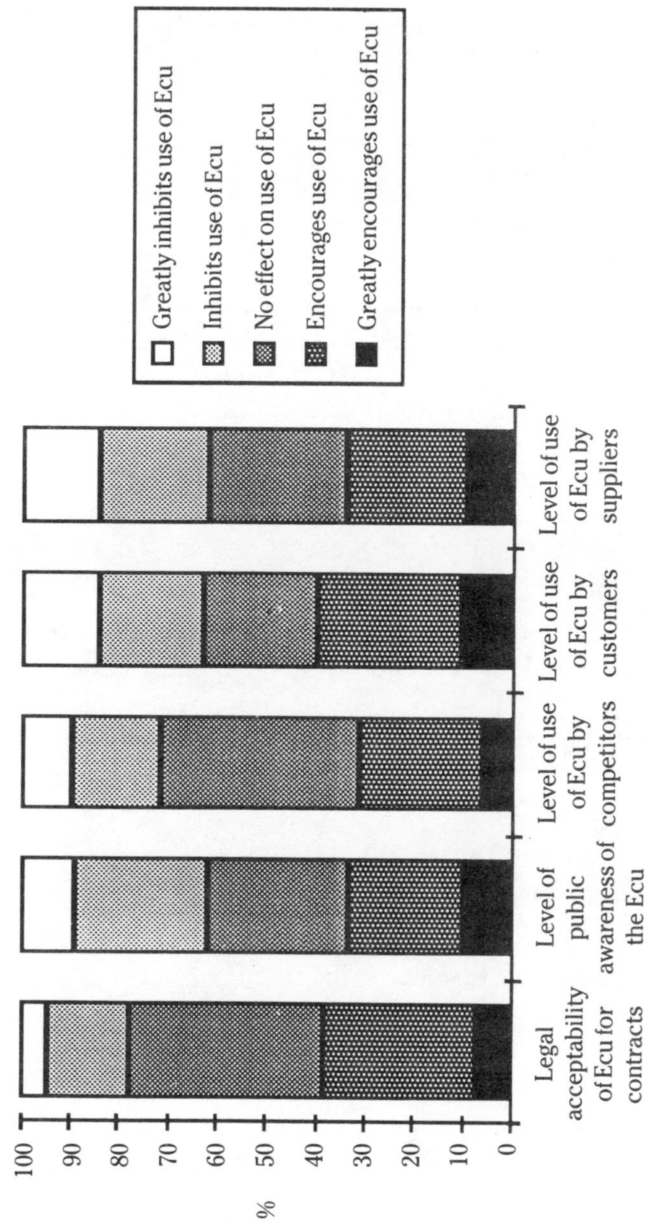

Figure 13: To what extent do the following factors encourage use of the Ecu?

6.3 Belgium

6.3.1 Regulatory obstacles to the private use of the Ecu

Legal tender

As a general rule, the Ecu has no status as legal tender in Belgium. It has foreign currency status, and it is possible to open Ecu accounts and to obtain Ecu loans in the same way as for any other foreign currency.

The exceptions are the gold and silver Ecus which were issued by the Belgian government in 1987 and 1989. These coins are legal tender, but were designed for investment or numismatic purposes.

Company law and stock exchange regulations

The share capital of companies incorporated in Belgium must be denominated in Belgian francs (Bfr). Shares are quoted on the Brussels stock exchange in Bfr.

Companies are allowed to issue guarantees in Ecu, to take out local insurance policies for foreign trade transactions in Ecu and to discount Ecu instruments with commercial banks

Accountancy standards

Companies are obliged to publish their accounts in Bfr. However, they may prepare a parallel set of accounts in Ecu for information purposes if they so wish.

For accounting purposes, transactions in Ecus are treated as for any other foreign currency.

Fiscal policy

All tax calculations and settlement in Belgium are denominated in Bfr. There are no exceptions to this rule.

Customs and excise treatment

Imports and exports can be cleared in customs against Ecu invoices, in the same way as against invoices prepared in any other foreign currency.

Banking system

The Belgian banking system is on the whole neutral towards the Ecu. Thus cheques in Ecu can be accepted by banks in certain circumstances, the charges on Ecu transactions are similar to those on other foreign currencies, the clearing system works efficiently and smoothly, and Belgian banks do provide information on Ecu products.

However, the central bank rediscounts only in Bfr, there is a lack of certain products such as FRNs' bonds with warrants, treasury paper and short-term instruments, and there are few end uses of the currency. Ecus are very rarely used as a transaction medium.

6.3.2 Perceived obstacles to the private use of the Ecu

Inertia

Wait and see

Belgian leaders appear to be financially conservative rather than innovative: they told us that they would wait for usage of the Ecu to reach a certain minimum level before they include it more systematically in their financial options. All of the companies responding to our questionnaire stated that they would be encouraged to use the Ecu more if it were widely used by all sections of commerce for day-to-day transactions.

Not all currencies in EMS

The Belgian private sector consulted in our survey perceived the Ecu as lacking credibility due to the fact that not all EMS currencies are part of the ERM and that certain currencies have wider margins. They were consequently not convinced that the Ecu offers valid and reliable cover against exchange and interest rate risks.

Political nature

It is also quite clear that a number of respondents felt that the Ecu is purely a political symbol which holds little real value for profit-orientated companies. This was borne out by the high level of responses indicating that employment of the Ecu was mainly useful for furthering European union.

Furthermore, it was felt that there was a lack of official encouragement for the Ecu, (the government does not accept Ecu, payments between governmental supranational bodies are not conducted in Ecu, etc.) which further detracted from its credibility.

Habit

Cultural and national habits were found to be a major inhibitor to development of a new currency.

Although the US dollar and the Deutschmark are still the most used foreign currencies in Belgium, there is a generally positive attitude towards further development of the private Ecu. Thus Belgium is the only country which has gone through the highly symbolic act of issuing Ecu coins.

US stake in economy

Many Belgian companies are affiliates or branches of US companies. In a large number of cases, financial policies are initiated by central management in the US and therefore local management does not have the opportunity to use the Ecu or influence central management on this issue.

Lack of end uses

Limited Ecu circuit

Companies responding to our survey stated that they were not keen to use the Ecu because of its limited end usage. For example, almost half of the questionnaire respondents stated, that customers' and suppliers' use of the Ecu currently inhibited their own use of the Ecu for invoicing, whilst almost all stated that the quotation of raw materials and commodities in Ecu on world markets would encourage them to use the Ecu for invoicing.

Currency status and liquidity and availability

No lender of last resort

Our respondents identified uncertainty caused by the absence of a lender of last resort.

Lack of a European central bank

The combined results of questionnaires and desk research showed that the lack of central bank backing for the Ecu is considered to be a major obstacle to its wider use in transactions.

Ecu basket

The basket nature of the Ecu and the fact that it does not exist as a tangible currency unit was perceived to detract from its credibility, and hence to inhibit its use.

Illiquid Ecu market

The lack of Ecu products and end uses both causes and reflects the lack of liquidity of the market and its lack of sophistication. It was felt that other currencies such as the US dollar, yen, sterling or the Deutschmark offered a wider variety of instruments, maturities and yields than the Ecu. The market was not considered to be sufficiently liquid for large capital flows, such as those demanded by Japanese institutions.

The technical difficulties and uncertainties linked to bundling and unbundling, and the nature of private Ecus contribute further to the market's lack of liquidity, especially when compared to the relative technical ease of using other international currencies.

Strong/weak economies

Hegemony of the US dollar

The hegemony of the US dollar in world currency trade was regarded as a major factor inhibiting use of the Ecu in Belgium: in comparison, the Ecu was perceived as lacking in international prestige.

Strength of the Deutschmark

Our survey revealed that companies trading internationally preferred to fund in Deutschmark rather than Ecu, because the Deutschmark interest rate was lower than the Ecu interest rate; the Deutschmark also had a more stable exchange rate against the Belgian franc.

Pockets of ignorance

Lack of clear information and understanding of pros and cons

We found that awareness and understanding of the Ecu was still quite limited in the Belgian business community. The existing information was considered to be excessively academic and theoretical and the practical motivations for using the Ecu were rarely made clear. Over one third of the companies responding to our questionnaire stated that the current level of knowledge of the Ecu in their purchasing departments inhibited its use.

Internal administration

Administrative costs of using Ecu

Roughly one-half of companies responding to our survey stated that internal administrative costs currently inhibit the use of the Ecu.

Use of Ecu for procurement/purchasing

Approximately one-third of Belgian companies responding to our questionnaire had been discouraged by the extent to which administration of a purchasing transaction was complicated by the use of the Ecu as a source of procurement/purchasing.

Other legal

Perceived limitations of the Ecu's legal status

A large majority of Belgian companies responding to our questionnaire stated that the Ecu's current legal status made it difficult/very difficult to use the Ecu in settlement of domestic transactions, to issue share capital, to assess and pay taxes or for cash management purposes.

Ability to impose Ecu as means of payment

Almost 50 per cent of Belgian company respondents also stated that their inability to impose the Ecu as a means of payment had, in the past, discouraged their use of the Ecu for invoicing.

6.4 Denmark

6.4.1 Regulatory obstacles to the private use of the Ecu

Legal tender

The Ecu has foreign currency status in Denmark, but is not legal tender.

Company law

Share capital in Danish companies must be denominated in Danish krone (Dkr). However, there are no restrictions on raising long-term debt in Ecu, using other Ecu-denominated financial instruments, or holding short-term Ecu accounts.

Stock exchange regulation

The market value of Danish stocks and shares is quoted in Dkr, although it is permissible to make a joint quotation in Ecu.

Some Danish government bonds are registered in Ecu.

Accounting standards

All financial and accounting statements must be published in Dkr, although a parallel statement in Ecu is permissible.

Tax, customs and excise duties

For assessment and settlement of tax, customs and excise duties, the Ecu is treated as a foreign currency.

Central bank and banking systems

There are no specific regulations regarding clearing of the Ecu; it is dealt with in the same way as all other currencies.

6.4.2 Perceived obstacles to the private use of the Ecu

Inertia

Low level of use

There was an overwhelming response from companies indicating that they would be greatly encouraged to use the Ecu if their customers, suppliers and competitors used the Ecu for day-to-day transactions.

Almost all company respondents said that if the Ecu were more widely used by customers they would be encouraged to use it more frequently, whilst *all* respondents said they would be encouraged if the Ecu were more widely used by all sections of commerce for day-to-day transactions.

Lack of end uses

Quotation of raw materials

The vast majority of companies participating in our survey stated that they would be encouraged to use the Ecu for invoicing if raw materials and commodities were quoted in Ecu world markets.

Liquidity and availability

More than three-quarters of companies responding to our questionnaire stated that the availability of efficient current account banking in Ecu would encourage its use.

Strong/weak economies

Dkr's lack of bargaining power

Danish companies felt that they were obliged to accept contracting parties' currency settlement requirements in order to win their order/contract, because the Dkr is not a major or prevalent currency in international markets.

Ecu too volatile

Companies said they would use the Ecu more if its interest rate and exchange rates were attractive compared to other EC currencies and stable over a long period. For example, almost all company respondents stated that they would use the Ecu more for funding in the future if the Ecu interest rate was lower than the domestic rate, and a similar number said they would be encouraged to do so if the Ecu interest rate were less volatile than other rates.

The thought was also expressed that interest rate differences between individual EC countries need to be reduced.

Pockets of ignorance

Corporate ignorance

Companies responding to our questionnaire felt that there was a lack of knowledge and a lack of background material available about the Ecu. Most companies had not evaluated the pros and cons of using the Ecu because they lacked information and only conducted a small amount of transactions in Ecu.

Other legal

Perceived limitations of the Ecu's legal status

Over half of the Danish companies responding to our questionnaire stated that the current legal status of the Ecu made it difficult for them to use it for cash management.

A large majority of Danish company respondents also stated that the Ecu's current legal status made it difficult/very difficult for them to settle domestic transactions in Ecu, issue share capital in Ecu, assess tax liability in Ecu or pay taxes in Ecu. The tax-related obstacles were perceived to be the most difficult to overcome.

6.5 Federal Republic of Germany

6.5.1 Regulatory Obstacles to the private use of the Ecu

Legal tender

The Ecu has had foreign currency status in the Federal Republic since 1987, when some restrictions on its use, including exchange controls, were lifted. Further restrictions were removed in January 1990, enabling long-term loans to be raised and bonds to be issued in Ecu without prior Bundesbank approval. A number of short term Ecu instruments are now also available.

Company law

Shares in West German companies may not be denominated in Ecu.

Companies may now raise long-term debts in Ecu, use other Ecu-denominated financial instruments and hold short-term Ecu accounts.

Stock exchange regulation

The *Handelsgesetzbuch* stipulates that German companies must report their annual results in the German language and in Deutschmarks. An additional set of results may be issued in Ecu.

Financial services legislation

Any special requirements with respect to holding or trading Ecu products have now been abolished.

Tax customs and excise duties

The Ecu is treated as any other foreign currency with respect to tax, customs and excise duties.

Central bank and banking system

Three large banks in West Germany are clearing banks for Ecu products. These are the Deutsche Bank, Dresdner Bank, and Commerzbank.

Some smaller banks do not use the three main German clearing banks for Ecu clearing, but use foreign banks with whom they have a commercial relationship.

6.5.2 Perceived obstacles to the private use of the Ecu

Inertia

Competitive advantage sought

The consideration of competitive advantage featured strongly among our respondents as a motivational factor for the initiation of corporate change and investment.

Neither banks nor companies were willing to increase their use of the Ecu or invest in systems and training to facilitate its greater use unless the same course had been adopted by their competitors, clients and suppliers. Since companies are familiar with dealing in many currencies and possess advanced technology and expertise in this area, a move to use of the Ecu as a thirteenth currency would present no problems, but conversely would offer no financial gain.

Of those companies who responded to our postal survey, 90 per cent expressed the view that if Ecu purchasing provided a competitive advantage they would be encouraged to use the Ecu in future. All of the banks consulted felt that if their customers perceived the Ecu as a competitive product, use of the Ecu would be greatly stimulated.

Centralization

Questionnaire response demonstrated that almost two-thirds of those questioned would be encouraged to increase their use of the Ecu if a strategic decision to do so was taken by central management. (This was a response factor peculiar to the Federal Republic and The Netherlands: in other countries it did not feature as a decisive factor.)

Low level of use

At present, Ecu balances held within the banking system in West Germany account for less than one per cent of total balances. Over two-thirds of companies responding to our questionnaire stated that they had not considered using the Ecu, whilst the vast majority had never used the Ecu for a range of functions listed.

This obstacle presents a *Catch 22* situation. Both banks and companies say they would use the Ecu more if those around them did, but nobody was willing to make the first move. Our survey results suggest however, that once use becomes widespread, the current trickle of Ecu transactions could become a flood. Of those companies responding to our questionnaire, 70 per cent said that if the Ecu were widely used by all sections of commerce, then they would be encouraged to use it too, and most banks stated that increased customer use of the Ecu was an incentive to them to offer more Ecu products.

It is encouraging to note that half of the banks consulted foresaw 'rapid growth' for Ecu bond products and two-thirds were actively planning to develop long-term loans and swaps in Ecu.

Lack of end uses

Raw materials quoted in Ecu

Over 60 per cent of those companies responding to our postal survey stated that if raw materials were quoted in Ecu on the world markets, then they would be encouraged to use the Ecu for invoicing.

Currency status

European central bank

Three-quarters of the banks replying to our questionnaire stated that the creation of a European central bank would greatly encourage the use of Ecu instruments.

Lender of last resort

Half of the banks consulted stated that the absence of a lender of last resort inhibits them from offering Ecu-denominated products.

Strong/weak economies

Strength and dominance of the Deutschmark on international markets

The nature of the Deutschmark was perceived by our respondents to present an obstacle in two ways: firstly because its bargaining strength within the EC reinforces its acceptance and, secondly, because it negates any financial incentive for use of the Ecu.

The strength of the West German economy and the fact that the Deutschmark is the strongest currency in the Ecu basket discourages use of the Ecu, because German companies are in a position to insist that international transactions are denominated in Deutschmarks. This argument has been borne out not only by the stated preference of West German companies for billing subsidiaries and clients in Deutschmarks and conducting their purchasing in Deutschmarks, but also by the comments made by companies in countries with less dominant currencies to the effect that they would settle in the currency preferred by their client because they are aware that their currency offers them no bargaining leverage.

The strength of the Deutschmark also means that Ecu interest and exchange rates are insufficiently attractive to the German private sector. In its present form, the Ecu will never be as strong as the strongest currency within the Ecu basket. Of the respondents to our survey, 70 per cent stated that if Ecu interest rates were lower than all other interest rates, they would be encouraged to use it. Furthermore, almost two-thirds of questionnaire respondents stated that Ecu weakness compared to the strength of the Deutschmark had discouraged their use of the Ecu in the past.

Pockets of ignorance

Corporate ignorance and lack of relevant skills

The majority of companies responding to our survey had not analyzed the costs associated with handling several European currencies, had not considered using the Ecu and had never used the Ecu for a variety of purposes. Almost two-thirds of companies stated that the presence of the necessary skills within their organization would encourage use of the Ecu.

Large- and medium-sized banks sensed the need to raise awareness of the Ecu and one bank told us that attempts to launch Ecu products had failed because of corporate ignorance. The banks themselves felt that their level of knowledge of the Ecu was more than adequate to cope with customer demands and enquiries regarding Ecu-based products.

Internal administration

Cost

The companies consulted in our survey expressed the view that there was no advantage to themselves in using the Ecu, since its foreign currency status meant that bank transaction fees were higher for the Ecu than for the Deutschmark. Almost all West German respondents to our questionnaire stated that if the cost of using the Ecu were lower than the cost of using their domestic currency, they would be encouraged to use it. More specifically, two-thirds of respondents said that a decrease in banking fees for foreign exchange in Ecu would encourage their use of the Ecu, while the same proportion stated that a decrease in banking fees for Ecu transfers would encourage use.

Ease of transition

A significant minority of around one-third of West German company respondents felt that use of the Ecu inhibited or greatly inhibited the difficulty of making internal changes.

Current accounting systems

Almost 50 per cent of West German companies replying to our questionnaire stated that their current accounting systems inhibited use of the Ecu.

Other legal

Perceived limitations of the Ecu's legal status

In response to a question on ease of use of the Ecu with regard to its legal status, a substantial majority of West German companies stated that they found it difficult to use the Ecu for:

- Settlement of domestic transactions;
- Issuing share capital;
- Assessing tax liability;
- Paying tax; and
- Publishing reports and accounts.

6.6 France

6.6.1 Regulatory obstacles to the private use of the Ecu

Legal tender

Transactions between companies on French soil must be executed in French francs. However, if both parties agree, a transaction can be made in Ecus.

The Ecu has the same status as any other foreign currency. It can be used as a means of payment in dealings with non-resident companies subject to the same constraints as other currencies.

Company law

French companies have to use French franc-denominated share capital. They cannot use the Ecu or any other foreign currency as part of their capital requirements.

However, French companies can use Ecus for issuing *titres participatifs* (quasi-equity funds). Since June 1989 it has also been possible for French companies to issue commercial paper in Ecus or US dollars.

Stock exchange regulations

There are no particular restrictions on the types of financial instruments available in Ecu. The products available in Ecu at the moment are comparable to those which can be denominated in other currencies (most types of short- to long-term bonds, convertible bonds, variable- and fixed-interest instruments).

Financial services legislation

There are no special conditions or constraints on the use of the Ecu. Operations in Ecu are treated by banks in much the same way as operations in other currencies.

Fiscal and accounting standards

According to present legislation, French companies' accounts must be published in French francs. It is, however, possible to publish consolidated accounts in Ecus or hold an internal parallel set of accounts in Ecus. Neither of these possibilities is ideal because both cause problems in choosing the appropriate exchange rate for conversion into francs.

For both fiscal and accounting purposes the Ecu is treated in the same way as other foreign currencies.

Central bank and banking system

The Bank of France is very active in its support for the development of the private Ecu. The private Ecu is a listed currency and the Bank of France participates in the market.

French banks are also very interested in the Ecu and Paribas, for example, is the world's most active lead manager of Ecu bond issues.

6.6.2 Perceived obstacles to the private use of the Ecu

Inertia

Anticipated EMU changes

A number of companies interviewed felt that recent progress towards EMU might actually be restraining development of the Ecu, as the private sector may be waiting for oncoming changes before doing anything.

No profit from Ecu use

Most big companies, which have their own foreign exchange risk department and dealing rooms, feel that they are capable of managing multi-currency exchange risks, and can add to profit from currency management. However, they do not see the Ecu as a useful currency in this respect.

It was also felt that billing in Ecu implies exchange and transaction costs for both buyer and seller which is not the case if a domestic currency is used.

Less support for Ecu at grass roots

Although the French banking system generally takes a positive stance in favour of the Ecu, our survey revealed that senior level government and banking support for the Ecu has not yet reached trading floor and branch level staff.

Lack of end uses

Lack of final users

The lack of final uses of the Ecu was a major problem encountered by our respondents. This means that most Ecu-denominated operations are usually associated with a swap into some other usable currency.

With very few exceptions, the Ecu was rarely used as an internal invoicing currency. It was felt that if two subsidiaries invoiced each other in Ecus there would be a double exchange risk. In our survey, almost 90 per cent of the companies involved stated that the level of their suppliers' use of the Ecu had discouraged them from using the Ecu for invoicing.

The Ecu was perceived to be useful to small- and medium-sized enterprises (SMEs) as a cheap, not too complex intra-European exchange risk management tool.

Lack of liquidity and availability

Lack of liquidity

The lack of Ecu liquidity and the absence of a real commercial- and transaction-based foundation for the Ecu was cited as one of the most important obstacles to its development.

Pockets of ignorance

Ignorance of pros and cons of Ecu

There was clearly very little understanding or awareness of the advantages and disadvantages of the private Ecu among French companies consulted.

Internal administration

Administration costs

Three-quarters of the French companies responding to our questionnaire stated that the administrative cost of using the Ecu currently inhibits or greatly inhibits their use of it.

Other legal

Perceived limitations of the Ecu's legal status

A large majority of French companies consulted in our survey expressed the view that the current legal status of the Ecu made it difficult/very difficult for them to:

- Use the Ecu to settle domestic transactions;
- Settle international transactions in Ecu;
- Issue share capital in Ecu;
- Assess tax liability in Ecu;
- Pay taxes in Ecu.

The strongest negative response emerged with regard to the difficulty of assessing tax liability.

6.7 Greece

6.7.1 Regulatory obstacles to the private use of the Ecu

Legal tender
The Ecu has foreign currency status. It is freely convertible into drachma and is accepted as a deposit currency account in major financial institutions operating in Greece.

Company law
Companies incorporated in Greece are obliged to denominate their share capital in drachmas. Companies operating in Greece may raise long-term finance in Ecu and they may hold chequing accounts in Ecu of up to 10 per cent of the value of their exports.

Stock exchange regulation
Shares of companies listed on the stock exchange are denominated only in drachmas.

Financial services legislation
It is not permissible under present Greek law to use the Ecu for swaps, options, futures or LIFFE contracts.

Since entering the EC, the country has liberalized its capital operations, especially regarding the free purchase of Greek securities by EC countries and nationals, but it will not lift capital controls until 1994–5.

Accountancy standards
Annual accounts must be published in drachmas but there is no restriction on publishing them in Ecu as well.

Tax, customs and excise duties
The Ecu is treated as any other foreign currency.

Central bank/public authorities
The government has issued Ecu-linked bonds on the stock market.

Banking system
There is at present no Ecu clearing system in Greece. Although the current low level of Ecu usage is such that the lack of a clearing system does not present a hindrance or additional cost to its use, if volumes were to increase, this would become a major obstacle.

Financial products such as options, futures, LIFFE contracts and swaps are still not available in Greece.

6.7.2 Perceived obstacles to the private use of the Ecu

Inertia

Low level of use
None of the Greek companies who participated in our survey had ever used the Ecu for sales or purchasing outside the EC, management accounting, investment appraisal or inter-company transactions. Only 5 per cent of respondents had used the Ecu for raising funds and sales and purchasing within the EC, while 16 per cent had used the Ecu for investment purposes. All of the Greek companies responding to our questionnaire stated that they would be encouraged to increase their use of the Ecu if it were more widely used.

The current low level of use of the Ecu means that when Ecu deposits are accepted by banks, the entry value threshold is much higher than it would be with other, more extensively-used currencies such as the US dollar.

Habit of using other currencies
From research, we identified that overseas traders have dealt in US dollars, sterling and Deutschmarks. Such habits are hard to change.

Companies dealing internationally and in raw materials had a history of dealing in the US dollar and perceived that this practice would be very difficult to change. Others stated that they preferred the stability and *acceptability* of the Deutschmark as opposed to the Ecu and that they generally used the former for intra-European transactions.

Wait for official backing of the Ecu
Greek companies appear to be waiting for an authority guaranteeing and promoting the Ecu. They told us they had neither the knowledge,

confidence in the Ecu nor the influence to be proactive in encouraging its use. The private sector respondents would first look to their competitors and react to customers' demands, rather than pre-empting them.

We were told that companies normally look for specific financial incentives from the government before undertaking change which has no first-mover advantage.

Centralization

For subsidiaries, the decision of the parent company was felt to be important in encouraging/discouraging use of the Ecu. Almost 80 per cent of company respondents, for example, stated that a central management decision to use the Ecu would encourage them to use it in procurement transactions. A high degree of centralization currently persists within the Greek economy.

Strong/weak economies

Greater influence of Greek trading partners

The Ecu was not yet accepted and used by the trading partners of Greek companies surveyed. As the majority of Greek firms are small, they have little bargaining power. They are also highly dependent upon imports.

Pockets of ignorance

Domestic nature of business/high number of SMEs

The companies in Greece are mostly small- and medium-sized enterprises (family concerns). Many had not considered using the Ecu (three-quarters of those companies responding to our questionnaire had not done so) and were unable to address the issue of estimating the costs of doing so. Generally they did not have a specialized treasury function and those which had used the Ecu for financial investment tended to be those with foreign parent companies.

There was an overall lack of awareness as to the function of the Ecu and its potential benefits among our respondents; in particular there was ignorance as to what is available and permissible in Greece regarding use of the Ecu and its products. Companies noted a lack of skills within their organization to deal competently with the Ecu.

For example, there was a great deal of ignorance as to the use of the Ecu as a source of finance and financial investment. An illustration of this is the case of a Greek company which wanted to take out a currency loan: it did not consider the Ecu, neither was it offered such a loan by banks, despite the fact that it wanted to use a stable currency. The company accepted that the Ecu should have been a prime currency to consider because of its stability but dismissed the possibility on the grounds that such a facility was not yet available in Greece. The company was surprised to hear that it was both available and legal.

One bank did actually want to introduce the use of the Ecu in Greece but found public awareness to be almost zero.

With the weakness of the drachma and lack of sophistication regarding treasury functions within Greek companies, it could be expected that the Ecu should be an obvious choice as an investment currency. In fact, the government's Ecu bonds offer the highest interest rate yield in Athens at the moment. The latest issue pays interest at the rate of 12 per cent a year, compared with 10.5 per cent yielded by Ecu bonds issued by other European governments.

Lack of information from banks

A lack of suitable banking and support services for the Ecu was noted by companies participating in our survey.

Internal administration

Transaction cost

The administrative cost of using the Ecu for no apparent benefit was perceived as a further obstacle to its use.

Current accounting systems

One-third of Greek companies participating in our survey stated that their current accounting systems inhibit/greatly inhibit their use of the Ecu.

Other legal

Perceived limitations of the Ecu's legal status

Half of the Greek company respondents stated that the current legal status of the Ecu made it difficult/very difficult to them to assess and pay tax in Ecu.

Legal acceptability of the Ecu for contracts.

Almost 50 per cent added that the current lack of legal acceptability of the Ecu for contracts inhibits/greatly inhibits them from using it.

6.8 Ireland

6.8.1 Regulatory obstacles to the private use of the Ecu

Legal tender

The Ecu has foreign currency status and, as such, is subject to exchange controls, which are operated by the central bank. This means that Irish resident persons in general cannot hold balances in Ecu. Exchange controls are due for abolition by 1992. The Ecu is not legal tender.

Company law

Provided that exchange control permission is obtained, companies are allowed to:

- Denominate their share capital in Ecu;
- Raise long-term debt in Ecu;
- Use other Ecu-denominated financial instruments; and
- Hold short-term Ecu accounts.

Stock exchange regulation

Ireland is part of the UK stock exchange and bound by its regulations.

Financial services legislation

Annual accounts may be published in any currency including the Ecu, although this is seldom the practice.

Tax

The Ecu is treated for tax purposes as any other foreign currency.

Banking system

The central bank does not appear to have an explicit official policy on the use of Ecu.

The clearing system is mainly geared to IR£ transactions.

6.8.2 Perceived obstacles to the private use of the Ecu

Inertia

Low level of use

The low level of suppliers' use of the Ecu was perceived by three-quarters of company respondents to be the most discouraging factor, but the low level of use amongst competitors and lack of acceptance by customers were also felt to be significant by a large majority. On the supply side, banks stated that they were only likely to be encouraged to use the Ecu by greater demand for it from their customers.

Once again the *Catch 22* situation is identified: the private sector is discouraged from using the Ecu because its general use is low, but no-one is prepared to make the first move in order to change the status quo.

Currency status

Lack of legal enforceability of contracts
Our research showed this to be a minor obstacle to use of the Ecu.

Pockets of ignorance

Significant lack of corporate knowledge
Corporate respondents generally lacked practical knowledge about the Ecu. This was especially the case among purely domestic and smaller companies. It seems that this may be a significant obstacle, since in the interviews conducted with Irish companies it emerged that the more familiar companies were with the Ecu, the more they supported its use.

Low public awareness
Over two-thirds of respondents said that the level of public awareness inhibited use of the Ecu.

Internal administration

Administrative/current accounting systems/ease of change
Over one-third of Irish company respondents to our questionnaire expressed the view that the administrative cost of using the Ecu, current accounting systems and the ease of change to using the Ecu in their company inhibit/greatly inhibit them from using the Ecu.

Other legal

Perceived limitations of the Ecu's legal status
The vast majority of Irish companies participating in our survey said that the Ecu's legal status made it difficult/very difficult for them to:

- Settle domestic transactions in Ecu;
- Issue share capital in Ecu;
- Assess and pay tax liabilities in Ecu;
- Complete annual reports and accounts in Ecu; and
- Use the Ecu for cash management.

It was considered most difficult to issue share capital in Ecu.

Legal acceptability of Ecu for contracts

Over half of the Irish companies involved in our study stated that the lack of legal acceptability of the Ecu for contracts currently inhibits/greatly inhibits their use of it.

6.9 Italy

6.9.1 Regulatory obstacles to the private use of the Ecu

Legal tender

The Ecu has foreign currency status.

Financial services regulations

The use of Ecus and other foreign currencies for various types of short-term financial services, in the past, has been inhibited by the Bank of Italy through the Ufficio Italiano Cambio (UIC). One reason for this is that the UIC attempts to balance foreign currency debits with credit positions on a daily basis.

Private Italian residents can purchase an unlimited amount of foreign currency and hold it over a minimum of 60 days and a maximum of 120 days, but they must show a good reason. Furthermore, private citizens cannot have a foreign currency account or savings book with a foreign national or international bank (although this restriction will be lifted by July 1990).

It is only recently that Italian companies have been allowed to hold foreign currency for over 120 days – and this has to be justified by a sale of goods or services abroad.

Italian companies cannot invest directly in foreign currency via swaps or currency futures/options unless investment is channelled through a bank authorized by the Bank of Italy. Banks were, until recently, only able to operate swaps and currency options in local currency but are now entitled to operate directly in foreign currencies and for speculative purposes.

Speculative operations are still under the strict control of the Bank of Italy, which demands that Italian banks balance the exposures against the currency assets for each foreign currency on a bi-weekly basis. Given the nature of the regulations and from a commercial viewpoint, the use of the Ecu is therefore inhibited because exposures in Ecu have to be matched by an equal hedge in the same currency. This places the Ecu at a disadvantage as compared to other currencies, such as the Deutschmark, which have wider commercial use.

Accountancy standards
It is not permitted to report in Ecu.

Tax, customs and excise duties
There is a lower withholding tax on interest on Ecu certificates and treasury bills than on domestic lira certificates and treasury bills for foreign residents. For Italian residents the withholding tax is the same for the former as for the latter. On the former, the withholding tax rate is 12.5 per cent for Italian residents and zero for foreign residents, whereas on the latter the withholding tax is 12.5 per cent for Italian residents and from 10 to 30 per cent for foreign residents (according to the existing tax treaty with the specific foreign countries).

6.9.2 Perceived obstacles to the private use of the Ecu

Inertia

Low level of use
The Italian companies surveyed did not tend to be proactive in use of the Ecu and thus the low level of use by customers, competitors and suppliers inhibits their own use of the Ecu, as does lack of encouragement by the trade associations and lack of use of the Ecu by the European Commission itself. One-third of the companies responding to our questionnaire stated that the level of use of the Ecu by customers had inhibited their own use of the Ecu, while almost all companies stated that they would be encouraged to increase their use of the Ecu if it were widely used by all sections of commerce for day-to-day transactions.

No competitive advantage
The use of the Ecu was perceived as an unnecessary burden which obliges the commercial partner and oneself to deal in an extra financial currency which will eventually have to be exchanged for another currency.

Companies identified no operational advantage in the use of the Ecu in consolidated balance sheets. Most Italian companies consolidate their balance sheet in Italian lira. Those who filed their balance sheets in a foreign currency for international marketing purposes tended to use US dollars as they are more widely known.

The Ecu is not considered advantageous for inter-company sales. This is because the administrative savings are not easy to forecast, whereas the financial cost can increase two-fold because of intermediation and extra exchange operations. The Ecu is not perceived as a natural intermediary.

Traditional dealings in US dollars

Research revealed that there is wide use of the US dollar for cross rate fixings, especially on extra-EC currencies.

Lack of end uses

Raw materials and commodities not quoted in Ecu on world markets

Companies told us that they were not accustomed to using the Ecu, especially as raw materials and commodities are rarely quoted in Ecu on world markets. In fact, 80 per cent of those responding to our questionnaire stated that if raw materials and commodities were quoted in Ecu on world markets, then they would be encouraged to use it for invoicing.

No commercial transactions in Ecu

The Ecu was regarded as a useful currency for financing, but not for investment or hedging, since respondents reported that it did not seem natural to a company to use a currency which is not supported by commercial transactions.

Currency status

Desire for European central bank

We found a strong consensus in Italy that EMU will work only with central controls over member states' budget deficits – mainly because of Italy's need to tackle a huge budget deficit. Phase one of EMU, which involves the elimination of capital controls, is expected to worsen Italy's budget problems of monetary control if the relatively low level of financial intermediation rises.

Liquidity and availability

Lack of Ecu products

Companies told us that other use of the Ecu and other foreign currencies was inhibited due to lack of suitable banking and support services and lack of availability of Ecu products such as documentary credits.

Concern about processing time

Italian companies questioned told us that payment from abroad takes from a few days to weeks to be credited to a domestic account. Italian respondents were concerned that the use of an extra currency (Ecu) would lengthen the time lag.

Underdeveloped secondary market

Companies feared that if they commit themselves to Ecu payments they would have greater difficulties raising the Ecu funds to cover the exposure. They considered that the secondary market was not well enough developed to supply short-notice and short-term requests in Ecu.

Strong/weak economies

Volatility of Ecu/EMS fluctuation

It was claimed by some respondents that volatility of the Ecu due to the fluctuations of sterling and the wider band of oscillation of the Italian lira in the EMS, has contributed to reducing companies' usage of Ecu financing.

The fluctuations of the EMS currencies against the Ecu were considered to be too frequent and two wide, forcing prices to change quite frequently and subjecting the prices to exchange risk. Hence the prices are perceived to be more cumbersome to manage.

Competitive domestic loans

The level of interest rate charged on Ecu-denominated loans was attractive to many Italian companies for medium-term financing, but in the last two years the interest charged on domestic loans had decreased to the point of being competitive with Ecu loans.

Pockets of ignorance

Lack of skills, knowledge and habit of using Ecu

Italian companies found that the transaction currency in commercial agreements was generally determined according to the preference of the commercial partner and the negotiating parties' respective power. Low acquaintance by either partner with use of the Ecu, often the case in Italy, drastically reduced the use of the Ecu as a transaction currency.

This lack of familiarity with the Ecu, its value or use on national financial markets created a psychological barrier: clients preferred to have a quotation in a known currency, and suppliers, anxious to please their clients, tended to comply.

Companies felt that further use of the Ecu was discouraged due to a lack of the necessary skills within commercial organizations.

Internal administration

Administrative cost/current accounting systems

There was a fear that the use of the Ecu will lead to double accounting, thus incurring additional costs. Approximately two-thirds of Italian companies responding to our questionnaire stated that both the administrative cost of using the Ecu and current accounting systems inhibit/greatly inhibit their general use of the Ecu.

Companies feared too that the administrative savings from the use of the Ecu would be low, because procedures are highly automated and strict labour laws hinder personnel reduction.

Other legal

Perceived limitations of the Ecu's legal status

All Italian company respondents expressed the view that the current legal status of the Ecu made it difficult/very difficult for them to use the Ecu for:

- Settlement of domestic transactions;
- Issuing share capital;
- Assessing and paying tax liabilities; and
- Completion of reports and accounts.

A large majority also found it difficult to use the Ecu for cash management while two-thirds found it difficult to use the Ecu for the settlement of international transactions.

6.10 Luxembourg

6.10.1 Regulatory obstacles to the private use of the Ecu

Legal tender

The Ecu in Luxembourg does not have legal tender status and has limited use in transactions. It is, however, considered as a unit of account along with other foreign currencies.

Throughout an experimental period, shops, restaurants and hotels displayed prices in Ecus, indicating the level of official support in banking and government circles for the use of the Ecu.

Company law

Luxembourg is the main secondary market for Ecu bonds, most of which are quoted on the Luxembourg stock exchange.

Luxembourg law allows share capital to be denominated in any currency, including Ecus.

One listed commercial company and a number of financial institutions report in Ecus.

Investment

There are over 100 investment funds (UCITS) listed in Ecus; many of these are sub-funds operating under an umbrella fund. The investment strategy of these funds is normally either investment in European securities, in Ecu-denominated debt securities, or geographically within Europe.

There is no discriminatory legislation specific to Ecus with regard to the following:

- Raising long-term debt in Ecu;
- Using Ecu-denominated financial instruments; or
- Holding short-term Ecu accounts.

Stock exchange regulations

The Luxembourg stock exchange allows quotation in Ecus. There are no special requirements other than the normal listing regulations. However, as with any non-franc issue, a prospective issuer is required to justify their choice of currency denomination.

Fixed-interest securities

Fixed-income securities are the largest category of securities officially listed on the Luxembourg stock exchange. They are quoted, dealt in and settled in the currency of issue, which includes Ecus: there are currently 496 such issues.

In 1988 66 per cent of Ecu Eurobond issues were quoted on the Luxembourg market. The Ecu is the third most popular currency of issue in Luxembourg with 6.2 per cent of the total amount outstanding, ranking the Ecu behind only the US dollar and the yen. However in terms of market trading, the Ecu sector took first place with over 27 per cent transactions. This indicates the level of acceptance of the Ecu as a unit of transaction in bond trading.

Equities

There are currently seven securities quoted on the exchange in Ecu; quotations are also available for Ecu options and Ecu warrants.

In general terms the Bourse is seen as strong supporter of the Ecu and participated in the recent Luxembourg experiment.

Financial services legislation

There is no identified legislation which discriminates against Ecu products at the expense of the products of the other currencies, although as would be expected there is regulatory legislation concerning all areas of financial services.

Accountancy standards

Luxembourg reporting requirements conform with generally accepted international accounting standards and the relevant EC directives. It is permissible to publish accounts in Ecus, although the practice is limited to the banks, collective investment funds and listed companies, mentioned earlier in this analysis.

Tax customs and excise duties

For tax, customs and excise purposes, the Ecu is treated as any other foreign currency.

Banking system

The indigenous Luxembourg banks see themselves as strong supporters of monetary integration and the use of a single unit of currency. The recent Ecu experiment was actively supported by three of the top four Luxembourg banks. This support extends to the holding of Ecu-denominated financial instruments; in 1988 4.3 per cent of Luxembourg bank assets and 3.4 per cent of their liabilities were in Ecu products.

The retail banking sector offers most products in Ecus, including mortgages and saving schemes, and Luxembourg banks were among the first to arrange Ecu loans in the early 1980s. An explanation for this enthusiasm for the Ecu is straightforward. Luxembourg banks concentrate on private banking and retailing their profits from forex transactions and are not significant as compared to UK, French or German banks.

In addition the Ecu is seen as a vehicle for penetration of other markets, particularly in the pan-European context, equalizing the disadvantage of a stable but poorly supported currency.

Political influence is of significance. Gaston Thorn, former Luxembourg prime minister and European Commission president is also chairman of Banque Internationale à Luxembourg.

Clearing system

There are no obstacles to the use of the Ecu derived from the clearing system. Cedel, which is based in Luxembourg, is the main clearing institution for financial instruments denominated in Ecus in Europe. All transactions on the local exchange are cleared through Cedel.

6.10.2 Perceived obstacles to the private use of the Ecu

Inertia

Reluctance of trading partners to use Ecu

Inertia was perceived by some respondents to be the major barrier to use of the Ecu.

Over 90 per cent of Luxembourg's consumption is imported, and a similar level of internal production is exported. Responding companies were not likely to be in a position to dictate the transaction currency but would instead accept the currency imposed by their trading counterparts – normally francs or Deutschmarks.

Lack of pan-European political will to proceed to EMU

Luxembourg is probably the Community's most enthusiastic proponent of the Ecu, but there is a sense that progress on this front is dependent upon the political will of other member states, such as FRG to progress towards EMU.

Habit

Companies referred to the force of habit (i.e. traditional use of US dollars or Deutschmarks) as a further barrier to use of the Ecu.

No competitive advantage

Luxembourg already deals in many currencies and perceives its flexibility on this front to represent a competitive advantage. Respondents considered that the Ecu would not enhance this position.

Currency status

Absence of a physical currency unit

The absence of a tangible Ecu currency unit was felt by a number of companies interviewed to be a factor inhibiting greater private sector use of the Ecu.

European central bank

Companies participating in our survey stated that the presence of a European central bank would greatly encourage their use of the Ecu.

Strong/weak currencies

Long-term strength and dominance of the Deutschmark

The Deutschmark has a history of long-term strength and stability as compared to the Ecu, and for many operators was perceived as the natural choice as a vehicle or investment currency.

Dominance of the dollar

The US dollar is another dominant and accepted currency for foreign currency transactions conducted within Luxembourg. It was noted in one interview that even the *European* Airbus is priced in US dollars.

Pocket of ignorance

Still some ignorance

Despite Luxembourg's leading position in Ecu use, those companies consulted in our survey still rated lack of knowledge as an obstacle.

Internal administration

Transaction costs

The use of a thirteenth currency was perceived to incur marginal additional costs.

6.11 The Netherlands

6.11.1 Regulatory obstacles to the private use of the Ecu

Legal tender

The Ecu enjoys foreign currency status, but is not legal tender.

Company law

The share capital of Dutch companies must be denominated in Dutch guilders. However, share return payments can be made in a foreign currency and regulations have been introduced with regard to the applicable exchange rate.

Stock exchange regulation

Dutch companies listed on the Amsterdam stock exchange ('ASE') must have Dfl denominated share capital. Foreign companies listed on the ASE may have quotations and share capital denominated in a foreign currency, including the Ecu, if the legislation of their own country permits.

At present no companies with Ecu-denominated shares are listed on the ASE.

Financial services legislation

There are no special requirements or restrictions with respect to holding or trading in Ecu products; the Ecu is regarded in the same way as any other foreign currency.

In view of the liberalization of capital movement as of 1 July 1990, most of the current restrictions will be lifted. This will apply especially to the holding of short-term accounts and financing of international investment portfolios.

Accounting standards
Annual accounts may be published in Ecu. Accounting rules in the Netherlands are laid down in the civil code. Article 362, clause 7 of the *Second Book* stipulates that the annual accounts (including consolidated accounts) or only the consolidated accounts may be in a foreign currency if the activities or international links of a company justify such reporting.

A further clause stipulates that if the annual accounts are published in a foreign currency, the issued capital, expressed in Dfl, must be recorded in the accompanying notes.

Tax, customs and excise duties
The Ecu enjoys exactly the same status and treatment as other foreign currencies with regard to tax regulations, customs and excise duties.

Central bank and banking system
The Dutch central bank displays a neutral stance towards the Ecu.

An efficient multilateral Ecu clearing system operates within The Netherlands, due to the membership of the country's two largest banks – Amro and ABN – of the Ecu Banking Association.

6.11.2 Perceived obstacles to the private use of the Ecu

Inertia

Banks' conservatism
It was felt the Dutch central bank does not actively encourage use of the Ecu and discounts any suggestion that it should play such a role. Dutch banks echo this conservatism and are also wary of the financial losses they expect to incur as a result of the introduction of a single currency. One large bank, for example, considered that the expected reduction of income as a result of having the Ecu as a single currency (i.e. loss of revenue from currency trading) would be higher than the reduction of costs involved in switching to a single currency.

Political nature
The Ecu and its promotion were perceived by several firms to be political in nature, rather than the inevitable result of free economic dynamics.

Dutch private sector representatives consulted considered that the Ecu as a single currency in Europe was unrealistic at present because there is no political commitment within the EMS from national governments. They considered completion of the internal market and a fixed exchange rate within the EMS to be prerequisites for any move to monetary union and were consequently apathetic towards the Ecu.

Wait and see

Current use of the Ecu was very low in companies questioned. We were told that companies would only increase their use of the Ecu if their customers or suppliers demanded it: they would be reactive rather than proactive. Almost 90 per cent of companies which responded to our questionnaire said that the Ecu becoming more widely used would encourage them to use it more frequently too.

Centralization

More than two-thirds of the Dutch companies responding to our questionnaire stated that a decision to use Ecu made by central management would encourage their use of the Ecu for future funding.

Lack of end uses

No incentive for Ecu life insurance

We were told that for an insurance company there is no incentive to use the Ecu because many of its activities are in life insurance. Since this is mostly pension insurance, the Dutch customer is not interested in an investment in any currency other than the guilder because he cannot pay his day-to-day expenses in any other currency.

SMEs see no need for Ecu

Smaller companies, which deal mainly in their domestic currency and have little to do with other currencies, feel that the Ecu is irrelevant to their operational needs or income.

Currency status

Basket nature of Ecu

The Ecu is felt to be a high-risk currency because of its basket nature and companies actually advise their clients against using it.

Strong/weak economies

Stability of the guilder/dominance of the Deutschmark

As opposed to other foreign currencies, including the Ecu, the stable guilder or Deutschmark were preferred for financial transactions. Currencies of southern European countries were regarded as presenting too high a risk, with the guilder both stable and offering high real interest rates. All but one of the companies responding to our questionnaire said that they used the guilder for these reasons. The only other currencies which companies were inclined to use are the Hong Kong and US dollar.

Evidence from our postal survey of companies suggests that Ecu interest rates are currently too high to attract Dutch business. Forty per cent said that the Ecu interest rate compared to their domestic rate discouraged use of the Ecu, and 90 per cent said that if the Ecu interest rate was lower than all other interest rates, they would be encouraged to make greater use of it for funding. A similarly large proportion of respondents would also be encouraged to use the Ecu for financial investment if the Ecu interest rate was lower than the domestic rate.

One Dutch company consulted in our survey trades in guilders outside West Germany and in Deutschmarks inside Germany. Its foreign trading companies collect in their own currencies and pay the production company in The Netherlands in guilders – with the exception of the West German one, which pays in Deutschmarks. This favoured role of the Deutschmark is not exceptional – many companies allow their German customers to settle in it.

As well as the strength of the Deutschmark, the geographical and trading proximity of The Netherlands and West Germany appeared to be an influential factor. Historically, the guilder has followed the Deutschmark very closely and has been a natural vehicle currency for the Dutch to use.

Generally speaking we found that the Dutch private sector did not assume that the Ecu will necessarily become the single currency of the future; indeed the Deutschmark seemed an economically more viable alternative to some respondents.

Internal administration

Transaction costs

Since the Ecu has foreign currency status, banks charge a transaction fee for dealing in it and consequently it is cheaper to use the guilder for which there is no charge.

The Ecu is unattractive to Dutch insurance companies as an investment currency because of the amount of commission that has to be paid.

Private loans would also be more expensive to run in Ecu.

Current accounting systems/ease of change

A significant minority of the Dutch companies participating in our survey stated that current accounting systems and the problems of change to using the Ecu inhibits them from using it. The majority of respondents, however, felt that these factors had no effect on their use of the Ecu.

Other legal

Perceived limitations of the Ecu's legal status
A large majority of Dutch company respondents found that the Ecu's legal status made it difficult/very difficult for them to settle domestic transactions or assess and pay tax liabilities in Ecu.

A smaller yet significant proportion stated that the Ecu's legal status also made it difficult to issue Ecu-denominated share capital.

Ability to impose the Ecu as means of payment
More than one-third of Dutch companies said that their inability to impose the Ecu as a means of payment discouraged their use of it for invoicing.

6.12 Portugal

6.12.1 Regulatory obstacles to the private use of the Ecu

Legal tender
The Ecu has foreign currency status in Portugal and is only used in international contracts for specific products, such as oil, and as a currency for opening a credit. Its domestic use is virtually non-existent.

Company law
Share capital has to be expressed in Portuguese escudos.

Accounting standards
Accounting must be carried out in Portuguese escudos, although the shareholders of larger companies would probably accept Ecu accounting.

Tax, customs and excise duties
Tax calculation and settlement must be conducted in escudos.

Central bank and banking systems
There are no Ecu products.

6.12.2 Perceived obstacles to the private use of the Ecu

Inertia

Habit

Our research showed that the force of habit of using the US dollar or the customers'/suppliers' national currency for business transactions was a major obstacle to use of the Ecu. It also reflected a very low level of private sector initiative in promotion of the Ecu, as witnessed by the fact that there is no political or entrepreneurial group actively involved in encouraging use of the Ecu. All companies responding to our questionnaire stated that they would be encouraged to increase their own use of the Ecu if it were more widely used for day-to-day transactions by all sections of commerce.

High-level state influence in the economy

The Portuguese economy is still greatly influenced by the state, which determines pricing, banking credit ceilings and fiscal and monetary policies. Moreover, many of the largest companies and financial institutions are still state-owned. As a result many Portuguese companies were waiting for a lead from the public sector before acting in favour of the Ecu themselves.

Response to our company questionnaire illustrated the effect of this state influence upon the private sector. Of those responding to our survey, 90 per cent stated that if national government used the Ecu for stamps, payment of excise duties etc., they would be encouraged to make greater use of the Ecu themselves.

Currently, public procurement is only conducted in escudos and there are no policies to increase use of the Ecu.

Centralization

The degree of centralization within a Portuguese enterprise was felt to be important in the decision to make ultimate use of the Ecu.

Lack of end uses

High number of SMEs – no need for Ecu

Since the vast majority of Portuguese SMEs only trade intra-nationally, they perceive no need to use the Ecu.

Non-EC trading partners

Although it was felt that EC trading partners are beginning to accept transactions in Ecu, non-EC partners were reluctant to do so.

Currency status

Non-existence of Ecu in physical terms

The non-existence of a tangible Ecu was felt to be an obstacle to its use.

Liquidity and availability

No Ecu products

Research from our national offices in Portugal concluded that there are *no Ecu products*.

Some commercial banks obtain credit from the EIB in Ecu, but when they supply credit to corporates they usually contract in Portuguese escudos.

Strong/weak economies

Exchange profits

Some companies contacted were making significant exchange profits from the instability of exchange rates at present. They therefore felt that they would make a financial loss as a result of use of the Ecu as a 'single European currency' and were consequently disinterested in active promotion of it.

Domestic economy lacking bargaining power

The Portuguese economy is largely composed of SMEs, many with family management, and GDP per capita is one of the lowest in Europe. As a result, Portuguese companies cannot yet enforce their position in the international or European markets. The tradition of dealing in the US dollar or the trading partners' preferred currency appeared likely to continue, until the Portuguese economy develops a stronger stance within European and/or an external impetus is given which would provide commerce and industry with a reason to challenge the present status quo.

Pockets of ignorance

High number of SMEs

Whilst some large companies and multinationals are beginning to use the Ecu, SMEs were not aware of its uses and advantages and did not appear interested in finding out what they are.

Lack of information from banks

There was felt to be a definite lack of information from banks about the Ecu, and almost all company survey participants pointed out that suitable banking and support services would encourage its use.

Lack of experience of Ecu products
There is a general lack of experience in working with the Ecu and providing financial services denominated in Ecu.

Lack of awareness amongst non-EC trading partners
Portuguese companies stated that their non-EC trading partners might be more willing to accept the Ecu as a business transaction medium, if they were better informed about it.

Other legal

Perceived limitations of the Ecu's legal status
More than 50 per cent of Portuguese companies completing our questionnaire stated that the Ecu's legal status made it difficult for them to use it for the settlement of domestic transactions.

6.13 Spain

6.13.1 Regulatory obstacles to the private use of the Ecu

Legal tender
The Ecu has foreign currency status within Spain, but is not legal tender.

Company law
Share capital in Spanish companies must be denominated in pesetas. A Spanish company taking a foreign currency short-term loan must first place a non interest-bearing deposit with a bank. In this the Ecu is treated as any other foreign currency.

Stock exchange regulation
Joint stock companies must publish their accounts and report in pesetas.

Financial services legislation
There are no restrictions on the use of the Ecu as a financial instrument. Ecu products which may be used include long-term loans, derived instruments (futures, swaps and options) and, since 1 July 1989, short-term accounts.

Accounting standards
Account reporting and publication must be in pesetas.

Tax, customs and excise duties
The Ecu is treated as any other foreign currency.

Central bank and banking system

On 30 September 1989, the Bank of Spain authorized the right of resident individuals and companies to hold credit accounts, saving accounts and term accounts in Ecu at any of its branches 'without the need for prior authorisation'. This indicates that favoured status has been given to the Ecu as compared with other foreign currencies.

6.13.2 Perceived obstacles to the private use of the Ecu

Inertia

Wait and see

Three-quarters of companies stated that wider use of the Ecu by their competitors would encourage their use of it in the future, while 85 per cent stated that they would be encouraged to follow suit if the Ecu were more widely used by all sections of commerce for day-to-day transactions.

A large majority of responding companies also stated that they would be encouraged to increase their use of the Ecu for funding if lenders were more willing to lend in Ecu than any other currency.

Strong statements were made indicating that supplier use, customer acceptance of and demand for the Ecu, as well as trade association policies would all encourage greater use of the Ecu if these groups were favourably disposed towards it.

Low level of use

We found that the amount of business transactions currently conducted in Ecu is low. It is mainly used as a means of payment for important operations, while internal accounting, published accounts or sales invoicing in Ecu is virtually unheard of. Only 0.03 per cent of Spanish trade flow is denominated in Ecu, although 60 per cent of foreign trade is inter-EC.

The present low level of Ecu transactions is partly due to the fact that Spanish companies are not highly internationalized. Almost two-thirds of Spanish companies who responded to our questionnaire stated that the current low level of use of the Ecu by customers inhibited their use of the Ecu, while a similar number stated that suppliers' level of use was also inhibiting.

Liquidity and availability

European central bank

Presence of a European central bank would encourage use of the Ecu.

Low availability

The lack of availability of Ecu instruments from banks was felt to inhibit its use by companies.

Eighty-five per cent of the banks questioned stated that if the minimum size of transactions was lowered they would be encouraged to offer Ecu loans in the future.

Respondents considered that there are too few market-makers – almost all banks questioned said that more market-makers would encourage them to offer Ecu loans in the future.

The banks responding to our questionnaire felt that, overall, there were too few banks offering Ecu loans for their use to be encouraged and increased.

Clearing system

A number of banks claimed that the current difficulty of joining the Ecu clearing system is a major factor inhibiting banks from offering more Ecu products. Medium-sized banks are unable to obtain membership of the clearing system and consequently have to settle transactions through one of the two Spanish banks which are members.

Strong/weak economies

Domestic nature of SMEs

The majority of Spanish companies were unable to impose the Ecu as a currency of choice in negotiations because of their size and because they lack the support of trade associations. In our survey, over three-quarters of companies who responded said that their inability to impose the Ecu as a means of payment has discouraged their use of it for invoicing.

Higher interest on inter-bank investment

Returns on investment in the inter-bank market are roughly 4 per cent above the Ecu interest rate at 13 per cent. Thus, only a restricted amount of business transactions are conducted in Ecu at present. In the short term at least, there is little prospect of a shift in these interest rates.

Pockets of ignorance

Lack of awareness

Spain is a relatively new member of the EC. Her economy is more domestic in nature than that of longer-standing EC members, with a large number of SMEs and, consequently, Spanish companies' awareness of European issues and their practical commercial experience of trade within the EC is limited. Moreover, almost 70 per cent of the companies who responded to our questionnaire stated that the current level of public awareness of the Ecu in Spain inhibits its use.

There is low awareness of the Ecu amongst Spanish banks, especially at branch level. Two-thirds of the banks responding to our questionnaire stated that the level of knowledge of the Ecu in the bank's retail department inhibited them from offering Ecu-denominated products.

Questionnaire evidence indicated that while companies were looking to banks to provide encouragement and incentives for greater use of the Ecu, banks perceived a lack of customer demand to be a major obstacle to its wider use. Over three-quarters of companies said that the presence of suitable banking and support services would encourage their use of the Ecu, whilst 70 per cent of banks said that the level of demand for the Ecu by their customers inhibited them from offering Ecu-denominated products.

Internal administration

VAT calculation only in pesetas increases cost

Invoicing in Ecu is discouraged because VAT cannot be applied to the Ecu and hence the necessity of an intermediate calculation between the Ecu and the peseta again means higher administrative costs.

Transaction/transition costs

Companies were concerned about the administrative cost of using the Ecu. At present the Bank of Spain collates and classifies all currency data centrally, which means that companies incur administrative costs as a result of related communications.

Spanish banks considered that they were discouraged from using the Ecu by the size of the training costs involved to enable their staff to deal capably with the Ecu. Furthermore, some companies were concerned about the extra cost involved with using the Ecu because of the changes to their accounting, administrative and software systems. More than one-third of the companies responding to our survey stated that the problem of changing to the Ecu inhibits/greatly inhibits their use of it.

In response to our questionnaire, 90 per cent of companies stated that if fees for dealing in Ecu were lower than for other borrowing they would be encouraged to use the Ecu generally. With regard to purchasing and procurement, 80 per cent said that a decrease in banking fees for foreign exchange in Ecu would encourage them to use the Ecu, and a similar number stated that a decrease in banking fees for Ecu transfers would encourage them to increase their Ecu use.

Current accounting systems
More than one-third of Spanish company respondents said that current accounting systems inhibit/greatly inhibit their use of the Ecu.

Invoicing
Fifty per cent of the respondents stated that they were discouraged from using the Ecu by the lack of extent to which invoice preparation is simplified.

Other legal

Perceived limitations of the Ecu's legal status
A large majority of those Spanish companies involved in our survey felt that the Ecu's legal status made it particularly difficult to:

- Settle both domestic and international transactions in Ecu;
- Pay taxes in Ecu; and
- Use the Ecu for cash management.

Legal acceptability of Ecu for contracts.
A quarter of the respondents stated that the lack of legal acceptability of the Ecu for contracts inhibits their use of it.

6.14 The United Kingdom

6.14.1 Regulatory obstacles to the private use of the Ecu

Legal status
The Ecu has foreign currency status, but is not full legal tender. Agreements for value denominated in Ecu are permitted, but enforcement is dependent on the wording of the agreement itself.

Company legislation
Companies are allowed to:

- Denominate their share capital in Ecu;
- Raise long-term debt in Ecu;
- Use other Ecu denominated financial instruments; and
- Hold short-term Ecu accounts.

Stock exchange regulations

Companies are permitted to issue shares denominated in any currency. However, all stock exchange quotations and transactions are denominated in sterling. Settlement is through brokers, who may accept any currency by agreement, but are legally required to accept sterling in the absence of any binding contract for an alternative currency.

Reporting requirements

Companies must issue accounts in a 'reporting currency', which is defined through objective tests of their business activity. For most companies the reporting currency is defined by historic major cash flow. Therefore any company having its major cash flows in Ecu would publish Ecu accounts. Annual accounts may additionally be published in any memorandum currency.

Tax, customs and excise duties

There are no withholding tax implications relating to the Ecu, and no tax credits available – so in practice the tax use of the Ecu differs greatly from other currencies. Ecu is treated for tax purposes as a foreign currency.

6.14.2 Perceived obstacles to the private use of the Ecu

Inertia

Apathy

Low level of use and lack of end uses are the paradox of the present Ecu market. We found that the true obstacle is organizations' tendency to be followers rather than leaders (i.e. if competitors and suppliers used Ecu, companies would follow). A large majority of companies involved in our survey said that their customers' level of use of the Ecu inhibits/greatly inhibits their own use of it, and all companies stated that they would be encouraged to increase their use of the Ecu if it were widely used by all sections of commerce for day-to-day transactions.

This lack of pioneering spirit was combined with political apathy. UK organizations reported no feeling of obligation or inclination to assist government in achieving political ends, even if those ends could realize substantial benefits for themselves.

Traditional investment relationship with the United States

The UK has a high-value investment relationship with the United States, a link which was strengthened by North Sea oil revenues realizable in US dollars, the international oil trading currency.

Cross-investment with the United States has created an unusually high value of UK-US business transactions, and UK organizations reported that they were more familiar than other European organizations with the use of the US dollar as an international trading currency, or as an intermediary between two other currencies. The Ecu was considered to be a latecomer to this pattern of financial transactions.

Lack of end uses

The lack of end uses was identified as one of the principal obstacles to use of the Ecu. Companies identified few end uses because their customers and suppliers do not use the Ecu, but companies would use the Ecu if their trading counterparts did so. Respondents found it difficult to differentiate between lack of end uses and low level of use ('apathy') in considering the Ecu as a transaction currency.

Currency status

Basket nature of Ecu

The Ecu was perceived to be attractive as a technical hedging currency, but its development as a separately traded currency, or as a single currency, would remove some of the technical obstacles bestowed by the present basket. Respondents were very concerned at the effect on volatility of the Ecu against the US dollar if it became a traded currency, as the smoothing property of the basket would be lost.

Status

In the course of the interviews, we were told that the Ecu's credibility is reduced by the fact that it currently has no 'home' economy through which it can be enforced, and no 'home' government to provide status. Therefore all Ecu agreements are dependent on the legal quality of the agreement itself.

Liquidity and availability

The lack of liquidity of the Ecu market was identified as another major obstacle to its use within the UK. The impact is increased by the absence of end uses, since if the Ecu is only to be a trading medium, one must at least be able to trade in it freely. All companies responding to our survey stated that suitable banking and support services would encourage/greatly encourage their general use of the Ecu.

Pockets of ignorance

Low public awareness

Ninety per cent of the companies involved in our study claimed that the current level of public awareness of the Ecu inhibits/greatly inhibits its use. Again, respondents found it difficult to distinguish between the low level of present use and the low level of public awareness of the Ecu.

Internal administration

Anticipated cost of transition/need for official confirmation of Ecu role

The costs of transition to a single currency were perceived to be high. Accordingly, interviewees reported that they had no intention of making investments in systems, training and operations until the identity of the future European currency and the timetable for its introduction are firmly announced by all EC governments.

Current accounting systems/ease of change

More than one-third of UK companies participating in our study found their use of the Ecu inhibited by current accounting systems and the difficulties involved in change to using the Ecu.

Other legal

Perceived limitations of the Ecu's legal status

All of the UK company respondents stated that the Ecu's legal status made it difficult/very difficult for them to use it for assessing and paying tax liabilities.

A large majority said that the Ecu's legal status made it difficult/very difficult for them to issue share capital in Ecu, complete reports and accounts in Ecu or use the Ecu for cash management. Almost two-thirds felt that the Ecu's legal status impeded its use for the settlement of domestic and international transactions.

Legal acceptability of the Ecu for contracts/means of payment

Half of the UK companies responding to our questionnaire stated that the legal inacceptability of the Ecu for contracts inhibits their use of it and that lack of ability to impose the Ecu as a means of payment further discouraged its use.

7: A Strategy for the Ecu: Macroeconomic Considerations

A Paper by the National Institute of Economic and Social Research

7.1 Purpose of the analysis

The purpose of this paper is to provide an analysis of the major macroeconomic issues affecting the issue of the Ecu as a means of achieving monetary union in Europe. It was written in order to provide the background understanding for the recommendations produced in a joint research project with Ernst & Young on *A Strategy for the Ecu*, financed by a grant from the Association for the Monetary Union of Europe. It has three specific objectives:

1. To identify the macroeconomic obstacles to monetary union in Europe;
2. To explore the possibilities of the use of the Ecu by the private sector to eliminate these obstacles; and
3. To recommend what steps should be taken to improve the chances of success in achieving monetary union by removing the macroeconomic obstacles.

Governing all this discussion is the need to find politically feasible solutions. Although the report outlines the costs and benefits of the various possibilities in economic terms, and decision makers will act in the light of those, the recommendations for action have to be within the plausible bounds of European negotiations.

The work is stimulated by the Delors Report on Economic and Monetary Union and its endorsement by the European Council in Madrid in 1989. Under that agreement an inter-governmental council is to be set up, probably by the Dublin summit in mid-1990, to sort out what legislative changes are necessary to achieve monetary union. The Delors Report sets out a three-stage procedure to achieve monetary union by *institutional* change. As part of that process the report concludes: 'Although a monetary union does not necessarily require a single currency it would be a desirable feature of a monetary union ... the Ecu has the potential to be developed into such a *common currency*'. (The five paragraphs referring to the Ecu (45–9) are reproduced in Appendix 1.) Although the Committee explicitly rejects the use of the Ecu as a *parallel currency* (a genuine currency in its own right rather than the 'basket' of existing currencies that it currently forms) it did recommend that 'there should be no discrimination against the *private use of the Ecu* and that existing administrative obstacles should be removed'. The Madrid summit also required that by the time of the Dublin Council further more detailed proposals are required to establish what obstacles need to be removed to enable the Ecu to be used without discrimination.

The basic contention which our work here seeks to substantiate is that without making the full transition to a single currency in Europe many of the gains from monetary union will not be reaped. Problems of transition and political sensitivities mean that the best candidate for such a single currency is the Ecu. The path to monetary union will be substantially eased by the early announcement of the clear decision to move to the Ecu as the single currency of the European Community by a firm but feasible end date, in the manner so successfully exemplified by the inauguration of the 1992 programme for the completion of the internal market. Our work therefore starts from the presumption that monetary union is the objective and seeks to establish what role the wider use of the Ecu can play in achieving that objective.

7.2 Structure of the paper

In the pages which follow we begin by setting out the gains which could be achieved by the use of a single currency in the European Community. We then examine how far these gains are likely to be realized under the framework envisaged in the Delors Report. We examine in particular the risks and difficulties that this approach seems to offer by use of the National Institute's model of European and other international economies, *GEM*. The rest of the report is concerned with addressing how these risks and difficulties can be reduced.

We investigate four alternative scenarios. The first is to allow the EMS to be rather more flexible in the short run, permitting more frequent realignments so as to allow all the member states to participate fully. The second is to follow the even more flexible solution which is widely referred to as a currency competition, allowing market forces to determine how monetary union will come about rather than seeking to ensure change by the institutional steps envisaged in the Delors Report. We then consider the other end of the spectrum, by exploring the gains from a much more rapid progress to monetary union, eliminating any extended transition period.

Many of the problems faced occur during the process of transition. The next section therefore examines these, particularly those involving the use of the Ecu as a currency by the private sector. The remaining sections consider the advantages arising from the early wide use of the Ecu in Europe and the means which are available for encouraging that use. We end by forming recommendations for changes necessary to advance the pace of monetary integration in Europe and remove macroeconomic obstacles to the use of the Ecu as a single European currency.

7.3 The advantages of a single currency

There are several forms of monetary integration, but the eventual structure envisaged in the Delors Report is that there should be just one currency in the European Community, administered by some coherent authority. We shall describe this arrangement as 'monetary union', although some less close arrangements are sometimes awarded this title. (The Werner Report, for example, did not suggest that a single currency was a central requirement of MU.) Two of the major advantages of monetary union only occur if there is a single currency – namely, the removal of transaction costs between currencies and the elimination of uncertainty due to exchange risk. Therefore if a lesser arrangement is entered into where existing currencies remain, even if they are linked with irrevocably fixed exchange rates and a 'common currency' which is usable in all member states, the full benefits are not realized. The advantages of a single currency can be summarized as follows:

1. Decreased transaction costs;
2. Decreased uncertainty in returns from international transactions and need to take costly forward positions;

3. Decreased cost of capital;
4. Improved allocation of capital;
5. Cost of gains from use as a vehicle currency;
6. Pooled reserves can be used more effectively;
7. Reduction in inflation losses;
8. Improved macroeconomic management as a result of cooperation;
9. Improved stabilization of the EC economy.

However sincerely governments may sign 'irrevocable' agreements, their permanence in practice is perceived to be limited. Whatever the specific treaty obligations, governments cannot successfully bind their successors. It does not need to be dramatic events on the scale of recent upheavals in eastern Europe to change their wishes – elections or even 'U-turns' are sufficient. If national currencies are maintained it is inherently easier for members to break away if the alternative is politically unpleasant. The example of the ease with which the Irish punt was able to break away from a fixed exchange rate with sterling after over 50 years of parity is a very instructive case in point. If the institutions of separate monetary existence are removed, then breaking away will be a less plausible option.

Admittedly there are costs of moving to a single currency: for firms and banks in converting their procedures; for owners of coin and note operated machines; for governments in reprinting and minting; and for the public at large in adopting a new system. The lifetime of banknotes is in any case limited, and some coins may be able to continue in circulation with an equivalent value over quite a prolonged transition period (many florin and shilling coins are still circulating without any difficulty in the UK, 20 years after decimalization of the currency.

The costs at issue therefore are largely those which fall on the private sector. While aggregate calculations will be appropriate for assessing the impact on total welfare it is the balance of cost and benefit for the individual organization which will effect the acceptability of these changes. For companies involved in overseas trade there will be a balance between their reduced transaction costs and their conversion costs. Nevertheless conversion costs are a once-and-for-all cost while the transaction cost reduction endures indefinitely. For companies which are not trading internationally, there may be little to offset the costs, especially if they operate vending machines. Governments may wish to consider who should bear these costs.

7.3.1 The wider macroeconomic benefits

Focusing on specific direct costs is a mistake. There are other advantages of moving to a single currency. One arises simply from the decreased cost of capital in much of the union – under monetary union, convergence of inflation rates over the medium term is assured and hence the risk premium of countries which have previously shown higher inflation is eroded. The risk associated with the individual enterprise or indeed public authority will continue to be reflected in their credit rating and the relative interest rates which they are obliged to pay. Nevertheless this will entail a more efficient allocation of capital and lower capital cost on average.

This change in costs does not occur simply at the last stage of monetary union but progressively as countries show their ability to reduce their inflation rates to that of the 'anchor' currency, which is the Deutschmark at present. Only full monetary union will eliminate the differential altogether, and the fall in the risk premium on the way will reflect not the revealed success in having narrowed the differential but the expected differential in the future. Naturally past performance affects that expectation and influences the market's assessment of the government's credibility.

Given the size of the European Community, the adoption of a single currency is likely to offer further benefits in international transactions as a 'vehicle currency'. At present it is still the US dollar which tends to be preferred in international transactions, in part because of history but also because of the large US share in world trade. Even ignoring intra-EC trade, the EC is the world's largest trader. It is therefore to be expected that the Ecu will rapidly develop its role as a world currency in invoicing. This reduces the transaction cost for EC companies still further – although it does not necessarily reduce the exchange risk.

Most of the remaining benefits tend to be macroeconomic, although we have concentrated on the role of the single currency as a means of transaction rather than as a 'store of value' or a 'unit of account' – the other two textbook uses of a currency. Firms will of course also be concerned with these other two uses.

One of the most straightforward of the macroeconomic benefits is that without the need to provide a margin of reserves for 12 different currencies the reserves of the unified central banking system can expand their use.

However, monetary union is not normally considered on its own. It requires a measure of economic union or economic convergence for its achievement. That convergence takes a number of forms. Firstly, nominal convergence (convergence of price inflation); secondly, real convergence (convergence of standard of living); thirdly, convergence of policy; and lastly, a measure of convergence of economic structure. None of these requirements for convergence is absolute. Many other countries, particularly large ones, have continued satisfactorily with wide regional disparities in GDP per head, as Delors in his own background paper to the Committee shows (see Table 1). It will therefore be largely an empirical matter to determine how much convergence in each of these respects is required in the EC in order to permit the successful operation of a monetary union.

Table 1: Spread of GDP per head (average = 100)

Country	*Poorest region*	*GDP/head*	*Richest region*	*GDP/head*
EC (country level)	Portugal	47	Luxembourg	129
US (regions)	South-East	77	West Coast	111
EC (regions)	Iberia	66	Germany/ Denmark	122
US (states)	Mississippi	66	Alaska	131
EC (local areas)	Rural Greece	45	Groningen	237
Canada	Newfoundland	60	Alberta	123
Switzerland	Obwald	76	Zug	160
West Germany	Saarland	91	Hamburg	165

Source: EC (1989) pp. 84–5.

Since the process of convergence to monetary union involves the reduction of price inflation towards the level of the anchor country, this will provide a benefit for those who suffer from inflation. It may of course make the position of the government more difficult in so far as it used to finance some of its activities through an inflation tax. However, this gain may have had its offsets in the *de*flation that may have been required of countries to permit this convergence. We shall return to this question of relative benefit in our discussion of transition problems. At this stage, it is important to distinguish the costs and benefits which occur when monetary union is in operation from those which occur in the process of transition to it.

It is a common finding that the move to new systems which are clearly better than the current ones do not take place because of the costs of change. In extreme cases the costs of change exceed the discounted benefits from the new state. In which case it is clearly not beneficial to change. However, the more usual problem is that the costs appear first, and are both tangible and quantifiable, whereas the benefits are yet to occur and hence are more uncertain. Political decision-makers have to live with the immediate costs and have difficulties in persuading their electors of the validity of the future benefits. In the case of monetary union this is complicated because transition and ultimate costs and benefits are unlikely to be shared equally by the participating countries. Unless the relative and, most importantly, absolute losers are compensated by the gainers during the period of transition and prospectively in the proposed monetary union, the scheme is likely to fail as all must agree to the process. It cannot be enforced on a minority by the others.

The problem of assessing the wider advantages of a single currency and monetary union in general is that it is difficult to separate them from advantages stemming from other aspects of economic integration. Successful monetary integration requires a degree of co-ordination of macroeconomic policy. It is generally accepted that if countries co-operate they will achieve jointly better outcomes than if they do not. Furthermore, in the unfettered system, countries will tend to compete rather than co-operate so that they can achieve an advantage over their competitors.

This is a standard 'Prisoner's Dilemma' type of problem. If all can agree to co-operate they get the optimal outcome, but if the others do not co-operate then the best strategy is to look after one's own interests even though the total outcome for everyone taken together is worse. Thus the EC countries could gain from co-ordinated policies anyway, but monetary union and the agreed path to it is a means of making the co-operation a firmer commitment.

In the same way, monetary union assists stabilization policies within the European Community because it makes the transfer of resources to those areas experiencing difficulties automatic – internal balance of payments deficits are met. However, stabilization policies of this form are achievable by other agreements and monetary union is not a necessary requirement – it is, however, one of the most credible ways of ensuring that the process takes place.

7.3.2 Disadvantages

It is worth listing the various disadvantages of monetary union which have emerged from this discussion as a counterweight to the gains, as it may be possible to reduce or eliminate them by appropriate action. They fall into two categories: those which are endured in the transition to monetary union and those which continue once monetary union is in operation. Transition costs are:

1. Deflation
2. Conversion costs
3. Loss of seignorage revenues.

Enduring costs are:

1. Loss of sovereignty
2. Increased cost of adjustment to shocks
3. Slower rate of economic growth.

Costs of conversion are relatively minor: alteration of computer and accounting systems; alteration of machinery; and alteration of practices etc. Nevertheless, for individual companies these may be considerable. Someone has to bear them. They may be passed on to the customer. They may appear in part in inflation. Since the benefits occur in the main at the end of the process – and not necessarily to the same people who incur the costs – there are problems of redistribution both across time and between people.

However, the major costs are macroeconomic. Two of these relate to the transition process. The first is simply that since a low level of price inflation is an objective for the monetary union, those countries with the higher rates of inflation have to restructure their economies in order to achieve sufficient nominal convergence. It is not a symmetric arrangement and there is no corresponding pressure on low inflation countries to aid convergence by pursuing a more inflationary policy. It is thus convergence towards one extreme rather than towards the mean. These higher inflation countries have several means of trying to achieve this. While it might be ideal to hope to achieve such change entirely by improving the supply side of the economy, this will take some time, during which period inflation will continue to exceed the target level. A fall in the exchange rate would help compensate for this. If exchange rates are fixed or difficult to alter, then the options are reduced. Much more extensive use will have to be made of fiscal deflation to reduce the pressure of demand. This holding down of the standard of living is not politically popular.

A second macroeconomic problem accrues to those countries like Spain and Italy whose governments get a substantial proportion of their revenue from the impact of inflation – often known as seignorage. The transition to MU means that they have to lose much of this revenue. Since tight, budgetary policy is required in the transition (probably a tightening of policy), this poses a problem as other sources of income may be both more difficult to tap and politically unattractive. Increases in direct and indeed indirect taxation may have a net deflationary impact, compounding the problems of inflation reduction.

Even if the costs of transition are bearable, what is required of the state in MU itself may prove unbearable. It may simply be that governments are unwilling to see themselves constrained. So far, under the Delors Committee plan, not only do governments lose control of monetary policy to the ESCB but they have major constraints imposed on their fiscal policy as well. This loss is not important if the objectives of MU policy coincide with those of the particular member state. Indeed it may very well enable them to achieve their objectives quicker and at a lower cost. In these circumstances pooled sovereignty offers gains not achievable by states on their own. The loss of sovereignty becomes important if a member state is not convinced that its aims coincide with those of the union. This will occur particularly if a state feels that restricting the available responses by fixing exchange rates increases the cost of adjusting to unanticipated shocks. Not all economies adjust at the same rate. Those which have more difficulty in achieving nominal adjustment may have found in the past that exchange rate adjustment lowered the real cost of change.

Taken together these difficulties may mean that a country experiences not just a lower rate of growth relative to its fellow members but lower than it would have achieved without monetary union. The justification for membership in these circumstances will have to come from the gains from other aspects of EMU. However, long-term growth potential may be unaffected by these problems of adjustment and be responsive only to changes in supply-side factors such as technology, productive capacity and skills. The question is then about the degree to which the transition to EMU and behaviour within EMU may affect such factors.

7.4 The likely future under the Delors Plan[1]

The question at issue at this stage is whether the proposals put forward in the Delors Report for the specific form of monetary union and the path towards it seem likely to succeed and yield the full range of possible benefits.

The National Institute's latest forecasts, published on 28 February 1990, take account of the information on the likely future of the world available up to mid-February. The rate and scale of change in Eastern Europe is such that any detailed assumptions can become rapidly outdated. Forecasts for the European Community, particularly for West Germany, are fundamentally affected by these changes. Three effects have been incorporated; (i) the influx of migrants from the East into West Germany; (ii) a switch round in the Eastern bloc's balance of payments, moving into a trade deficit and a capital influx from the West; and (iii) a diversion of expenditure from the military to the consumer goods sector, particularly in the United States. Thus, unification of West and East Germany is not incorporated as such, and figures quoted for West Germany relate to the area inside current West German boundaries.

Among the EC countries, forecasts are only shown for France, West Germany, Italy, the UK, Belgium-Luxembourg (referred to as Belgium hereinafter) and The Netherlands. The *GEM* model also distinguishes the US, Japan and Canada as individual countries. The remainder of the EC is part of a bloc formed by the rest of the OECD countries and therefore cannot be distinguished. Any EC figures therefore refer to the EC(7) or EC(4). While the main four countries have 60 variable models to explain their behaviour, the Belgium and Netherlands models are much smaller.

The forecasts summarized in Table 2 show the world economy slowing over the next couple of years compared with the rapid growth of the last two years, and inflation also dropping. Thereafter growth continues fairly steadily with Japan remaining the fastest growing country at 4½ per cent a year compared with US growth of 2½ per cent. German and French growth come into line also at 2½ per cent while the Italian position continues to improve with growth at 3 per cent a year. The UK, however, continues to diverge with growth at 1½ per cent. Inflation shows considerable convergence (as measured by consumer prices).

The US reaches 1½ per cent and Japan 2 per cent. The EC countries range from this, with France and Germany at around 2 per cent, and the UK and Italy 1½ per cent a year higher.

On the basis of these figures there is very considerable nominal convergence by the second half of the decade among the EC countries.

Table 2: Forecasts for the world economy 1990–1999

(a) GNP growth (% p.a.)

	US	*Japan*	*FRG*	*France*	*Italy*	*UK*	*World trade*	*Manu-facturing trade*	*OECD industrial production*
1988	4.6	5.8	3.6	3.4	3.9	3.9	9.8	10.1	5.9
1989	2.9	5.3	4.2	3.1	2.9	2.2	7.2	8.4	4.1
1990	2.0	6.2	3.0	2.3	2.5	1.5	5.3	5.9	3.4
1991	2.4	5.1	3.1	2.2	2.7	1.4	6.4	6.0	3.8
1992	2.1	4.4	3.0	2.4	3.0	1.4	6.3	5.6	3.5
1993–5	2.3	4.5	2.7	2.6	3.2	1.4	6.6	6.0	3.6
1996–9	2.5	4.3	2.4	2.4	3.3	1.6	7.0	6.6	3.6

(b) Consumer price inflation (% p.a.)

	US	*Japan*	*FRG*	*France*	*Italy*	*UK*	*World manufacturing prices*	*Oil price*
1988	4.2	0.0	1.2	2.7	4.6	5.0	4.4	−18.7
1989	4.5	1.6	3.5	3.4	6.2	5.3	0.2	18.7
1990	4.0	2.0	1.5	3.1	6.0	5.8	7.0	12.1
1991	3.7	1.6	2.0	3.1	4.3	5.4	1.4	1.8
1992	3.2	1.8	2.3	3.0	4.0	5.4	2.2	5.3
1993–5	2.4	2.3	1.7	3.0	4.0	5.4	2.2	5.3
1996–9	1.4	2.1	2.1	2.2	2.7	2.6	2.3	5.4

(c) Exchange rates (% change p.a.)

	Nominal						
	DM/$	*Y/$*	*£/DM*	*Ffr/DM*	*L/DM*	*Bfr/DM*	*Dfl/DM*
1990	−9.4	5.2	10.6	0.5	3.1	−0.5	−0.5
1991	0.3	−1.8	3.4	1.4	2.7	0.0	0.0
1992	−0.3	−2.1	3.4	1.1	2.1	0.0	0.0
1993–5	1.4	−2.6	2.0	1.0	2.0	0.0	0.0
1996–9	−2.0	−2.5	2.0	1.0	2.0	0.0	0.0

	Real				
	DM/$	*Y/$*	*£/DM*	*Ffr/DM*	*L/DM*
1990	−7.2	7.3	6.7	−1.0	−1.3
1991	1.9	0.3	0.1	0.3	0.4
1992	0.6	−0.8	0.2	0.3	0.4
1993–5	−1.3	−1.8	0.4	0.8	0.9
1996–9	−2.7	−3.2	1.5	0.9	1.4

(d) Interest rate differentials – nominal (% points)

	DM/$	*Y/$*	*£/DM*	*Ffr/DM*	*L/DM*
1990	−0.1	−2.2	6.3	2.1	5.0
1991	−0.6	−2.2	6.0	1.6	4.2
1992	−1.1	−2.8	3.5	1.5	4.0
1993–5	−2.2	−3.2	3.0	1.5	4.0
1996–9	−2.5	−3.0	3.0	1.5	4.0

The picture on real convergence is more mixed with the UK continuing to diverge. As a consequence this forecast does not see the final stage of monetary union being reached by 1999. Complete fixity of exchange rates is achieved between Germany, Belgium and The Netherlands this year, while France reaches a steady 1 per cent depreciation relative to them by 1992, the lira a 2 per cent depreciation by 1993 and sterling a 2 per cent depreciation by 1995.

This therefore implies that there would need to be realignments within the existing EMS system approximately every two years or so to keep all the currencies within the 2¼ per cent bounds. If sterling were to join the ERM of the EMS early in the period, this would increase the rate of realignment or, alternatively, would require a wider band like that of the peseta. It is thought unlikely that sterling would join with a wider band and since the UK government has laid down two requirements for membership ('when the level of UK inflation is significantly lower' and 'there is capital liberalization in the Community and real progress has been made towards completion of the single market, freedom of financial services and strengthened competition policy' (HM Treasury 1989)) entry could be delayed very considerably. The general prejudice in the UK at present suggests that joining before the last quarter of 1990 is unlikely.

It is therefore a little difficult to date the stages of the Delors proposals in terms of these forecasts, but the implication is that stage one begins soon and lasts until the middle of the decade and that stage three is unlikely this century. However, what is clear is that part of the EC could move to EMU much more quickly and if Italy, the UK and any of Ireland, Greece, Spain and Portugal which also had problems, were to be excluded, nominal and real convergence would be adequate by, say, 1995.

There is some lack of attractiveness in moving backwards towards more frequent realignments of the EMS central rates. As is clear from Table 3, there has been a clear trend to fewer realignments: three years elapsed before the most recent realignment in January 1990 and that was relatively minor, including a narrowing of the bands of permissible fluctuation for the lira to 2¼ per cent as for the other existing participants.

Table 3: Changes in EMS central rates (per cent change)

Dates of realignments

	24/9 1979	31/11 1979	2/3 1981	5/10 1981	22/2 1982	14/6 1982	21/3 1983	21/7 1985	7/4 1986	4/8 1986	12/1 1987
Bfr	0.0	0.0	0.0	0.0	8.8	0.0	1.5	2.0	1.0	0.0	2.0
Dkr	−2.9	−4.8	0.0	0.0	−3.0	0.0	2.5	2.0	1.0	0.0	0.0
DM	2.0	0.0	0.0	5.5	0.0	4.25	5.5	2.0	3.0	0.0	3.0
Ffr	0.0	0.0	0.0	−3.0	0.0	−5.75	−2.5	2.0	−3.0	0.0	0.0
Punt	0.0	0.0	0.0	0.0	0.0	0.0	−3.5	2.0	0.0	−8.0	0.0
Lira	0.0	0.0	−6.0	−3.0	0.0	−2.75	−2.5	−6.0	0.0	0.0	0.0
Dfl	0.0	0.0	0.0	5.5	0.0	4.25	3.5	2.0	3.0	0.0	3.0

However, we do not yet know what the impact of removing the remaining French and Italian exchange controls later this year will be. It has been argued by Giavazzi (1990) for example that the effects will be small because the most important controls have already been relaxed.

The UK, Germany and The Netherlands have had no direct controls on capital movements for some time, and controls are minimal in Belgium and Luxembourg. (However, prudential regulations on the currency composition of institutional portfolios in these countries may have similar effects.) Denmark has already removed most of its controls and the remainder are due to be removed by 1992. Until recently French companies faced restrictions on their foreign exchange dealings, and individuals still face restrictions on holding bank accounts abroad or in a foreign currency (except Ecus). All controls will be removed by June 1990. Even when controls existed, it was always possible for companies to find channels through which funds could flow. The laxity of French controls may be reflected in the small size of the average uncovered interest differential.

Italian controls have been more stringent. For the 32 years up to September 1988 there were considerable restrictions on all foreign currency operations of both banks and companies. All transactions had to receive permission from the Bank of Italy. Controls were considerably relaxed in 1988. The only requirement now is that all foreign transactions go through a recognized bank. It is still forbidden to hold lira deposits abroad, to open credit lines to external residents, or to purchase short-term foreign securities. These restrictions will change portfolio composition but are unlikely to prevent large-scale capital flows. The persistence of a large uncovered differential on Italian international interest rates in 1988/89 (in the absence of significant capital controls) suggests that there may still be a risk permium on the lira. The Italian government is determined to remove all remaining controls by July 1990. However, the removal of capital controls, which has effectively already taken place at least among the larger economies, has not destablized the ERM and has not even necessitated a realignment of central rates.

Part of the problem in making judgements about how fast the exchange system can converge to fixity is that differences between interest rates seem to persist even when the difference in expected rates of inflation is allowed for. The normal presumption is that in a foreign exchange market where there are forward-looking operators who wish to make profits, the bilateral exchange rate expected for a period ahead will differ from the current exchange rate by approximately the difference in the interest rates on the two currencies involved. If expectations are on average correct, then in the past, interest-rate differentials will have been reflected in exchange rate changes. There are a number of reasons why this 'open arbitrage' condition for exchange rates may not have held. In particular, there may be a systematic 'wedge' between exchange rate changes and interest-rate differentials.

It is clear in Table 4 that the uncovered interest differential between France and Germany has averaged −0.3 since 1978, while that between Italy and Germany has averaged – 3.2. The differentials have been larger in the second half of the 1980s. The continuing differences in uncovered interest differentials may be explainable by 'risk premia' – people want to hold Deutschmarks so much that they are prepared to pay a premium to do so. A second possibility is that there has been a systematic underestimation of the likely success of Italian anti-inflationary policy. As a consequence inflation in Italy has consistently turned out to be lower than people thought it was going to be. Of course the mere existence of binding capital controls is likely to mean that higher domestic interest rates have to be offered than would be the case in an unconstrained market.

Table 4: Interest differentials

	Interest rate differentials			*Change in exchange rates*		*Uncovered interest differential*	
	FF/DM	*lira/DM*		*FF/DM*	*lira/DM*	*FF/DM*	*lira/DM*
1978	4.3	7.8	1979/78	3.3	7.3	−1.0	−0.6
1979	2.5	5.2	1980/79	0.2	3.9	−2.3	3.0
1980	2.6	7.8	1981/80	3.4	6.7	0.8	−1.1
1981	3.4	8.1	1982/81	12.5	10.8	9.1	2.7
1982	5.9	11.4	1983/82	10.2	6.7	4.3	−4.7
1983	6.8	12.5	1984/83	3.0	3.8	−3.8	−8.7
1984	5.8	11.4	1985/84	−0.6	5.4	−6.4	−7.0
1985	4.7	9.8	1986/85	4.7	5.6	0.0	−4.2
1986	3.2	8.8	1987/86	4.7	5.1	1.5	−3.7
1987	4.2	7.5	1988/87	1.4	2.8	−2.8	−3.3
1988	3.0	6.1	1989/88	0.0	−1.6	−3.0	−3.3
1989	2.1	5.1					

7.5 Risks in the forecast scenario

The foregoing discussion is just one view of how the next ten years may turn out. Others may no doubt disagree with it, so it is important to trace out what the sources of that disagreement may imply for revision of the forecast before arguing what actions might follow if our view of the future is believed. An assessment of the range of risks of deviation from the forecast path will give an indication of the plausibility of the results.

There are some who argue (Friedman, 1990, for example) that stage one of the Delors Committee's proposals is inherently unstable in that the combination of no exchange controls and fixed but adjustable exchange rates will permit the rapid build-up of market pressure if it becomes widely accepted that any currency is undervalued or overvalued. If this turns out to be true then more frequent realignments may occur, becoming perhaps so frequent that the hoped for increased fixity of the EMS has to be abandoned.

The evidence thus far does not support that fear, but the changes in Eastern Europe, particularly those involved in German reunification, may force further realignments. The influx of migrants into West Germany could cause a revaluation of the Deutschmark because the new workers drive down wages and eliminate some of the existing bottlenecks in the economy. However, reunification could result in a major diversion of resources from West to East increasing the need to borrow and weakening the Deutschmark. The results depend on the seriousness of the difficulties in East Germany, how they are dealt with and the markets' longer-term view of the competitiveness of a united Germany. In so far as the Deutschmark weakens and inflation rises, this helps EC convergence. However, if it strengthens, problems of convergence are extended.

The effects of the wave of immigration into West Germany which accelerated at the end of 1989 are hard to judge. The short-term consequence will be a boost to demand which will benefit both consumer goods and the construction industry. In the medium term, the new immigrants should also increase the supply potential of the economy, especially as many of them are young and well educated (although some retraining may be required). In particular, the increase in the supply of labour will put downward pressure on wages. In 1990 the boost to domestic demand produced will provide an additional counter measure to declining external demand. This is illustrated in Table 5.

Table 5: The effects on the West German economy of an influx of migrants from the east

	Income[a]	*Domestic demand*[b]	*Consumption*[c]	*Trend Labour costs*[d]	*Current account*[e]	*Current GNP ratio*[e]
1990	0.6	1.2	1.6	−0.17	−4.0	−0.5
1991	0.6	1.1	1.6	−1.23	−7.1	−0.5
1992	−0.3	−0.5	1.0	−1.5	−4.6	−0.2
1993	0.2	0.3	0.5	−0.7	−2.5	−0.1
1994	0.2	0.2	0.3	−0.4	−2.3	−0.1

[a] Per cent deviation from base, fourth quarter on fourth quarter.
[b] Points from base in the fourth quarter.
[c] Per cent difference in growth rate, fourth quarter on fourth quarter.
[d] US dollar billion difference from base, annual total.
[e] Deviation from base, per cent of GNP.

In this simulation the workforce in Germany is 500,000 above base in 1990/1, 750,000 in 1990/2, 1 million above in 1990/3 and 1.25 million above in 1990/4 and thereafter, and the exchange rate is fixed. Demand rises more than output and hence the current account worsens. An increased labour supply puts pressure on earnings and causes unit labour costs to fall.

Source: Simulation by Ray Barrell in the *National Institute Economic Review, no. 131,* February 1990.

The continued influx of immigrants from East to West Germany requires an urgent policy response. In early 1990 it appears that the governments of both states view monetary union as the most immediate step that they can take, as a prelude to political reunification within the next two years. A common currency combined with freedom to travel to the West would give East Germans easy access to goods and services not yet currently available in the East. It would also enable Western capital to invest in the East without having to do so in a currency which is not tradeable outside the GDR. In addition it would provide a strong signal from the East German government of its intentions to develop its links with West Germany. It should therefore considerably allay the fears that are fuelling the present migration. A reduction in migration is in the interests of both states, since the East cannot afford to lose important members of its population, and the West cannot easily absorb continued immigration on the present scale.

Further benefits from Eastern Europe lie in the possible liberalization of these economies, allowing greater trade and increased investment in Eastern Europe by Western companies. These benefits are, however, heavily contingent on political developments. It would be foolish and premature to expect that the demise of communism necessarily entails an orderly adjustment to democratic governments and a market-based economic system. Economic links between East and West can therefore be expected to evolve relatively slowly until the East achieves greater political stability. The political change in Eastern Europe will therefore have a fairly muted effect in later years, provided that the East negotiates the transition to economic liberalization successfully. In the medium term, the benefits of such a transition are likely to considerably outweigh those that might emerge from the establishment of the single European market.

At the time of writing it seems reasonable to expect German reunification within the next two years, as this appears to be in line with popular opinion in both states, and also seems to be acceptable to other governments in both Eastern and Western Europe. It is possible that significant steps could be made within the next few months, particularly following the elections which were held in East Germany in March 1990. Reunification will lead to a major reorganization of both economies as East German industry is restructured and West German firms seek to invest in the East. The forecast shows German domestic demand growth of around 4 per cent in 1990, 1991 and 1992, much of this due to high investment and domestic demand growth.

For German policy makers there is a problem of shaping policy to accommodate both the potential short-run and medium-run developments within the economy itself. The primary macroeconomic concern remains the need to prevent the recent economic upturn leading to 'overheating' and consequently to inflation. This concern led to the Bundesbank increasing interest rates by ½ per cent in January, April and June of 1989, and by a further 1 per cent in October. The aim was both to slow the growth rate of domestic demand and to increase the value of the Deutschmark, in order to dampen inflationary pressure. The most recent economic data suggest that the economy remains close to capacity.

It is worth tracing out the implication of a fiscal expansion in Germany to cope with the problems of reunification. This is illustrated over a ten-year horizon in Table 6. The implications for the prospects for monetary union are striking. While the real impact falls almost entirely on West Germany, there is a major nominal consequence for France and smaller ones for the UK and Italy, all of which will assist the process of convergence. Over the 10-year period, prices rise by 7 per cent in France and by 3 per cent in Italy and by 1½ per cent in the UK.

Table 6: Impact of a German fiscal expansion by 1 per cent of GNP

(a) GNP/GDP

Year	*US*	*Japan*	*Germany*	*France*	*Italy*	*UK*
1	0.0	0.1	1.1	0.0	0.0	0.1
2	0.0	0.1	1.1	0.0	0.0	0.1
4	−0.1	0.1	1.1	0.0	−0.1	0.1
6	−0.1	0.0	1.0	0.0	−0.1	0.0
8	−0.2	−0.2	1.0	0.0	−0.1	0.1
10	−0.2	−0.4	0.9	0.0	−0.2	0.1

(b) Consumers' expenditure deflator

Year	*US*	*Japan*	*Germany*	*France*	*Italy*	*UK*
1	0.0	0.0	0.2	−0.2	−0.1	0.0
2	−0.1	0.0	0.5	−0.4	−0.2	0.1
4	−0.2	0.0	1.1	−1.0	−0.4	0.2
6	−0.4	0.0	1.6	−1.7	−0.7	0.1
8	−0.6	0.0	2.1	−2.7	−1.0	−0.3
10	−0.9	−0.1	2.5	−4.0	−1.4	−0.7

(c) Effective exchange rate

Year	*US*	*Japan*	*Germany*	*France*	*Italy*	*UK*
1	1.0	0.1	−2.3	1.9	1.1	−0.1
2	1.2	0.2	−2.8	2.4	1.4	0.0
4	1.5	0.4	−3.9	3.3	2.0	0.3
6	1.9	0.5	−5.0	4.4	2.5	0.6
8	2.2	0.5	−5.9	5.6	2.9	1.0
10	2.5	0.4	−6.8	6.9	3.2	1.5

(d) Interest rate

Year	*US*	*Japan*	*Germany*	*France*	*Italy*	*UK*
1	−0.1	0.0	0.6	−0.3	−0.1	0.0
2	−0.1	0.0	0.6	−0.3	−0.2	0.0
4	−0.1	0.0	0.6	−0.3	−0.1	0.0
6	−0.1	0.0	0.5	−0.4	−0.2	−0.1
8	−0.1	0.0	0.4	−0.5	−0.2	−0.2
10	−0.1	0.0	0.3	−0.7	−0.2	−0.2

(e) Current account balance (% of GNP)

Year	*US*	*Japan*	*Germany*	*France*	*Italy*	*UK*
1	0.00	0.04	−0.62	0.09	0.09	0.05
2	−0.01	0.02	−0.54	0.07	0.05	0.09
4	−0.01	−0.01	−0.40	0.05	0.00	0.11
6	−0.02	−0.03	−0.27	0.03	−0.02	0.09
8	−0.03	−0.05	−0.15	−0.01	−0.04	0.02
10	−0.05	−0.06	−0.03	−0.07	−0.05	−0.07

1. Figures for GNP, consumers' expenditure, and effective exchange rate show percentage difference from base.
2. Figures for interest rates and current balance ratio show difference from base.
3. All figures are fourth quarter values in the relevant year.

While the last two changes may be small, this simulation suggests that a fairly minor adjustment in the West German fiscal stance, given a continuation of the strong anti-inflationary stance in France, would permit monetary union with France at an early stage. Taken together, therefore, the base forecast and the assessment of risks suggest:

1. There will be steady nominal convergence in the EC over the next ten years.
2. Belgium, Luxembourg, The Netherlands (and probably Denmark) have already reached the point where monetary union with West Germany is feasible.
3. That group could be joined by France by the mid-1990s.
4. A small tendency towards more inflationary behaviour continues in France indefinitely, but the nature of the structural change required to remove that either by France or by West Germany appears achievable.

5. The problems for the UK and Italy are more severe. Specific further structural adjustment would be required beyond a tight monetary policy to achieve adequate convergence.
6. The UK is a special case not just because it is not yet a member of the ERM of the EMS but because it shows steady real divergence under a tight monetary policy. It must therefore be a real worry that the UK will find it unattractive to participate in monetary union unless another mechanism to achieve major structural change can be found.
7. It is, however, possible that the UK will join the ERM within the next year or so.
8. As a result of UK membership and Italian problems, more frequent realignments of the ERM can be expected over the next five years than over the last four.
9. This greater instability of the EMS poses problems for a route to monetary integration based on actions only *after* increased stability has been demonstrated.
10. Coupled with the difficulties of Ireland and the newer members of the Community – Spain, Greece and Portugal – there is a real chance that a 'two speed' Europe may emerge with the 'northern' countries integrating faster and a question mark hanging over Italy and the UK (the larger question mark in the latter case.)
11. If the Delors Committee plan is followed without amendment, full monetary union seems unlikely this century.
12. One ironic benefit to the process is that developments in Eastern Europe may ease the problems of integration with West Germany, although in so far as it diverts investment from the 'peripheral' areas of the Community it will emphasize the 'two-tier' problem.

7.6 Means of improving upon the current system

It appears therefore that there is a real danger that steps towards monetary union may falter halfway as progress in convergence fails to meet its targets. In these circumstances the European System of Central Banks could become a relatively empty institution like the EMCF and the current initiative wane like the Werner Report 20 years ago. It is therefore appropriate to ask what alternative options there are for improving the prospects. Four are explored here:

1. A 'softer' EMS with more freely floating exchange rates;
2. Currency competition;
3. A more rapid move to a single currency; and
4. A two-speed Europe

7.6.1 A softer EMS

A major worry about the EMS is that in the early stages after the final freeing of exchange markets in the EC and the simultaneous development of the single market in financial services, there may be considerably greater fluctuations in behaviour and unpredictability of reactions to familiar stimuli. This has been the experience of other countries in the process of financial deregulation, clearly illustrated by the UK. In these circumstances monetary control becomes more difficult and its impact erratic. The simultaneous combination of these increased fluctuations with a tightening of the EMS bands could lead to a destabilizing of the EMS.

One response to this would be to allow the member currencies to fluctuate rather more freely in the initial period. Alternatively, a greater readiness to accept realignments without feeling that they represent a failure to move towards integration might help ease the difficulty. A third possibility is for central banks to be prepared to wait longer before intervening in the market, until the compulsory bounds are reached, because at that point the central banks of both the appreciating and the depreciating currencies have to act. Currently the propensity is for unilateral intra-marginal intervention by the depreciating countries before the compulsory margins are reached. That symmetric intervention may help to avoid unnecessary short-term realignments or excessive unilateral pressures.

However, lack of symmetry has been characteristic of exchange rate regimes since World War II, and there is no reason to think that surplus countries will feel any more inclined to ease the problems of adjustment of the depreciating countries. Indeed, since this would be inflationary in net terms, it is not surprising that this should be the attitude. The Delors Committee has quite specifically looked at the question and the first mandate of the ESCB is that 'the system would be committed to the objective of price stability'. The proposed structure underlines the West German approach with an 'independent' central bank firmly committed to inflation restraint. The Delors Report (paragraph 33) sees fiscal policy as the method of achieving of other economic policy objectives: 'The broad *objective* of economic policy co-ordination would be to promote growth, employment and external balance in an environment of price stability and economic cohesion.' There is widespread debate among economists about whether this rigid separation of instruments and targets is optimal. There is always the danger that such a halfway system, which is neither fully floating nor closely controlled, will lack credibility and will hence fail, making the long path to MU even less likely.

7.6.2 Currency competition

One of the features of the Delors Committee's approach to MU is that it appears to be institutionally rather than market driven. There are many who argue (Robert Triffin, for example) that a satisfactory MU has to be market led. Institutional change, accommodating and facilitating official action is of course necessary to permit this market development. It is clear that the EC is quite a long way from being an optimum currency area. While it has considerable integration, which may help lead to a fairly similar reaction across the various parts of the Community to external shocks, it does not in practice have sufficient labour mobility to help ease adjustment mechanisms and does not at present have a clear sharing of the risks among the partners.

An optimal path towards monetary union in these circumstances might therefore comprise two components. The first would be the continuation of the process of trying to create the conditions for an optimum currency area, by closer integration through the completion of the internal market for example. The second would be to allow greater development of the currency market in the expectation that the competition between currencies in a more open market would eventually lead to some currencies winning the competition and hence to progress towards a single currency through the market mechanism.

The removal of restrictions on what currencies can be held and where will obviously enhance the ability of people to use and hold one currency rather than another. Transaction costs between currencies are falling both as a result of increased international competition between financial intermediaries as the single market develops and as technology continues to improve. Some development of the market in this way therefore seems likely.

The UK Treasury (1989) argues that this process will go further. As the market develops and integration continues, the EC currencies will become increasingly interchangeable. In the early stages the low inflation country currencies will tend to be preferred as they are more predictable. This in itself will help put market pressure on countries to follow policies that will reduce inflation quickly and effectively.

In this process there is no compulsion to rigorous fixed parity through the rules of the EMS, nor constraints on the budgetary position of governments. It is felt that the logic of the market will force them 'voluntarily' into conformity because the consequences of failure will be increased costs for losers in the currency competition and the erosion of the importance of their currency.

The Ecu would be one of the currencies in this competition. As divergences narrow it could very well develop a major, if not the major, role because its use would cut down on the number of transactions that have to be made. The UK Treasury (1989) suggests that one means of encouraging this development would be to fix the composition of the Ecu permanently so that this source of uncertainty about the value of the basket is removed. This process has considerable appeal in the sense that it gets round many of the disadvantages listed earlier. There is no formal loss of sovereignty, merely its gradual loss as a result of the realities of the process of integration, which may be politically a much easier course to follow. The role of centralized institutions is reduced, maintaining the principle of 'subsidiarity'. Adjustment mechanisms, including exchange rate depreciation, are available to the member states in the process of transition if they prefer that balance of costs.

This proposal also faces problems. It is not clear that all the member states would welcome a wider international role for their currencies. The greater that role, the less control the central bank can exercise and the greater the chance of divergence between the domestic and international requirements of monetary policy. Secondly, it is not clear how far the process would go as the market alone is very unlikely to drive out domestic use of the domestic currency. While domestic transactions dominate, there will always be a cost in moving into other currencies which will be less worth paying as currencies move closer.

This development of the use of the Ecu in international transactions perhaps shows how its role could develop as a means of avoiding transaction costs. Under these circumstances, the Ecu could gradually move into domestic transactions as acquirers of Ecu go on to make these transactions, where it would be less costly to avoid changing currency. This pattern of increasing penetration would follow the typical path of any new product for which there are 'system' costs. Domestic Ecu transactions will tend only to take place if both parties can avoid incurring an exchange cost. Initial growth would thus be slow but as more and more people avoided the need to exchange Ecu for other currencies the use would expand very rapidly.

The idea that a lot of currencies would be used freely in various markets seems unlikely. Not just because there are considerable information costs but also because the holding costs for the individual would rise. Certain currencies would only be suitable for some purposes. The more one moves towards discussing household transactions, the less plausible the prospect becomes. There are difficulties in using Scottish pound notes in England, for example, not just because they are fairly rare and many people would not known if they had a forgery (that would be overcome by familiarity), but also because there are no pound notes in England and hence ticket machines will not take them.

Overcoming these problems points strongly to the use of a common currency rather than other EC currencies, and ultimately to that common currency becoming the single currency. In this case it is not possible to ignore the question of who issues such a common currency. It could develop privately or be issued by central banks, but an unfettered development might be confusing, unstable and difficult to regulate. European central bankers would want to act in co-ordination in these circumstances and some central institution seems inevitable. Otherwise one might have competition between various different Ecus, each issued by a different bank, which need not even be exchangeable one-for-one, their parity depending upon who issued them. Most previous examples of monetary unions, where the same currency was issued by several different banks without the supervision of a single central bank, were based on a metal standard so that the coins which backed up any paper issued were quite literally of the same value and hence could be traded at parity.

Currency competition might thus be a route towards monetary union although increased central bank co-operation and action seems inevitable despite the claims of the literature on 'private money'. However, it has the major drawback that there is no guarantee that it would actually encourage moves towards union or indeed do it at a reasonably rapid rate. This is only a drawback, of course, if monetary union is the required destination, rather than finding the most effective market-led form of monetary integration which fits the prevailing state of economic union.

7.6.3 A rapid move to a single currency

The major gains from monetary union only occur with implementation of the single currency appropriately administered. There is, therefore, a serious temptation to say that the correct approach is to move rapidly towards a single currency and face the problems this poses, head-on.

The major problem is straightforward. The ability to change exchange rates and interest rates relative to other countries is an important facet of being able to absorb external shocks. If those mechanisms are not available a monetary union must be able to offer compensating adjustment mechanisms to prevent the shocks appearing intolerable. One hypothesis is that monetary union forces the pace of structural convergence. Another, which in our opinion holds considerable force, is that commitments to change in the long run have far less credibility than commitments to achieve change in the short run. Credibility makes the achievement of an objective a great deal easier. To achieve credibility, especially where this involves a change in policy, requires an over-reaction by governments. The 1992 programme is an excellent case in point. Cutting through the wealth of virtuous statements in the past about the wish to achieve full economic integration in the EC, it produced a comprehensive plan with specific legislative objectives to be achieved with a tight timetable. It was clear to many from the beginning that it was over-ambitious, and that parts of the programme were unlikely to be agreed as originally intended. Nevertheless, aided by a concerted marketing campaign, it has changed attitudes and the whole expectation of the pace of change in European integration has been altered. This, therefore, stimulates investment and the receptiveness of suppliers and purchasers to integration and hence makes it much easier to achieve. Forcing the pace has bred its own success.

Could forcing the pace of monetary union have the same effect? The danger is that the approach makes obstacles, which might have been soluble given enough time, insuperable, and hence leads to failure instead of success. Attempts to repair failures may be much harder than pursuing the course of slow change, even though it is the course of lesser ambition.

By using our *GEM* model to simulate forcing the pace of monetary union we can expose the extent of the adjustment problems and the plausibility of their solution. We can also look specifically at the problem of the UK because that provides the greatest adjustment difficulties and, using our much larger model of the UK economy

(*NIMODEL*), we can examine how choosing the timing and exchange rate at which to enter the ERM can ease the problem of adjustment.

The choice of date for forcing the pace is difficult and largely arbitrary. We have therefore taken as an illustration a timetable with a similar length to that of the successful single market programme. In the case of MU, 1990 was taken to be the start year, equivalent to 1985, when the White Paper was published outlining the proposals for the completion of the internal market. Hence the end of 1997 would be the year, seven years ahead, which corresponds to 1992 as the target date for achievement of full monetary union. As *GEM* only explicitly deals with West Germany, France, Italy, the UK, Belgium and The Netherlands, we assume that they define the EC and show results only for the first four as they have the fuller models.

Pursuing the parallel with the single market timetable, we assume that agreement on MU is achieved in 1990 and that exchange rates are declared to be irrevocably fixed as from the first quarter of 1991. As a result of this commitment, we expect that interest rates will fall immediately towards the German rate, although, in the case of Italy, the commitment is treated as not being totally 'credible' and a 2 per cent risk premium is maintained.

This illustrates the problem very clearly. If on the way to monetary union there are important external shocks, adjustment is eased by reneging on the union commitment. The longer the period of transition, the greater the chance of an adverse shock. However, once inside a truly irrevocable union the problems do not vanish. Either the economies must have changed so that they converge more closely or there needs to be offsetting flows to mitigate the less favourable response. To create the union, fiscal policy also needs to be changed. At present Italy and France run larger government deficits than Germany. Monetary union will involve some tightening of the policy stance in order to bring inflation down to the (post-union) German level. These deficit reductions will also reduce the balance of payments deficits that would otherwise emerge for these countries. Payment flows still have to be financed outside a union, and deficits still imply the transfer of assets to non-residents.

The reduction of interest rates to German levels increases demand in these economies, even given the concomitant reduction in inflation and real rates of interest. Fiscal policy has to be used to constrain increases in consumers' expenditure in France, Italy and the UK. Equilibrium savings and investment flows are produced if: (i) the Italian budget deficit is progressively reduced from its current 10 per cent of GDP to around 3 per cent by 1997; (ii) French fiscal policy is progressively tightened, reducing the deficit by 2 per cent of GDP; and (iii) the UK tightens fiscal policy in the early 1990s in order to reduce demand growth and ensure that savings and investment flows return to equilibrium by 1997.

This forced route to MU appears successful because inflation does converge to German rates, and averages only 1¼ per cent per annum throughout the Community between 1991 and 1997. Table 7 describes the union in terms of deviations from the base forecast.

Table 7: Consequence of faster path to monetary union

		GDP	*Domestic demand*	*Current balance ($bn)*	*Unemployment (percentage points)*	*Consumers' expenditure deflator*	*Export market share*
Germany	91	0.0	0.0	−1.7	0.0	0.0	0.3
	93	0.6	0.3	−1.4	−0.2	0.2	1.0
	95	1.2	0.6	−2.8	−0.5	0.8	1.6
	97	1.1	0.4	−5.9	−0.5	1.4	1.8
France	91	−0.4	−0.8	5.4	0.6	−0.3	−0.4
	93	−0.5	−0.5	0.9	0.6	−1.1	−1.4
	95	−0.3	−0.1	−1.9	0.3	−2.3	−2.0
	97	−0.5	−0.4	−3.6	0.7	−3.1	−1.8
Italy	91	−0.3	−0.4	0.8	0.4	−0.3	−0.5
	93	0.0	0.6	−6.6	0.0	−1.3	−1.2
	95	−0.3	0.1	−7.6	0.3	−2.7	−1.7
	97	−0.8	−0.4	−10.8	0.8	−4.5	−1.9
UK	91	−0.2	−0.4	4.1	0.3	−1.0	−1.0
	93	0.0	1.3	−3.7	0.0	−5.4	−1.5
	95	0.3	3.4	−20.2	−0.4	−9.8	−1.6
	97	−0.7	1.8	−7.6	0.6	−13.6	−3.6

Note: Deviations from base levels in per cent except current balance and unemployment.

Inflation in Germany is around ¼ per cent per annum higher, while in France it is about ½ per cent lower. German output is a little higher and the French a little lower. However, the lagged reaction to continually changing fiscal policy appears to be long. The base forecast had German competitiveness deteriorating relative to that of France, but with a fixed exchange rate this tendency is less marked, and the Germans gain export market share while the French lose it.

The UK and Italy make more significant inflation reduction gains than do the French as a consequence of the faster path to union. Italian inflation falls by almost 1 per cent a year, while that in the UK falls by 2¼ per cent a year. Lower interest rates in both countries raise domestic demand, despite the tighter stance of fiscal policy, but output is below base because competitiveness relative to Germany causes some loss of export market share. Unemployment is likely to be marginally higher as a consequence.

These results suggest that a more rapid monetary union would not be costly to create, and would produce substantial anti-inflationary gains, especially in the UK and Italy. This result has been produced using an historic model and hence does not depend upon any gains made through structural change consequent on the union. These favourable results rely on two factors: (i) the credibility of the announcement of 'irrevocably fixed exchange rates'; and (ii) the lack of a long-term trade-off between inflation and unemployment. In this case, they get an inflation gain with little employment loss.

What this illustration has explored is the ability of member states to move rapidly to MU. However, for such a monetary union to be successful it must also be sustainable. Rapid attainment of MU would not be helpful if it broke up soon thereafter because it could not cope with unanticipated shocks. Adequate nominal convergence to achieve MU does not automatically give sustainability. Other facets of convergence, such as similarity of economic structure, also matter. We therefore looked at a second set of simulations which examines how the EC countries, with their current structures, respond to external shocks under the rules of behaviour implied by MU. If these results appear unacceptable, it would imply that further integration of the European economy is necessary before MU can realistically be achieved.

The pattern of the effect of external shocks depends upon the policy reactions of the authorities and on the reactions of other market participants. It is assumed that the European central banking system operates essentially like an expanded Bundesbank, aiming to keep German inflation in check. (The exchange rate equation, which obviously reflects the behaviour of market participants as well, is an adapted version of that for Germany, but takes into account the Community deficit as a percentage of Community GDP rather than that of Germany alone.) Two shocks are simulated: a doubling of the oil price to $30 per barrel and an increase in US spending of 2 per cent of GDP.

Oil price shock

Table 8 gives the results of an oil price shock on the monetary union and Table 9 the results without a union. The responses of the individual economies are diverse even with monetary union. The deterioration of the union's balance of payments produces a depreciation of the dollar exchange rate. This, in combination with the rise in the oil price, causes the rate of inflation to rise in the short run and the price level to rise in the long run. Prices rise most in Italy and least in Germany. The Italian economy has in the past reacted more quickly to external pressures than the rest of Europe and real wages have been more responsive to change. This may of course change under monetary union.

However, the long-run structural differences may not be the only source of divergence in our model. A monetary policy reacting to slowly evolving German inflation raises nominal rates by only 1 per cent in the short run. The faster speed of price responses in Italy, France and the UK

Table 8: Shocks with a monetary union – oil price rise (per cent differences from base levels)

		GDP	*Domestic demand*	*Unemploy-ment*	*Consumers' expenditure deflator*	*Balance of payments ($bn)*	*Dollar rate*	*3-month[1] interest rate*
Germany								
Years	1	0.9	0.1	−0.3	1.4	−11.0	0.8	0.9
	2	1.0	0.1	−0.4	2.1	−9.0	3.2	0.9
	3	1.0	−0.1	−0.4	2.7	−7.8	2.2	0.6
France								
Years	1	−0.3	−0.6	0.3	3.2	−13.0		
	2	−0.5	−1.4	0.6	5.9	−6.5		
	3	−0.8	−1.9	0.9	7.2	−1.3		
Italy								
Years	1	−0.1	−0.6	0.0	4.0	−9.7		
	2	−0.6	−1.5	0.1	5.9	−5.0		
	3	−1.4	−2.2	0.2	7.2	−3.7		
UK								
Years	1	0.4	−0.6	0.0	2.6	2.0		
	2	1.1	−0.8	−0.1	5.0	8.5		
	3	1.5	−0.4	−0.1	6.4	11.3		

[1] Percentage point differences from base rates.

implies that real interest rates there will fall under a monetary union, expanding demand and causing prices to rise. There are, however, two other structural differences. Inflation itself has a greater effect on domestic demand in Italy than elsewhere, reflecting the influence of the import content of exports. The UK and Germany benefit most from the increase in holdings of non-interest bearing assets. The rise in oil price also affects countries differently, reflecting their dependence on oil exports, with France showing the least response. GDP is higher than base in Germany while domestic demand is lower, reflecting, in the long run, both this gain and the effect of a smaller rise in prices on competitiveness.

The effects of the oil shock without a monetary union depend upon policy responses. The most marked difference is for the UK, because of its relative dependence on oil exports. The rise in the oil price improves the UK balance of payments, causing the UK to appreciate.

Table 9: Shocks without a monetary union – oil price rise (per cent differences from base levels)

		GDP	*Domestic demand*	*Unemploy-ment*	*Consumers' expenditure deflator*	*Balance of payments ($bn)*	*Dollar rate*	*3-month[1] interest rate*
Germany								
Years	1	0.9	0.1	−0.3	1.4	−8.7	0.8	0.9
	2	1.2	0.1	−0.5	2.3	−10.7	3.4	1.0
	3	1.2	0.0	−0.5	2.8	−8.7	2.6	0.7
France								
Years	1	−0.4	−0.7	0.0	3.2	−12.5	−0.1	1.6
	2	−0.7	−1.7	0.1	5.5	−5.6	−0.2	2.3
	3	−1.1	−2.2	0.1	6.4	−2.0	−0.2	1.6
Italy								
Years	1	−0.2	−0.8	0.0	4.0	−7.8	−0.4	2.4
	2	−1.3	−2.6	0.2	5.4	−2.1	−0.3	2.1
	3	−2.3	−3.5	0.4	6.5	0.6	−0.4	1.3
UK								
Years	1	0.4	−0.6	0.0	2.1	3.2	−2.8	1.6
	2	0.9	−0.5	−0.1	2.8	8.9	−5.1	1.0
	3	1.2	0.3	−0.1	2.0	13.2	−9.5	−0.2

[1] Percentage points difference from base rates.

Inflation in the UK initially rises, but the appreciation reduces the price level to below base, and as a consequence interest rates fall relative to base. The lower inflation rate is associated with a smaller rise in income above base levels. Given revealed policy preferences, this is probably better than the effects in the union.

The other European economies no longer benefit from the improved UK trade account. As a result Germany depreciates more than in the union and takes on more inflation. The depreciation, especially relative to France and Italy, improves competitiveness and raises output. Given revealed German policy preferences, this might be considered a worse outcome. Without the union both France and Italy show faster interest rate responses to inflation and as a consequence their exchange rates do not depreciate, and their inflation rates are lower. Without the union, and with policy independence, the Italian price level is 5 per cent lower by the end of our simulation than the union, and the French price level is

Table 10: Shocks with a monetary union – US government spending (per cent differences from base levels)

		GDP	*Consumers' expenditure deflator*	*Current Balance ($bn)*	*Dollar rate*	*Interest rate*[1]
Germany						
Years	1	0.4	0.1	2.6	−1.1	0.02
	2	0.5	0.2	2.8	−1.0	0.12
	8	0.4	0.6	7.2	−5.2	0.07
France						
Years	1	0.0	0.1	0.5		
	2	0.1	0.3	1.3		
	8	0.0	0.5	−1.5		
Italy						
Years	1	0.2	0.4	0.4		
	2	0.2	1.1	0.7		
	8	0.0	2.8	−3.8		
UK						
Years	1	0.1	0.2	0.2		
	2	0.1	0.5	−0.1		
	8	0.3	0.5	−5.0		

[1] Percentage points difference from base.

4 per cent lower. Both display lower output as well. As with the UK, the effects of the oil price rise seem to be better without the union.

Table 11: Shocks without a monetary union – US government spending (per cent differences from base levels)

	GDP	*Consumers' expenditure deflator*	*Current Balance ($bn)*	*Dollar rate*	*Interest rate*[1]
Germany					
Years 1	0.4	0.1	2.7	−1.2	0.02
2	0.5	0.2	2.7	−1.1	0.11
8	0.3	0.5	5.4	−5.5	0.05
France					
Years 1	0.0	0.2	0.2	−0.1	0.09
2	0.1	0.7	1.4	0.0	0.31
8	0.0	2.6	4.7	−0.1	0.40
Italy					
Years 1	0.2	0.3	0.3	−0.2	0.13
2	0.3	0.7	1.3	−0.1	0.60
8	0.2	3.5	8.2	−0.2	0.62
UK					
Years 1	0.1	0.3	0.3	−1.1	0.11
2	0.1	0.4	0.2	−2.1	0.12
8	0.1	−7.5	−3.9	−12.4	−0.73

[1] Percentage points difference from base.

US government expenditure shock

The US government expenditure shock produces similar results throughout the Community with a union except, as Table 10 shows, Italian inflation responds more noticeably to the higher level of world demand. However without the union, responses are more divergent. Our estimated exchange rate equations produce a considerable appreciation of sterling and hence a lower level of prices. This reflects the much stronger links between the dollar and sterling than the other currencies. The Deutschmark also appreciates more than the French franc or the lira, reflecting its role as an international currency that is affected more than the others by the higher US deficit.

Easing the entry path for the UK

In the case of the simulations for forcing the pace of monetary union we had to neglect one of the most important costs, namely the possible existence of a long-run trade off between inflation and employment. In the case of the NI domestic model of the UK (*NIDEM*), that is not necessary. Using optimal control methods we have therefore tried to select an entry method to the ERM which makes the transition to MU as satisfactory as possible. We saw in the base forecast that the UK is inflating faster and will continue to do so in the slow transition to MU. Any attempt therefore to enter the EMS at an exchange rate close to current levels would be unacceptably costly.

We therefore present three simulations which show the costs of rapid entry.[2] The first simulation (A) assumes that the government only has the objective of lowering inflation. The second (B) adds the objective of trying to avoid falls in output. Both of these (see Table 12) result in highly restrictive fiscal policies in 1990 and 1991 with £6–7 billion contractions, £11–13 billion in the two years combined. This, we think, is politically implausible. We therefore experimented with a more gradual entry (C) allowing a depreciation by 8 per cent against the Deutschmark after entry up to 1995. Here the contractions are of the order of £2 billion in 1990 and 1991 compared with the base, although it creeps up to £4 billion again in 1992.

Table 12: Fiscal deflation in the UK required to support ERM entry (£bn)

	Case A	*Case B*	*Case C*
1990	6	4	2
1991	7	7	2
1992	3	2	4

Note: These are changes from an indexed base. Thus in case A, if income tax remains unchanged public expenditure has to fall by £6bn in 1990 and a further £7bn in 1991.

Table 13 reports the optimal entry levels for sterling, all substantially below current levels of around 2.80 DM/£. Thus a successful path for the UK would involve an initial devaluation for entry into the ERM followed by a series of small realignments. If immediate fixity has to be achieved, the initial devaluation has to be higher. The ultimate DM/£ rates are approximately the same in all cases as this is a requirement of long-run equilibrium (a feature of the NI model).

Table 13: Alternative entry rates for the UK into the ERM

	Case A	*Case B*	*Case C*
Average annual inflation 1990–5 (%)	5.0	6.0	5.5
Effective exchange rate 1991 Q1	77.0	74.0	82.0
Implied DM/£ rate 1991 Q1	2.4	2.35	2.6

In these examples therefore we have explored how harsh a transition period is feasible and seen that it is possible to achieve MU in 1995[3] if the UK is allowed a flexible transition path. No doubt Italy and the newer EC members would find a similar phased transition beneficial. Nevertheless, by announcing at the outset that 'swift' transition to the MU was intended and hence imposing credibility on the whole arrangement, completion could be achieved by the mid-1990s, whereas under the Delors Committee plan, where a specific time path is unstated, it is unlikely to be achieved by 1999 and still requires a fundamental structural adjustment in the UK and Italy, laying the system open for longer to adverse unanticipated shocks which would encourage countries to renege.

It does appear therefore that on these macroeconomic grounds a faster route to integration with an end-date before 1999 is both feasible and necessary if the process is to have enough credibility to affect expectations. However, operating from the outset of the adjustment period with virtually fixed exchange rates and no central rate alignment as was achieved between 1989 and 1990 is too harsh a requirement. Coupled with the main benefits only being realizable when transition to the single currency is complete, the course of faster progress to MU has clear attractions.

7.6.4 A two-speed Europe

One of the problems of integration is that the implementation of many aspects depends upon the pace of the slowest country. The more 'positive' the move towards integration then the more likely this constraint is to bind. The single market was in many respects an attempt to get round this problem in the case of economic integration. The areas on which positive agreements and harmonization are required have been minimized while most of the actions are aspects of 'negative' integration – removing the barriers to integration rather than eliciting any specific response.

The currency competition route is a similar response in the field of monetary union. However, in this case a number of positive steps are required even if the framework is more minimalist than that envisaged by the Delors Committee. One way of progressing faster is to allow those members of the Community that can agree to move rapidly towards monetary union to do so, and to permit the others to join when they too can manage the transition. In general, except when forced to do so, the Community has tried to avoid arrangements in which only some participate. Even if some members are opposed, qualified majority agreements are binding on all. Monetary measures are an exception to this. Not everyone joined the 'snake' and membership fluctuated; not all countries have been in the ERM of the EMS, or formed part of the Ecu basket. Those that were in the full system did not necessarily face the same intervention bands. It would not therefore be an illogical step to continue this asymmetry.

Many of the benefits would still accrue if the MU bloc was at all substantial; it is merely that a rather larger number of their external transactions would have to be in 'foreign' currencies. However, assuming that this bloc has the Ecu as its single currency, it is likely that its use would be very considerable in the Community non-participants. Not only will the prospect of the gains encourage them to try to enter the system, but the use of the Ecu will automatically integrate them to a considerable extent. This two-speed approach therefore has significant attractions. It prevents those with greater adjustment problems from holding the others back and acts as an encouragement for them to continue to move closer.

However, one of the problems of the process of convergence to achieve the necessary structure for participation is that it tends to be asymmetric. It would be much easier for the EC to converge towards the mean rather than towards the lowest inflation countries. The more help those in difficulty can obtain from the union bloc, the easier that process of adjustment is likely to be. Trying to stick to the principle of complete agreement across the EC will tend to encourage mutual assistance in order to get that agreement. Forming a two-speed system where the slower group has the lower standards of living may help exacerbate the differences and assist fragmentation rather than unification.

Any agreements on slower-speed adjustment to MU for some member states would therefore be better served if they lay within a timetable of gradual change, such as those laid down for new EC members, rather than being timeless expressions of hope for full membership in the future. However, having more than one speed for transition may aid the objectives of widening the Community.

Most worrying, however, is the possibility that a two-speed Europe will not be a deliberate move to ease integration but an involuntary result of attempting to move to monetary integration too fast. If some countries fail to adjust in time they will have to withdraw from the agreement or it will need to be slowed. Slowing the timetable, particularly if the evolutionary period already appears to be long, will lose credibility and may endanger the achievement of MU.

7.6.5 Implied improvements

Some clear themes have emerged from the examination of possible improvements that could be made to the base forecast of the path of monetary union over the next ten years.

Firstly, there are clear benefits in an early announcement of a specific date for the completion of European monetary union within the planning horizon of the main agents in the market. This gives credibility to the intention – firms in particular are not likely to react in the short run to long-term expressions of intent by governments with no fixed date of completion, especially if it is plain to all that there are considerable problems *en route*. Costs are incurred in preparing for MU and firms will not wish to incur them unnecessarily. Also, an announcement exerts pressure on the member states in relation to actions to achieve convergence that have to be taken immediately. Most importantly a credible announcement will result in a fall in interest rates in the short run in the expectation of generally lower rates of inflation in the future. It will not lower them immediately to the ultimate levels because some measure of uncertainty is bound to remain. This has two major advantages: first of all it lowers the cost of capital at a time when investment is at a premium because of the need to restructure in order to respond effectively and reap the benefits from the single market programme; and, secondly, it eases the problem of transition for the more inflation-prone countries. Not only can high interest rates contribute to inflation directly but they require that the process of transition is more deflationary. That not only makes it more difficult to achieve real convergence but it is politically more difficult to implement.

Secondly, the announcement at the outset that the Ecu is to be the single currency of the MU will avoid unnecessary costs and enable the market to prepare for the change in good time. Markets will continue to evolve whatever decisions governments take. If the Ecu is not announced as the end point there will be continuing competition among currencies for a role in inter-country transactions. If the Ecu is nominated then its role will increase during the transition period, both cutting costs and easing the process of familiarization to its use in MU. Many changes in accounting, invoicing and cash machinery, such as tills and vending machines, take a long time to plan and implement so the end point of the change to the Ecu needs to be clear from the outset.

Thirdly, the removal of capital controls, the completion of financial integration and the possible consequences of German reunification make it likely that the EMS will experience more fluctuation than has been the case recently. The system should accommodate that instability and not move to ever closer rigidity. The problem is to retain credibility. Unsustainable rigidity and excessive flexibility both bring the achievability of MU into question. The ability of markets to respond to shocks is being increased. Previous experience with financial deregulation shows that traditional control methods become more difficult to apply. Also, it is impossible for some countries, particularly the UK, to achieve the necessary convergence to MU without some realignments. An unwillingness to be flexible will slow rather than advance the process of MU.

Finally, there are problems of control in the internationalization of currencies which have to be addressed during the period of transition. The internationalization of existing currencies means that national central banks have less control over their currencies as a lever on domestic inflation. Development of the Ecu as a substitute needs a framework for control if it is to operate well.

7.7 The problems of transition

It has become clear from the preceding discussion that it is the transition to MU which provides the most intractable problems. The advantage of a single currency in MU is clear. Except under fairly special circumstances, that single currency is going to be a new 'European' currency rather than that of any one of the member states. Although the current role of the Ecu as a basket may confuse the picture of that future, as convergence increases this problem will diminish. There are no obvious substitutes in the form of new European currencies and the development of an existing currency to perform the task is not only politically a very sensitive matter but poses major problems of control in the transition.

Many of the macroeconomic transition problems which have been identified do not involve the Ecu as such, although use of the Ecu might be helpful in solving some of them. Two major problems emerge. The first is one of responsibility and the other is the distinctive nature of the Ecu.

The Ecu is a basket currency composed of the member states' currencies in a predetermined proportion. It is nobody's domestic currency, so it is not issued by any central bank. There are in practice two types of Ecu. The 'official' Ecu, used by central banks, which forms part of the EMS system, and the 'private' Ecu, held by the private sector. The two are separate and the official Ecu is quite explicitly not to be used for creation of 'high-powered' deposits by central banks to develop a private Ecu based on the official Ecu.

The private Ecu has developed very rapidly in recent years but as a financial asset rather than as a transaction medium. In 1988, the Ecu ranked sixth in importance for bond issues among all Euromarket currencies. In the early 1980s, use of the Ecu rose rapidly but peaked, although activity has increased again in the last two years. The principal users have been in Italy and France (non-EC institutions) although substantial use of the Ecu has also been made by countries outside the EC. London is the most active Ecu market and use has also been made of Ecu treasury bills, particularly by the UK.

The Ecu, by providing an automatic portfolio of European currencies, fulfils a useful role as a financial asset. It is not sufficient on its own of course, because for many holders the Ecu weights will not provide an ideal portfolio. Because of its special nature the number of financial instruments denominated in Ecu is limited and as time passes and the market becomes bigger this will no doubt develop in-line with other currencies. Thus, although the Ecu will continue to be attractive as a portfolio asset, it is not likely to sweep aside the role of national currencies in the short run. The more it is used in transactions and the closer MU approaches then the more private market will also expand.

The very attraction of the basket nature of the Ecu for financial holders is the source of its unattractiveness for transactions. Unless the Ecu itself is the currency for both parties to the transaction the chances are that their subsequent transactions will be in different currencies, necessitating further exchange costs. Outside Community institutions, the Ecu is nobody's currency.

It would appear *prima facie* sensible, if the Ecu is the ultimate destination of MU, that it is used increasingly *en route* to facilitate the change – if only to familiarize an increasingly large proportion of people with it. There appear to be several options. The first is to allow Ecu markets to continue as at present until monetary union has been reached, and then switch to the Ecu as the single currency in a single move. This appears to be the approach of the Delors Committee. Full EMU would be achieved, and the ESCB could establish how a single currency should be managed with a view to implementing it at some later date. Here the Ecu is very much a follower, not a force for change. Existing administrative obstacles to the private use of the Ecu are to be removed (paragraph 49) but no more extensive proposal is made.

The second option is to develop the use of the Ecu as a parallel currency during the period of transition. This could be unfettered, allowing central banks to behave as they thought best by co-ordination between themselves through the ESCB or, indeed, centrally via a European central bank. In this case, the Ecu would not change its basket characteristics. One of the problems of this approach is that having a thirteenth currency adds complications and costs to the system which may not be outweighed by the benefits. There will need to be institutions to handle the transactions; it becomes necessary to hold a wider range of balances. It may even increase the number of transactions which have to be undertaken. If the path to MU is to be followed by the market, the Ecu should appear attractive not a burden. Financial intermediaries will not, of course, object to such complications because they earn their livelihood from the complexity and demand for transactions. Indeed the demise of a large portion of the foreign exchange markets under MU will result in some of their employees losing their jobs.

A more radical proposal is to create a new Ecu altogether, separating it from its basket role. This would involve an attempt to launch the Ecu as the most attractive currency in Europe in the hope that not only would it be the destination of MU but that its use would increase during the process of transition thereby automatically easing the process. The basket Ecu has the disadvantage that it will, by definition, not be the strongest currency in Europe. Hence although it may appear relatively attractive compared with the weaker EC currencies it will appear less attractive in the stronger currency countries (except of course as a means of payment). If a separate Ecu is created this could artificially be made the strongest currency in the EC by, say, guaranteeing that it will never fall in the realignments of the EMS, always moving with whatever happens to be the strongest currency. Instead of moving from 12 currencies to 1 we would move from 12 to 13 currencies and then to 1 – the thirteenth ultimately taking over.

In some respects this seems attractive. Transition involves progressively greater use of the common currency. However, the comments about increased cost may also apply to the independent as well as the basket Ecu. It is confusing in so far as two meanings, and indeed rates, will develop for the same currency. It also requires that someone must issue it. This could be commercial banks, but to achieve its role as the strongest currency this should be implemented by central banks. This would involve advancing the institutional pace of MU and, in effect, having the process of discussion about management first, which could take several years to agree, thereby slowing the pace of integration. However, the strongest argument is that the central banks themselves have argued against this route. It was explicitly rejected in the Delors Report and this forms the basis for future progress. Despite its merits therefore, we consider it inappropriate as a way forward at present. Although later on, when the basket weights are fixed and convergence is close and the single currency ceases to be a distant prospect, it might again become a realistic option.

Advantages of early use of the Ecu

It is clear from the earlier discussion that the pace at which the Ecu can advance, first as a common currency, and then towards its ultimate role as the single currency of the EC, is rather limited. Nevertheless, it will grow both as a financial asset and as a means of transaction as the market develops. Early use of the Ecu will help reinforce the commitment to its ultimate use as the single currency and, hence, any steps which can be undertaken by the authorities to encourage that use and remove barriers to it will be welcome.

7.8 Means of advancing the use of the Ecu

1. We have already noted that the most important single act that the member states can take to advance the private use of the Ecu is to announce as soon as possible that it is to be the single European currency – along with a credible timetable for completion of MU. That credibility will not be established unless governments and other public institutions within the Community also act as if the Ecu is the destination. Indeed, experience of establishing credibility suggests that, if anything, governments have to overreact in order to persuade people to change their minds.

2. In the first instance therefore, the member states should take every opportunity to allow the Ecu to be used on an equal footing with domestic currencies. The microeconomic features of this requirement are set out in the associated report by Ernst & Young. Here we conclude that it is necessary for public institutions to accept transactions in Ecu at an early stage and to initiate them themselves where this is reasonably possible. There are some obvious examples. At the EC level all transactions could be denominated in Ecu, including payments to and from Community institutions. Secondly, all agreed lending on behalf of the Community, whether through the EIB or nationally, could be in Ecu. At the national level the requirements become more difficult, but an easy example is the invitation to tender for public sector contracts. They are already part of the single market programme and their expression in Ecu would help increase their integrating force. Another area frequently quoted is the payment of taxation in Ecu. This makes sense in so far as it relates to international transactions or transactions with firms or households which also deal frequently overseas. In many respects this may be largely symbolic but there is a need for symbols.

3. It is in international transactions that the greatest scope for the early private use of the Ecu may lie. Although emphasis has been placed on internal accounting procedures by multinational firms, there is scope in the case of external transactions as well. The potential role of the Ecu as an international vehicle currency is considerable given the great importance of the EC in international trading. While it may be difficult to force the pace it would certainly be unwise to encourage a role which would then have to be unwound. Central banks therefore also have a role to play in this transitional period, in addition to that set out in the Delors Report. By their management actions they can encourage the use of the Ecu and discourage substitution for it. In particular they can make greater use of the Ecu as against national currencies in their own foreign exchange dealings. Ultimately the Ecu will become a currency of intervention against the dollar and yen, not just for the EC central banks but for the US and Japanese as well.

4. Towards the end of the transition period, the Ecu can increase its role further by becoming legal tender in the member states so

that its domestic as well as its international position can develop. At this stage exchange rates will be much more closely aligned and the process of convergence between the economies will be close to that necessary for full MU. The Ecu basket would then be fixed and its various roles could be amalgamated. This will also require intervention by central banks because the currency will have to be managed. We think it important that MU should have a single currency from the outset. Although introduction in a single day is possible, many changes would in fact take place on that day, and it would be helpful if the transition can be phased.

5. Acting too early could perhaps be more dangerous to the success of MU than acting too late. In the early period we have already noted that the EMS may have to be looser rather than tighter, permitting more frequent realignments. The role of the Ecu cannot therefore be developed too fast. On the other hand, in just the same way that binding governments early on to the credible commitment to convergence will in itself increase their ability to achieve that change and stiffen their resolve to achieve it, so early steps to use the Ecu will tend to advance the move to its role as the single currency of Europe. There are always good arguments for caution, but a step of this dimension inevitably involves a passage through the unknown. There is no easy example to follow.

   Two things need to be borne in mind. The drive towards monetary union in the European Community is nothing new. It is an objective of the Treaty of Rome (Article 2) and, although of secondary importance in the early years, came to the fore again with the summit meeting in the Hague in 1969 and the Werner Report of 1970. However, that initiative lost its way by the mid-1970's. The lesson of that experience has to be learnt. It is easy to be too ambitious, but the major failing was not setting a tight enough timetable or a detailed enough path ahead to secure credibility. Secondly, we have examples from other countries on their path to monetary union, including those of Germany, the US and even the UK. The move is not straightforward and can involve steps back as well as forward, but the major gains are reaped by having a single strong currency with consistent sources of issue. A prolonged competition to resolve the currency of Europe could be destabilizing and slow the advent of monetary union. The Ecu is the only currency in prospect and the system of regulation agreed in the Delors Report is closely akin to that operated by the Bundesbank. Therefore, there may be a politically attractive prospect in a single currency as described to us by Deutsche Bank – with a French name, run under German rules, from London!

7.9 Principal conclusions

There are four main conclusions from our research.

1. It is important to announce at the outset of the agreed path to monetary union that the Ecu is going to be the single currency at the end of the day. For that announcement to be credible it should include a specified end-date for the process which is far enough in the future to permit sufficient convergence of the member states and yet close enough to be within the planning horizon. The Werner experience suggests that 10 years may be too long, while 5 years is not long enough for adjustment. The 1992 programme was credible with announcement in 1985, agreement in 1986 with the Single European Act, and completion by the end of 1992. While there is no necessary reason why the path to monetary union should be the same length, repeating the formula with a shift of five years could be plausible: i.e. announcement 1990; agreement 1991; and completion end of 1997. (We were persuaded by the view put to us by industrialists that no firm will act on vague promises of the future.)
2. It is important to familiarize the market with the use of the Ecu and to discourage the wider international use of the currencies of member states. To that end, central banks should increase their use of the Ecu and facilitate its use by others. In particular the Ecu should become an important medium of foreign exchange intervention. The part of this report produced by Ernst & Young sets out how all of the detailed obstacles to the use of the Ecu should be removed and it is assumed that there is no longer any discrimination against the use of the Ecu. Taking the use of the Ecu further by issuing an independent Ecu as a parallel currency, without the basket composition, goes too far. It is already firmly ruled out by the Delors Report and poses problems for the management of the currency in the transition to MU. Gradual increases in co-operation between the central banks has been emerging already, even before the implementation of the Delors

proposals. This process needs to continue to the point where there is a single competent system established for the issue and management of the Ecu before the currency's role develops further. This is likely to be when monetary union is established.

3. Towards the end of the transitional period the Ecu should become legal tender in the member states. There is no point in introducing this early on, first of all because it is inappropriate for a basket Ecu while exchange rates (and by implication inflation and interest rates) are not closely aligned. Secondly, there will be many functions that a second currency cannot perform until it has a full note and coin issue and it is important not to raise a false impression of usefulness as this would damage credibility. It is however important not to make other currencies legal tender as this will divert activity and may very well result in a regime which makes monetary union appear less attractive because of its complications. This step should reinforce the message that the Ecu is the end point of the progress to a single currency. (This rules out the currency competition route to a single currency.)

4. Community and national institutions should give a lead to encouraging the growing use of the Ecu by adopting it for their own activities. All payments to Community institutions should be acceptable in Ecu and where possible payments should be made in Ecu. This would include lending activities to non-EC countries in eastern Europe and elsewhere. The acceptability of the Ecu needs to be fostered in the international community outside the EC as well as for domestic transactions. National governments can also assist this process by using Ecu or permitting its use in a number of areas: payment of taxes, for example; quotation for major contracts; and other forms of supply to the public sector. This would of course be in addition to the types of microeconomic assistance that would be necessary to help firms adjust to the requirements of operating in a new currency. It will obviously assist this process if other multinational organizations, including firms, were to set an example by moving towards use of the Ecu where this made economic sense. While the development of the private use of the Ecu needs to be primarily market-led if it is to be successful, official institutions in the EC need to provide a favourable climate because the introduction of any such change is a difficult and expensive exercise for companies and households.

[1] This section draws on the World Economy chapter written by Ray Barrell, Stephen Dulake and Andrew Gurney in the *National Institute Economic Review, no. 131*, February 1990.

[2] These results are based on Wren-Lewis, Westaway, Soteri and Barrell, 'Choosing the rate: An analysis of the optimum level of entry for sterling into the ERM', *NIESR Discussion Paper no. 171*, February 1990.

[3] This is two years earlier than the end point used in the *GEM* simulations.

Bibliographical references

Delors, J. (1989) *Report on Economic and Monetary Union in the European Community*, Committee for the Study of Economic and Monetary Union.

Giavazzi, F. (1990) *Capital Controls are Gone: Will the EMS Survive?*, Centre for Economic Policy Research.

H.M. Treasury (1989) *An Evolutionary Approach to Economic and Monetary Union*, November.

Part III
External Contributions to the Study

8: The Private Use of the Ecu: A Comment on its Problems and Prospects

By Eirik Svindland, DIW, Berlin

8.1 Outline

As reproduced in Appendix 1, the Delors Report expresses three opinions in paragraphs 46, 47 and 49 about the future private use of the Ecu.

Below I argue that the basket Ecu is currently required, sometimes demanded, as an alternative to a commitment to a single national currency. Elementary theory of the market system tells us that a matching supply has a welfare-increasing effect. I therefore agree that everybody should have open access to Ecu services (paragraph 49 of the Delors Report). However, a transformation of the present semi-currency into a new, fully-fledged EC currency (or 'new Ecu') constitutes a fundamental discontinuity relative to the purpose of private, voluntary Ecu use. This discontinuity gives rise to scepticism about the possibility that the basket Ecu has the potential to be developed into a common EC currency (paragraph 46) and it implies that the current problems and prospects of the Ecu-market offer us little information about the introduction of a single new Ecu. Further, I indicate two additional reasons for being sceptical about the parallel currency approach to the introduction of a single currency (paragraph 47) and my recommendation is to agree on a traditional, one-step monetary reform approach.

8.2 Principles

8.2.1 Intra-firm use of the ECU

Cost accounting, bookkeeping and regular balance sheets are important components of a firm's commercial development. Their consistency and comprehensiveness – both conditions for their usefulness – rest on the use of a single monetary unit. Any well-defined money, for instance the Deutschmark, can serve as this accounting unit. The legal tender in the firm's home country is the natural, and usually also the sole legal choice. An expansion of business beyond national borders, and even the formation of subsidiary companies in other countries, will not usually affect this choice; the headquarters remains decisive in matters of communication patterns. The multinational character of the firm will rather imply a two-tier accounting system in the subsidiaries – one enforced by local law and one used for reports meeting the requirements of the head office.

If the firm goes truly multinational then it will sometimes change its choice of internal unit of account. The basket Ecu may be a rational choice if both the business and the finances have become truly European. The argument in this case is that the development of an Ecu balance sheet provides a mean of balance sheets in national currencies, and thus a compromise as far as information for holders of the firm's debt and equity capital is concerned. Another rationale for the choice of the Ecu is a reform of EC laws offering a choice between local currency and Ecu accounting. Multinationals will avoid the two-tier accounting of their subsidiaries. However, in both cases the use of a common EC currency provides a simpler and hence a better solution than the use of a variable currency basket. This means that every inter-firm use of Ecu provides evidence of demand for further monetary reform which would lead to the introduction of a new Ecu.

8.2.2 Inter-firm use of the Ecu

'Inter-firm use' means use of the Ecu in the selling of goods and services – at least as regards pricing them in Ecu – and its use also as an invoicing currency. What circumstances currently provide a rationale for this kind of use of the Ecu? As a general rule, sellers invoice in the same monetary unit they use for accounting. Exceptions to this rule mostly occur in international trade (e.g. commodities, minerals, oil, marine transport, etc. – in other words, staple commodities traded at international auction markets which are mostly quoted in sterling or US dollars).

A second exception concerns exports from small countries when invoicing in the seller's currency is difficult because small-area currencies have a correspondingly narrow, low-volume foreign exchange market. These currencies are (mostly) traded against a few important currencies, spreads tend to be wider and hedging opportunities are more restricted and expensive. The export proceeds from a small-currency area will therefore be transferred to another via the market of a vehicle currency and, in the case of a planned payment the importer, owing a certain amount in the exporter's currency, will need a chain of two forward contracts in order to hedge against the exchange rate risk. A debt in his own currency would of course be more convenient, but less so for the exporter.

Now, consider small-country exporters and importers who have trading partners in several countries. Their financial management can be complicated and costly and, the smaller the firm, the greater the problem. The tendency is therefore to try to simplify and lower transaction costs by concentrating foreign exchange positions in one major foreign currency, and to use it in price lists and contracts. Of course, an importer will prefer to have a commitment in his home currency, but he will accept the chosen major currency as a better solution than payment in the exporter's home currency. If the currency choice is not only led by attempts to minimize transaction costs but also by exchange rate expectations, then there is a case for using the Ecu. Its definition as a basket of several currencies implies the relative stability of the Ecu in comparison with its component currencies.

This stability also makes it a good choice in the third exception to the general rule that a seller will invoice in the currency he uses for accounting purposes. In this case, expectations about exchange rate movements cause a disagreement between buyer and seller. The seller prefers a currency which is expected to appreciate and, if the purchased goods will be paid for at a later time, the buyer prefers a depreciating currency. Invoicing in Ecu will provide a suitable compromise.

These two reasons for invoicing in a semi-currency like the basket Ecu would not exist within the EC if it had one common currency instead of its present multiplicity. Hence, with respect to this aspect of the Ecu market, it is correct to view the private use of Ecu as a first step on the way to the introduction of the new Ecu.

8.2.3 Private asset holdings

My suspicion about the thesis (the Delors Report, paragraph 46) that the Ecu can be smoothly transformed from a basket of currencies into a genuine currency centres on the use of the Ecu as a money standard in deferred payments – e.g. in loans.

A recent European Investment Bank Report says: 'The higher degree of intra-EMS exchange rate stability might explain part of the more limited interest for Ecu instruments among traditional Ecu investors who in the past had turned to Ecu investments notably because of their inherent characteristic of hedging the exchange rate risk. The considerable variability between the exchange rate of the Ecu and non-participating currencies, on the other hand, appears to have been an important reason for the increased buying of Ecu securities by Japanese investors.' This dependency on exchange rate variation reveals that market participants interpret Ecu denomination as a version of indexation of contractual payments: European investors demand this indexation in addition to the contractual rate of interest if they anticipate loss of value of their money across a long-term commitment, and the debtor accepts this index clause gladly if he expects relative price (exchange rate) changes to favour growth of his real money income.

The structure of the Ecu bond market fits in with these problems. It is known to be largely retail-oriented – towards individual purchasers who tend to hold securities until maturity. Japanese institutional investors do the same. They demand Ecu bonds as part of portfolio diversification which is well served with an 'index of far away Europe'. European institutional investors are better informed about the particular problems and prospects of their local capital market. They therefore have their own opinion about the optimal currency composition of their European portfolio, and they frequently and flexibly change this composition to take account of new information. Hence, they are not persistently dominating the Ecu market. This international bond market use of the Ecu resembles the proposition known as the Anti-Gresham-Law: good money drives bad money out, if both are only voluntarily accepted.

Now, imagine a convergence of monetary policy in Europe which gradually eliminates differences in inflation rates as well as expectations of exchange rate changes between EMS currencies. Against some EMS currencies, the Ecu will cease to be a better currency. The special demand for Ecu assets dwindles, but the motive for selecting the best currency will still exist and will eventually induce a demand for assets in a non-EC currency. For that reason a fundamental difference exists between the capital market preference for Ecu and the aim of establishing European monetary union, and thus there must be a discontinuity in a change from the present EMS-Ecu system to a new Ecu monetary union.

The essentials of this planned change are – from a capital market perspective – very much like a merger of democratic parties: you are living in a democracy, and you may be satisfied with the conduct of its administration. In this case you will vote for the ruling party, but you are glad to have at least one alternative. Sometimes you also join forces with the opposition. Now, imagine a merger of parties. If the merger leaves only one 'Einheitspartei', you may still be a supporter of the government, but now your choice of whether to stay in your country or leave is more important than before – to leave has now become your only way to demonstrate your opposition.

8.2.4 From old to new Ecu: Evolution or revolution?

There are three options concerning the appropriate method of substituting the present semi-currency Ecu basket with a new fully-fledged Ecu.

Option one

The first strategy consists of measures which will make the Ecu, as presently defined, competitive as a medium of transaction – notably to give it legal tender status in all EC countries. The argument runs like this: a common legal tender Ecu will be convenient as intra-European transaction money, and hence it will increasingly be used as a substitute for national currencies, thereby becoming instrumental in forcing national policies to converge towards stability of prices, interest and exchange rates, and carrying on the process towards monetary unification via market forces rather than through government regulation. This makes good sense given the supplementary assertion that the Ecu, remaining as a basket currency, will not – in a narrow sense – be a parallel currency, and that its use can therefore not interfere with national central banks' money supply – the national central banks keep full control of monetary policy.

My first counter-argument is to point to the contradiction between 'keeping full control of monetary policy' and 'being guided by market forces to conduct a certain policy'. The second goes deeper: who controls the expansion of the Ecu money supply? Using the Ecu instead of, for instance, the Deutschmark implies that the banks hold Ecu deposits instead of Deutschmark deposits and that they therefore will demand easily tradeable, short-term Ecu liquid instruments of high quality, like British Ecu treasury bills. If all EMS central banks continue to supply only their own currency, controlling the money supply as if it only consists of their respective domestic currencies, then there is no adequate control over Ecu supply expansion – or at least no adequate policy determination of the growth of Ecu stock. Someone will have to settle the following questions: Who supplies these liquid instruments usable throughout the EC? Who makes a decision about the Ecu amount supplied and about liquidity reserve requirements? Who controls this area of monetary policy? Remember: as legal tender, liquid Ecu instruments would be accepted by everyone – the central banks too! The problem resembles the liquidity creation in the Eurodollar market.

Option two

The Ecu as legal tender would interfere with national monetary policy like the legal tender use of the currency of a neighbouring country. The necessary agreement among the respective national monetary authorities would be very much the same as in the case of the second option: namely the issue of a new fully-fledged Ecu to be used as a parallel currency. The Delors Report has already turned this proposal down arguing (in paragraph 47) that the necessary agreements would 'complicate the already difficult endeavour of co-ordinating different national monetary policies' and that 'an additional source of money creation...could jeopardize price stability'. The last argument rests upon the implicit assumption that the parallel currency is legal tender. Gresham's Law then explains how an additional money supply source can endanger previous price stability.

I will therefore add two arguments against the parallel currency strategy applying to voluntarily accepted currencies. Both arguments are based on the assumption that an evolutionary explanation of the choice of a commonly accepted medium of exchange rests on the preference of a critical mass of transactors holding and using this particular currency. The critical mass is defined as a proportion of all transactions below which market forces will work against the medium of exchange. A new currency needs a kind of backing to hold and expand its ground. Historically, suspicion about the future value of current monies has provided the necessary (negative) backing for a new and trustworthy currency, but this backing mostly took the form of monetary reform (i.e. currency replacement) by a government holding a (regional) monetary monopoly. In the case of a parallel currency Ecu the scenario consists neither of a suspicion about other currencies, nor of a regional monopoly to be awarded. Thus, backing is to be provided by fiscal and/or administrative measures to the disadvantage of the national currencies (positive discrimination). The resulting payment system would therefore operate at higher cost and with less efficiency than the alternative systems of fully convertible national currencies. The rationale of a parallel currency system of this kind is not obvious.

Above the critical mass of transactors, the theory tells us, benefits from holding this new medium of exchange will outweigh the alternatives. Therefore, more transactors switch to this medium and effect a further increase in the sub-population of Ecu users, which in turn increases the benefits of belonging to this sub-population, and so on.

So far we have concentrated on the evolutionary explanation of the market selection of one common medium of exchange. However, in one essential respect this departs from the structure of a parallel Ecu competitive with national currencies: the national currencies are not supposed to be legally equal to the parallel Ecu. National central banks and their governments would (probably) not accept a complete loss of their regional monetary monopoly. That means that they would have to accept the existence of a parallel currency in voluntary use. The parallel Ecu then has to be the better – more worthy and appreciating – currency in order to be demanded as a standard of deferred payments. In this way, however, it cannot displace the national currencies as a means of payments (Gresham's Law). Rather, it will destabilize the monetary system.

Option three

For the sake of completeness, I should also consider the third case of a currency competition which is complete in the sense that all European currencies are accepted as legal tender in all other European countries. Every well known currency of unlimited convertibility would, in this case, be suitable as a standard of money asset holdings. There are two possible solutions to this kind of competition. One is the establishment of a system of stable parallel currencies, which would operate at higher total costs than the same multi-currency system minus one currency. The other solution is that only one currency remains. It is, however, not at all certain that the parallel Ecu would be the winner. Therefore, if politics rules the eventual competitive solution out (i.e. whereby one of the present national currencies becomes the currency of the Community), then the national currencies would have to be replaced in one politically administered step. This is my overall conclusion with respect to formation of a EC-currency union.

8.3 Answers to the NIESR questions

In this section I will give short answers to the questions posed by the NIESR (see Appendix 4).

1. What are the advantages of a common currency?
A simplification of multinational accounting and communication, which reduces information and transaction costs, and offers more security for international business in the sense that no monetary policy measures can interfere with the transfer of earnings and with the fulfilment of financial obligations. Overall these advantages favour more trade and hence greater economic ties between the countries using a common currency. In this respect, the formation of a currency union resembles the well known formation of a customs union – i.e. *ceteris paribus,* it also effects a revision of trade patterns (trade diversion and trade creation).

2. What is the plausible anti-monde against which to assess the use of the Ecu as the common currency?
Either the currency of a world-wide, highly respected and trusted central bank, which is at present obliged to serve the needs of a particular country, or a new Ecu issued by a similar new European institution.

3. What is the impact of 'announcing' that the Ecu will become the single currency?
Confusion: firstly because everybody in the bond market knows that the single currency has to be a fully-fledged currency which therefore cannot serve the indexation purpose of the present currency basket and, secondly, because nobody currently knows the future composition and value of the Ecu basket. Consider, for instance, the consequences of a German reunification: what will be the future weight of the Deutschmark in the Ecu basket? It would however make sense to announce a long time in advance that the current composition of the Ecu will be retained and so determine the future exchange rate for conversions of assets from national to EC currency.

4. Does it matter if the Ecu is a basket or an independent currency in its own right?
Yes. Only a fully-fledged currency will serve the purpose of a currency union.

5. What are the implications for monetary control?
All strategies towards a currency union imply monetary control problems which demand a consistent solution – either by co-ordination of the business of several national central banks or by leaving the whole business to a new European institution.

6. Would early development of a private market in Ecu ease the process of convergence among the European economies?

The commercial use of the basket Ecu is due to lack of a single currency. The Ecu capital market use is not. It does not have any importance for convergence other than being a special manifestation of currency convertibility, which indeed eases and enforces the process of convergence.

7. Would the use of the Ecu strengthen the influence of Europe world-wide?

The question currently has no obvious relation to the private use of the Ecu. The success of the EMS may be interpreted as emanating from the official use of the Ecu. A single currency, new Ecu would affect economic development in a way (see question 1) which may be interpreted as 'strengthening the influence of Europe', although I would not wish to take part in a debate about the precise meaning of this assertion.

8. What should the timetable be for the transition to a single currency?

A timetable should be confined to a short period between the foundation of a currency union and the time the union takes effect. With respect to the main problem (to figure out an agreement about the construction of the union) I cannot suggest any precise timetable. It may be advisable to announce simultaneously (a) the definite deadline for such an agreement and (b) the composition of the Ecu to be used in future currency conversion (question 3).

9: The Private Ecu: A Step Towards the Single European Currency?

By J. Le Cacheux, C. Mathieu and H. Sterdyniak, OFCE, Paris

A fairly broad consensus seems to exist today in Europe about the potential advantage of a single European currency. The coexistence of 12 distinct currencies, with exchange rates that may be altered from one month to the next, is in apparent contradiction with the completion of a single market in which large volumes of trade could probably not develop in the absence of a credible stability and predictability of relative prices. The functioning of the EMS has already achieved a significant reduction in exchange rate fluctuations among the currencies of the fixed-rate agreement. Parity changes were quite frequent during the early years of the system, but they have tended to become rarer more recently. In addition, they have always been in line with inflation differentials.

How to proceed? Some see the private Ecu as an embryonic common currency that would progressively grow in scope and could ultimately displace existing national currencies. Our contention is that such a process is unlikely and that, therefore, the institutional approach chosen in the Delors Report is the only realistic option for progress toward monetary union.

9.1 The advantages of a single currency in Europe

In the field of trade relations, the advantage of using a single currency as the unit of account and means of payment is obvious. Intra-European trade would be facilitated with the existence of a single currency: there would be no problem of conversion, so that transaction costs would be reduced and firms could economize on cash balances; with the complete disappearance of exchange rate fluctuation, there would be less uncertainty about the prospective returns on production and distribution investment.

From a macroeconomic point of view, a single currency would give the EC more weight in international monetary relations. A European currency would emerge, on a footing similar to that of the Japanese yen and the US dollar: the international monetary system would become truly triangular. A single currency would also entail unified interest rate structures: French and Italian rates would converge downward to the level of German rates, since the risk of a devaluation would have completely vanished.

Only if a single currency, controlled by a single European central bank, circulates in Europe could these benefits be reaped. So long as national currencies coexist, linked together only by a fixed exchange rate agreement, a risk of changes in parities still exists. National currencies cannot be perfect substitutes for one another; there cannot be perfect equalization of interest rates, with countries whose currencies have a positive probability of being devalued having to maintain higher interest rates; no encouragement is given to a wider international use of a European currency. For the realization of the expected benefits, it is necessary that existing monies disappear overnight and be replaced by the new, common currency, even though this abrupt change may upset the general public's habits.

9.2 Macroeconomic uncertainties

The existence of a single currency implies that the various participating countries agree to relinquish their national monetary sovereignty and transfer it to a supranational entity. Fiscal policy would therefore be the only instrument of macroeconomic policy to remain in the control of national governments. As for the last stage of the process of economic and monetary integration, the Delors Report proposes an original division of labour for macroeconomic policy-making: on the one hand, an independent central bank would see to the task of maintaining internal price stability in the EC; on the other, the 12 national governments would retain the responsibility for fiscal policy. How will the decisions concerning macroeconomic policies be made and coordinated?

The answers provided in the report are either vague or disturbingly one-sided. The European Central Bank System (ECBS), conceived as independent of all political authorities and only concerned with price stability, is bound to lead to a lack of coordination between monetary and fiscal policies: tight money to fight inflation and large budget deficits engineered by national governments trying to support domestic growth might then result in permanently too-high interest rates, as observed in the USA in the first half of the 1980s. This might exacerbate the world-wide 'interest-rate race' between the United States and Europe. Are national governments willing to forgo control over interest rates for the the benefit of central bankers who would not be politically accountable and might well lack any global macroeconomic vision?

Can anyone say for sure that the EC will never again in the future be faced with situations requiring parity adjustments? Suppose another oil shock strikes; suppose further that wages then increase sharply in France, while in Germany 'concerted action' successfully passes the burden of adjustment onto wage-earners. If France cannot make use of devaluation, it will have to suffer a prolonged phase of restrictive policies in order to reduce wage costs. A single currency means that individual countries cannot alter their exchange rate or, therefore, their competitiveness.

Some advocates of monetary union, most notably in France, see it as an opportunity for individual countries to pursue expansionary aggregate demand policies. Such policies are currently barred; if a single country tried to reflate, it would damage its external trade balance and trigger a capital flight that would make it impossible to maintain a fixed exchange rate within the EMS. In a monetary union, this external constraint would no longer exist, since national current accounts would become indistinguishable. Demand stimulation in a single country would no longer entail a domestic interest rate hike or an exchange rate crisis; it would be automatically financed by partner-countries, so that the increase in interest rates would be much less, being union-wide. The only remaining constraint would be that of solvency of individual states. From that point of view, monetary union is appealing, in so far as it allows differentiated regional policies tailored to the needs of the various zones.

So far, however, the major characteristic of the way the EMS has functioned is asymmetry: one dominant country, namely the Federal Republic of Germany, dictates the rules of the game. The success of the EMS is precisely due to the fact that participating countries have agreed to follow the German leadership. France and Italy have agreed to forgo their previous growth strategy, which was based on endemic devaluations aimed at re-establishing external competitiveness, together with low real rates of interest achieved through exchange control and a regulated domestic financial system; they have embraced a virtuous strategy based on 'healthy finance' (stable prices, reduction in the public sector borrowing requirement, and external balance). Monetary union would increase the authority of the Bundesbank, which favours domestic price stability and rejects any system in which external surpluses in some countries would serve to finance external deficits in others.

The FRG will not agree to a monetary union unless it is built according to their criteria. That is the reason why the Delors Report insists on instituting an autonomous ECBS, with European monetary policy managed by independent central bankers. This move would institutionalize orthodox monetary and macroeconomic policy: the European central bank would not be allowed to finance national budget deficits, while the European Commission would be entitled to enforce limitations on their amount. Will national governments then still be in a position to pursue stabilizing policies in the event of a macroeconomic shock requiring an increase in the budget deficit? Who will decide, and according to which criteria, that one deficit is excessive, while another is stabilizing? The limitations on national budget deficits are bound to contain fiscal policies in the various member states. While the EC budget will remain a small fraction of national budgets, it will have to take on stabilization policy. Will the supranational institutions be able and willing to take diversity into account? It is rather disturbing to note that the Delors committee is anxious to set limits on the size of budget deficits without even considering the possibility that some countries might pursue too tight fiscal policies.

Monetary unification may be a way of circumventing the impotence entailed as a result of a lack of policy coordination. But it is a risky enterprise: instituting a powerful and independent ECBS will undoubtedly strengthen the position of the advocates of orthodox economic policies and consequently weaken that of those who favour more growth oriented policies; individual countries might end up with no weapon left to fight macroeconomic disequilibria. It thus appears that there are three major prerequisites for monetary union: member countries have to be sufficiently similar and be united by sufficiently close political and social links so that macroeconomic evolutions will be parallel; fiscal and budgetary policy has to be unified along with monetary policy; both instruments have to be coordinated in such a way as to promote full employment as well as price stability.

9.3 How to achieve a single currency

Monetary unification may be realized either through a radical move or progressively. The 'big bang' method would undoubtedly be preferable but is in practice foreclosed for political reasons. The Delors Report thus realistically proposed a progressive unification. However transitory stages are potentially saddled with difficulties in so far as distinct national monies would continue to circulate during the transition. How would exchange rate stability be maintained without instituting a mechanism for financing persistent disequilibria in some countries – a mechanism that the FRG refuses to consider? The transition stages would be characterized by an uncertain sharing of responsibilities concerning monetary and fiscal policies, which would seem very difficult to manage. Will Brussels have a say in national financial and fiscal policies? Countries with higher than average inflation or with larger than average budget deficits would be likely to be forced to pursue tighter policies, which would reinforce the deflationary bias of the current system. The transition ought to achieve economic convergence, which boils down to alignment on German performance.

9.4 The parallel currency route to monetary unification: A mistaken approach

Ever since the first blueprints on monetary unification in Europe, two rival strategies have been proposed: the one that stresses institutional agreement amongst central banks, which is the strategy adopted in both the Werner Report and the Delors Report; and the parallel currency approach, whereby an additional currency would be created which would, owing to its intrinsic quality, displace existing monies through the free choice of private agents.

In the mid-1970s, a group of European monetarist economists on several occasions proposed the creation of a parallel currency, issued by a single European institution and price-indexed. These proposals were published in the *All Saints' Day Manifesto* (1975, reprinted in Fratianni and Peeters, 1979) and in the OPTICA reports (1975 and 1976). Following Hayek, Salin (1980) went a step further, advocating free competition among privately issued monies: market forces would then ensure the survival of the best monies – that is, those with the most stable purchasing power. In this perspective, creating a European currency is regarded primarily as an opportunity to reform the rules of the monetary game.

The proposals put forward in the *All Saints' Day Manifesto* and the two OPTICA reports are not radical enough and remain too vague. They advocate the creation of an indexed, parallel currency (the europa), the purchasing power of which would be guaranteed in terms of a basket of European commodities. The currency would then be an inflation-proof store of value; its diffusion would be left to market forces, with each country's residents being allowed to exchange their domestic currency for europas. Each domestic central bank would have europa liabilities and would cover the costs of indexation, which would weaken the public authorities' incentive to inflate. However, nothing guarantees that the europa would progressively come into use as a unit of account and a means of exchange in private transactions. Even its use as a store of value is attractive for investors only in so far as the rates of return on competing assets, denominated in national monies, could be less than the rates of inflation. In addition, the authors never mention credits in europa that private banks might grant along with their deposits: the project rests squarely on the goodwill of central banks.

Generally speaking, it would prove difficult for any parallel currency to acquire the three classical attributes of money that were first listed by Aristotle: unit of account, means of payment, and store of value. A money is primarily defined by its use as a unit of account. Its value stems from private agents' confidence in its role in transactions, in wage contracts and in extinguishing debts and paying taxes. In these various domains, a competitive process is hardly conceivable: private business and retail firms would have to chose the currency in which they would bill their customers; wage earners would have to bargain on the choice of the currency in which wages would be paid. All this would make transactions much more difficult and costly, and would initially increase uncertainty. There have been some real-world examples of coexisting monies, but they usually coincided with hyper-inflation: thus the 'dollarization' episodes in Argentina and Israel. In the current European situation, it is hard to conceive of a system in which customers would choose the currency in which to pay for their purchases according to the rate offered by the seller. Money is, in essence, a social choice, similar in this respect to the legal system and language.

It is therefore hardly conceivable that a parallel currency might develop beyond the stage of a pseudo-money, a store of value with no role in transactions. The various projects for a parallel currency would thus boil down to the creation of a new financial asset. But then how would its rate of interest be determined? The existence of a financial asset implies that some agents willingly issue it, while others willingly hold it. It has to prove superior to existing assets both for the issuer and for the holder, which is no simple business since their private interests are contradictory: from the issuer's point of view, for instance, equity shares are preferable to other liabilities, in so far as their rate of return depends on the firm's profits, and then the holder bears the risk; conversely the holders' preferred habitat is liquid, has a high rate of return and is riskless, which is costly for the issuer.

Hence the various projects for a parallel currency that would compete with the existing national monies do not appear to be realistic, essentially because there is hardly any reason why a debtor should issue an asset trustworthy enough and with a sufficiently attractive rate of return to displace publicly issued currencies.

9.5 Some other proposals

The project put forward by Professor Magnifico (1974) is another illustration of the consequences of neglecting the prime importance of the transactional function of money. Indeed he proposed the creation of a currency that would serve as an intermediary between existing European currencies and those outside Europe; the exchange rates of the various European currencies *vis-à-vis* this 'intermediate' money would have been fixed but adjustable, while the latter's external exchange rate *vis-à-vis* the dollar would have been controlled through joint interventions.

Such a project was intrinsically flawed, because there was no mechanism to guarantee the value of this artificial money: the European central banks had discretionary powers and could decide, for each single parity adjustment, the size of internal exchange rate variations as well as that of the external exchange rate. If, for instance, the European central banks decided to engineer a 10 per cent devaluation *vis-à-vis* the dollar, they could choose either to devalue the 'intermediate' money, or to keep the external rate fixed and lower the internal parities of the various European currencies *vis-à-vis* the 'intermediate' money. More recently, Edouard Balladur, a former French Minister of Finance, (*Le Monde*, 9 February 1990) proposed the creation of a common currency, issued by a European central bank, free of any reference to a basket of existing currencies, that would be offered to private agents. But how could the value of such a money be determined in the absence of any concrete transaction use? Who would accept the risk of issuing debt or holding such money?

9.6 The ECU as an embryonic parallel currency

Nowadays, the idea of a parallel currency is no longer an abstract concept, confined within academic circles; the development of the Ecu (see, in particular, Aglietta, 1986; Vissol, 1987) has led some observers to regard it as the sketch of the future European currency. However, whereas many analysts and politicians in Europe use the word 'Ecu' to refer to this future European currency, it is quite likely that they mean different things. Is it simply that the single European currency, once established with an autonomous and intrinsic value, will be labelled with a name that is already familiar? Or is the term used to refer to the existing Ecu – that is to a currency which, by construction, cannot but be the thirteenth currency in the system?

Prior to the creation of the current Ecu, the European unit of account (EUA), created in 1975 as a basket of the currencies of the various EC members, was used exclusively in EC public accounting. In 1979, along with the institution of the EMS, the 'official' Ecu was introduced, its use being limited to official transactions among central banks. The agreement founding the EMS stipulates that the central banks of the participating countries make a deposit of 20 per cent of their gold and dollar foreign exchange reserves at the EFMC (European Fund for Monetary Co-operation). These holdings are then converted into Ecus and counted as assets of the central banks. But this procedure of Ecu creation is nothing but an accounting convention. Indeed, central banks do not make Ecu deposits; they continue to hold deposits in gold and dollars, so that the value of an asset of one Ecu at the Banque de France does not have to be equal to one Ecu in the books of the Danish central bank. In particular, the national central banks, not the EFMC, continue to take the capital gains or losses resulting from the fluctuations of the dollar or gold exchange rates. For the 'official' Ecu to exist effectively as such, the national central banks would have to hold reserves in Ecu, that is to hold currency baskets in the same proportions as those entering the Ecu composition, whether they make the deposit at the EFMC or not. But in so far as the German central bank primarily monitors the dollar/Deutschmark exchange rate, interventions in Ecu would be extremely difficult to design. Hence, the essentially artificial character of the 'official' Ecu.

Rather unexpectedly, the major development of the Ecu has taken place within the private sector – hence the term 'private Ecu'. What are the motivations that could explain the use by private agents of a currency basket in various kinds of transactions? In some cases (the issue of Ecu-denominated bonds by national governments and Ecu accounting by some large multinational firms, which may have favourable public relations effects) the 'signal' appears to be overwhelmingly important: the use of a European monetary instrument testifies to the active support given to the process of monetary integration, of which the Ecu may be regarded as a symbol.

For the most part, however, the use of the Ecu must be due to the existence of transaction costs in the process of converting or exchanging one European currency for another. Indeed, the private Ecu does not possess any intrinsic monetary value: its nominal value is nothing but the weighted sum of its constituent currencies. Leaving aside transaction costs, private agents ought to regard as equivalent the use of the Ecu or of any other combination of its constituent currencies. This is especially true for portfolio diversification purposes and exchange rate risk hedging, since the institutionally determined weights in the Ecu basket are bound to differ from the optimal portfolio composition that may be calculated as a function of stochastic characteristics of the various anticipated returns. In addition, scale economies probably exist in the financial and accounting uses of currencies, which tend to favour existing instruments – in particular, the private Ecu, once established – relative to ad hoc combinations.

With transaction costs, even small ones, there cannot be perfect substitutability between the Ecu, (even though it is but a currency basket), and its constituent currencies. In the field of financial transactions, where the private Ecu has had its most spectacular development, such imperfect substitutability necessarily implies that there exists a specific preference for instruments denominated in European units; hence the existence of a specific supply of, and a specific demand for, Ecu-denominated assets. The rate of return on these assets, and consequently their market price, ought no longer to be strictly equal to the weighted sum of identical assets denominated in the constituent currencies: the Ecu rate of interest and the whole set of stochastic characteristics of returns on Ecu-denominated assets thus possess some degree of freedom (albeit possibly small) with respect to similar assets denominated in the various national currencies, which may make Ecu-denominated financial markets appealing to certain categories of investors and debtors in some circumstances (Le

Cacheux, 1987). Similarly, in food markets, one can choose to buy ready-made vegetable assortments for *pot au feu* or else decide to buy each vegetable separately, the costs and market prices being different.

During the first half of the 1980s, Ecu financial markets grew remarkably, especially in 1985 when the number and amount of Ecu denominated assets issued by public and private EC residents as well as international organizations and non-EC foreign institutions reached a peak. The rhythm of new issues then substantially receded, although 1989 again saw exceptionally large volumes issued by some EC member states (France, Italy and the United Kingdom) and by non-EC residents (foreign governments like Sweden, Austria) and foreign firms (especially Japanese banks and US-based companies).

Such developments are clearly related to the observed and anticipated changes in intra-EC and dollar exchange rates and interest rates, a relation that is supported by an examination of the geographical origin of supply and demand. During the first phase of development of the Ecu financial markets, most transactions have been between residents of countries – most notably Italy – plagued with exchange rate uncertainties and relatively high interest rates; in addition, favourable legislation tended, in those countries, to encourage the financial uses of Ecu-denominated assets. Again in 1985, the sudden increase in the volume of Ecu-denominated issues corresponded to a world-wide increase in interest rates, particularly in the United States, together with renewed volatility and uncertainty in intra-EC and non-EC exchange rates. So the advantages of Ecu-denominated assets appear to be, for investors, the need to diversify portfolios and, for debtors, the prospects of lower and less variable costs of borrowing. These factors have led to a situation in which financial markets in Ecu-denominated assets currently represent a significant share of total Euromarket transactions. The Ecu is now fifth on the list of currency denominations. But, as emphasized earlier, a period of lesser volatility and/or uncertainty of exchange rates and interest rates may cause a marked reduction in the volume of new issues, although banking activities in Ecus appear less sensitive to this kind of fluctuation, their growth being much more steady.

The use of the Ecu as a unit of account and for billing purposes has remained fairly limited (Ruffini, 1989), which is in broad agreement with the previous reasoning: indeed the need for diversification and risk hedging is relatively less in this area; it is also much easier to accomplish these tasks with existing instruments. In addition, the use of the Ecu to invoice exports corresponds to a sharing of exchange rate risk between the buyer and the seller, which differs from customary practices and may prove more difficult and costly to hedge against.

9.7 Prospects for the Ecu as now defined

Being a currency basket, the Ecu is founded on existing monies, which is an advantage; also, by construction, its purchasing power exactly corresponds to the weighted average of the constituent currencies' purchasing power. Ecu price stability is therefore necessarily less than that of the best currency in the basket, just as with some ready-made vegetable assortments, in which those vegetables at the bottom may be less fresh than those on top.

The Ecu's exchange rate stability within the EC, and therefore its attractiveness to EC residents, suffer in the current basket from the presence of currencies that do not participate in the EMS fixed exchange rate arrangement. On this account, the situation would improve if membership in the fixed rate system and basket composition coincided, either through sterling joining the fixed rate agreement or by excluding it from the composition of the basket. As it now stands, the Ecu cannot reap the full benefits of intra-EMS exchange rate stability and things may be made worse by the introduction of currencies into the basket from countries that do not fully participate in the EMS and which lack well developed Euromarkets.

The consequences on each country's monetary conditions of a wider diffusion of the Ecu are ambiguous: if firms in France and in the rest of Europe increase the share of their Ecu-denominated liabilities while French and other European investors willingly hold more Ecu-denominated assets, the impact on foreign exchange reserves in France and in other countries is unclear. Obviously though, this development would reinforce monetary policy interdependence: when monetary authorities in one country try to tighten their domestic policy more than average, domestic firms would tend to rely more on the issue of Ecu-denominated liabilities, which would partly offset the monetary squeeze; if, on the other hand, a country tried to pursue a monetary policy that is more expansionary than average, domestic savings would flow into Ecu markets. Such flows would be all the more significant as substitution between the Ecu and national monies is made easier. Note, however, that the situation is not perfectly symmetrical: indeed it is easier to resist a capital influx than an exodus, so countries pursuing tighter monetary policies are in a better position than those wishing to inflate.

Many people now regard the private Ecu as the future European currency and foresee a process of progressive substitution of existing currencies in both financial and commercial transactions. Faced with such a prospect, the various parties concerned have adopted widely divergent positions. The Committee for European Monetary Union supports the creation of a European central bank, the main role of which would be to encourage the private use of the Ecu and to maintain its value. Close in spirit to this committee, a number of major European firms have formed the Association for the Monetary Union of Europe which actively promotes the use of the Ecu in commercial transactions. This theme is often defended in British blueprints, but mainly as an alternative to monetary unification through institutional co-operation: thus the British Treasury claims to be supporting monetary unification by issuing Ecu-denominated treasury bonds. However, this very prospect is not welcome in the FRG, because the Ecu's purchasing power is, by construction, less stable than the Deutschmark's.

Nevertheless, the Ecu as it currently stands cannot be said to be a complete money. Quite apart from the distinction between 'official' and 'private' Ecus, the latter has, so far, essentially been used for financial asset denomination; its use for invoicing intra-European trade remains negligible and the US dollar is still, by far, the principal currency used in Europe for this purpose.

Recently, there have been a number of proposals for reforming the Ecu: for instance, Raymond Barre, the former French Prime Minister and EC Commissioner, has suggested that the Ecu ought to be indexed to the strongest European currency. But this proposal boils down to the introduction of yet another financial innovation: if the frequency of revisions dictated by the indexation procedure is low, the indexed Ecu will bear a close resemblance to the Deutschmark; if the frequency is high, the exchange value of the indexed Ecu will fluctuate widely with the various ups and downs of existing EMS currencies. Such a financial instrument is unlikely to develop.

This monetary unification scheme does not appear to be realistic. If a common currency is ever to exist, it will not be a currency basket. The Ecu is but an inferior substitute for monetary union and is in no way a necessary step toward monetary union. Monetary union requires that a radical step be taken, which is presently hard to envisage.

Some people recommend that certain EC payments be made in Ecus (for example, agricultural subsidies and EC taxes). However, this may, in the short run, make the management of EC finances more difficult and increase the cost of intra-EC monetary instability. As long as French firms pay their wages and set their prices in French francs, while German firms use the Deutschmark and British firms use sterling, any kind of intra-EC trade will bear an exchange risk which cannot be alleviated by the use of the Ecu in commercial invoicing. Quite the contrary indeed, since the use of the Ecu would be profitable; but then the exchange risk, transaction costs and costs of managing two different types of money holdings would have been shifted on to the wage earners.

As it now stands, the Ecu is hardly autonomous from its constituent currencies, be it in terms of exchange rate or in terms of interest rates; a central bank issuing Ecus would therefore have no degree of freedom. If it was decided to alter the definition of the Ecu and make it something other than a currency basket (the 'trans-substantiation' referred to in Aglietta, 1987), the difficulty would again be to establish credibility for a currency with no effective role in transactions and no legal tender status. Moreover, it would seem rather strange to initiate the process of monetary unification with the creation *ex nihilo* of the thirteenth currency, which is likely to increase monetary instability.

Bibliographical references

Aglietta M. ed. (1986) *L'écu et la vieille dame,* Economica, Paris.

Aglietta M. (1987) 'Des principes keynésiens pour un pôle monétaire européen' in Zerbato M. ed. *Keynésianisme et sortie de crise*, Dunod, Paris.

Allen P.R. (1987) *The Ecu and Monetary Management in Europe*, miméo, prepared for the ECU Conference-University of Leuven, Belgium, June 12-13.

Basevi G., Fratianni M., Giersch H., Korteweg P., O'Mahony O., Parkin M., Peeters T., Salin P. and Thygesen N. (1975) 'The All Saint's Day Manifesto for European Monetary Union', *The Economist*, 1 November.

Boissieu de Ch. (1987) 'L'Ecu et la libéralisation financière en Europe', *Revue d'économie politique,* July-August.

Committee for the study of economic and monetary union (1989) *Report on economic and monetary union in the European Community*, so-called 'Rapport Delors'.

Jean A. (1990): 'L'ECU, le SME et les marchés financiers', *Les Editions d'organisation*, Paris.

Le Cacheux, J. (1987) *Ecu et substituabilité des actifs financiers* miméo, OFCE, Paris.

Le Cacheux J., Mathieu C. and Sterdyniak H. (1989) 'Un chèque en blanc pour l'Europe monétaire?' *Lettre de l'OFCE*, May.

Mathieu C. and Sterdyniak H. (1989) 'Vers une monnaie commune en Europe?', *Observations et diagnostics économiques, revue de l'OFCE,* January.

Fratianni M. and Peeters T., (1979) *One Money for Europe*, Praeger Publishers, New York.

Magnifico G. (1974) *L'Europe par la monnaie, une nouvelle approche*, Lavauzelle, Paris.

OPTICA Report 1975 (1975) *Towards Economic Equilibrium and Monetary Unification in Europe*, Commission of the European Communities, Brussels.

Ruffini, P.B. (1989) 'Développement et limites de l'écu privé' *Revue d'économie financière, no 8/9, L'Europe monétaire*, March-June.

Salin P. ed., (1974) *L'unification monétaire européenne*, Calmann-Levy, Paris.

Salin P. (1980) *L'unité monétaire europééne: au profit de qui?* Economica, Paris.

Vissol Th. ed., (1987) 'Du dollar à l'Ecu' *Reflets et perspectives de la vie économique*, June.

10: Response of the Bank of Italy to NIESR Questions

By Lorenzo Bini Smaghi

10.1 What are the advantages of a common currency?

In a monetary union the advantages of a common currency can be valued both in micro and macroeconomic terms.

From the former point of view, for a monetary union to be complete, currencies have to be perfectly substitutable in the three-fold function of money. To fully satisfy the unit of account function legal tender status would have to be given to all currencies in the whole Community. Economic agents would thus face the cost of quoting prices and accepting payments in all currencies. Substitution in the means of payment function could be met by all currencies only if the Community cross-rates were the same over the whole area. It is necessary that this condition also applies for retail rates, not only for the official ones. Finally, even if fixed exchange rates are officially declared, substitutability relating to the store of value function requires the absence of any expectation of exchange rate realignment. As long as national currencies continue to exist, national authorities could be tempted, or could be forced, to leave the union. This may occur for two reasons.

Firstly, systems based on the monetary policy of the 'hegemonic' country tend to be asymmetric and fragile. Competition among countries can bring about continuous switching of the anchor role between currencies, thereby making the system indeterminate and endangering overall stability. Secondly, in the presence of real divergences, monetary authorities may have an incentive to manipulate parities in order to adjust imbalances. Economic agents can discount this possibility by pricing the same assets, denominated in different currencies, differently bringing about tensions in the system. For all these reasons it is highly unlikely that a multi-currency system performs as well as a single currency one.

From a macroeconomic point of view, a multi-currency system involves complications in terms of the conduct of monetary policy, both with respect to the definition of targets (in particular quantitative ones), and the instruments of intervention, since the distribution of the overall quantity of money in the different currencies is important. Conducting monetary policy in a single currency system implies simplifying things a lot.

The transition from many currencies to one is a complex process that requires time and a gradual approach. Changes will be needed in the habits and behaviour of economic agents, that will have to brought about in a smooth way.

To keep the cost of the change-over as low as possible the use of the Ecu among private agents should be encouraged in advance of full monetary union. This implies that the Ecu will have to coexist for some time with national currencies. In this context, it is necessary to help – but not to manipulate – market forces in their effort to develop a large and efficient market for the private Ecu. In recent years, the number and variety of private and public assets denominated in Ecus have increased and further progress is possible.

Finally, the good performance of the Ecu clearing system, which has given a strong impulse to the development of the private Ecu, can be seen as the embryo for a complete Ecu payment system.

10.2 What is the plausible anti-monde against which to assess the use of the Ecu as the common currency?

The choice of the single Community currency depends on several factors. The preferences of private agents will play a decisive role. Also, the problem is a political one because the issue of money is traditionally one of the privileges of the state.

The advantage of using one of the member currencies is that it already exists and, therefore, a large part of the Community market is accustomed to it. A likely candidate would be the Deutschmark. This approach has several disadvantages. Firstly, the increasing use of the centre country's currency can rest uneasily with the objective of price stability in the area, as has been discussed in the literature (the Triffin dilemma). The major currency should not play, at the same time, the role of system anchor and the means of international payments. Failure to acknowledge this problem led to the breakdown of the Bretton Woods system. Managing a system in which velocity is continuously changing, because of currency substitution, could be difficult and might cause inflationary (deflationary) pressures due to the creation of excess (insufficient) liquidity denominated in the single currency.

Secondly, it should be noted that Germany's present economic and financial role in the Community is much more limited than that performed by the USA in the Bretton Woods system. The share of US output during the 1950s and the 1960s was close to 50 per cent of world output and US foreign trade was around 30 per cent of the total. On the other hand, US exports represented only 5 per cent of its GNP, making the US economy a relatively closed one. Germany's output is about 24 per cent of the Community total and its share of intra-Community trade is less than 30 per cent, representing about 15 per cent of Germany's production. The relatively smaller dimensions of the Germany economy imply that it can be strongly affected by changes in the rest of the Community. This is even more true if we consider the size of the German financial market. While the US dollar market has always been very liquid with a great variety of instruments, that of the DM is still fairly small and not very liquid.

Thirdly, since the beginning of the EMS, the Bundesbank has always restricted the ability of other EMS central banks to increase their Deutschmark reserves. German monetary authorities have been determined to keep tight control on liquidity. This policy was required to ensure the Deutschmark's role as EMS anchor but, on the other hand, has restricted its ability to develop in international transactions.

Another problem that will arise in choosing one of the existing currencies is the distribution of seignorage. Seignorage will tend to fall for all the national monetary authorities, with the exception of the one whose currency is chosen as the common one. In the creation of an economic union, the renunciation of national sovereignty can be more acceptable if national monetary authorities transfer their autonomy to a supranational institution, rather than to one of the other national authorities. To avoid tensions between member countries the process towards a monetary union should, therefore, follow the basic principles of parity and joint responsibility on which the construction of Europe has traditionally been based.

10.3 What is the impact of announcing in advance that the Ecu will become the common currency?

The decision that the Ecu would be at the centre of the EMS has contributed remarkably to the system's development. The Ecu is essentially a market phenomenon: its open basket nature represents a strong link between private agents and the efforts of the European monetary authorities towards economic and monetary union.

The first effect of the announcement that the Ecu will become the future single currency of the union will be to further increase market confidence regarding the authorities' commitment to monetary and economic union. The move towards a common currency, as already mentioned, requires time because of economic agents' rooted habits in dealing with money; an early announcement on the new future currency will help to speed the process up. On the other hand, the announcement would appear weak and incomplete if all the remaining impediments to use of the Ecu are not eliminated. First, its legal tender status will have to be dealt with. Allowing for such legal use would enhance its role in commercial transactions. At the same time, the problem of the institution responsible for its value would inevitably rise. The private Ecu is currently just inside money that develops through market mechanisms.

The development of the Ecu requires a further stabilization of exchange rates. This objective could be attained first through the participation of every community currency in the ERM and then by implementing co-ordinated monetary policies aimed at achieving a higher degree of monetary cohesion in the system.

Once the announcement is made, the development of the Ecu would be facilitated by private financial institutions aiming to capture a larger share of the increasing market.

10.4 Does it matter whether the Ecu is a basket or an independent currency in its own right?

Given the basket nature of the Ecu, its value is determined by the value of the component currencies and its stability is therefore closely linked to that of the component currencies. This implies that the development of the Ecu is related to the promotion of exchange rate stability among EMS currencies.

As long as exchange rates are not irrevocably fixed, the basket nature of the Ecu should remain because it maintains a link between development of the Ecu and exchange rate stability. When exchange rates are irrevocably fixed, the basket nature of the Ecu will become irrelevant.

The Ecu is becoming more and more a currency in its own right and the implementation of the Ecu clearing system has brought about a large development of the market in Ecu-denominated assets. The process of transformation of the Ecu from a basket into a currency is a matter of habit that the market has to develop by itself.

10.5 What are the implications for monetary control?

As long as the Ecu remains as inside money, created by market mechanisms, its development should not pose major problems in terms of monetary control. Further, given its basket nature, national monetary policies can affect its value through the impact on component currencies. Monetary policy co-ordination therefore has an important role to play in influencing Ecu market conditions. On the other hand, the Ecu should not start to play a major role in the exchange rate mechanism. Given its basket nature, its value is a weighted average of the component currencies. Defining exchange rate policies aimed at stabilizing the value of the Ecu may entail a loss of the anchor for the EMS, and increase the rate of inflation in the Community. Only when exchange rates are irrevocably fixed will the Ecu play a major role in the conduct of policy.

Interventions in Ecu on the exchange market should maintain their technical purposes and should not be aimed at implementing an exchange rate policy for the Ecu.

10.6 What should the timetable be for the transition to a common currency?

The EMS and the Ecu have developed jointly. While the EMS is mainly a creature of the European monetary authorities, the Ecu is the product of market forces. We have already considered the conditions that would allow the change-over to a common currency. It should be added that the best time should be decided by market forces and by private agents. However, it will be a responsibility of the monetary authorities to provide the market with the necessary conditions to make the change-over feasible. The necessary changes in agents' habits regarding the use of money will be the result of the implementation of a legal and an economic environment that will pave the way for the use of a single currency.

The most important elements that will speed up the move from many currencies with locked parities to a common currency will be the creation of a European monetary authority that will conduct a single monetary policy for the whole Community and the development of a fully integrated financial market.

11: Response of De Nederlandsche Bank to the NIESR Questions

By Dr. Age Bakker

In this section I will respond to the questions posed by the NIESR (see Appendix 4).

A basic question underlying NIESR's questions seems to be the following: to what extent could a parallel currency provide a road towards a common currency which is less painful than the one requiring convergence of economic policy and performance and loss of sovereignty over economic decision making? This question has been examined in a contribution by Mr. Duisenberg to the deliberations of the Committee for the Study of Economic and Monetary Union, which has been published in the collection of papers supporting the Delors Report. The conclusion drawn is that the development of the Ecu as a parallel currency would be more of a burden than a panacea for the realization of economic and monetary union.

It would seem efficient in the final stage of EMU, which is characterized by irrevocably locked exchange rates, to have a single currency replace the other currencies. Of course, the present Ecu could well provide the name for the single currency, but its characteristics would be totally different from the Ecu as presently defined. National currencies will merge in the common currency which, by definition, will not be a currency basket.

Therefore, I have doubts about the likelihood of a spontaneous development of the Ecu into a parallel currency. NIESR's comparison with spontaneous 'standardization' in product markets seems to place too little emphasis on the essential value of a currency – i.e. the confidence people have in it. The minimum requirement in order for the Ecu to take over from all other ERM currencies is that people will have less confidence in their own currency than in the Ecu. The Ecu at present is an 'average'; the confidence in it can also be no more than average – which is clearly not enough.

The redefinition of the Ecu as an *independent* non-basket currency, which would never devalue relative to the strongest currency in the

ERM, would not overcome these difficulties. Rather, new difficulties would emerge. Such a currency would complicate even more the conduct and co-ordination of monetary policy in the ERM area. In addition, it raises pertinent questions as to the institutional responsibility for the issuance of Ecus and the determination and defence of its exchange rate and its interest rate. For all these reasons the Delors Report has discarded the development of the Ecu into a parallel currency.

In its background paper, the NIESR seems to take as the main presumption that the visible development of an actively-used European currency will confirm the expectation of future monetary union, which in turn will foster convergence in inflation rates now – thus accelerating the process to monetary union. It is, however, less clear by which mechanisms (besides the psychological one) that use of the Ecu will foster convergence.

The NIESR seems to place too much emphasis on *monetary* union, while leaving aside economic union. But, economic and monetary union are two sides of the same (common) coin. Convergence in economic policies is a prerequisite for the co-ordination of monetary policy. Excessive fiscal deficits and price stability are mutually inconsistent. Therefore convergence in inflation is not enough.

In our view, convergence to price stability and lower fiscal deficits will require further adjustment in most ERM countries. If the prospect of participating in an EMU lowers political resistance to such adjustment, then convergence will indeed be fostered. However, if increased use of the Ecu interferes with the effective conduct of monetary policy, the objective of EMU might fall into jeopardy.

We have always taken the position that the markets themselves must decide whether they feel that an expanded role for the Ecu is useful. Companies could make a major contribution to the development of the Ecu if they would increase their use of it for invoicing and settlement. On the part of the authorities, everything should be done to remove any impediments to such use. In The Netherlands there are no exchange controls and the Ecu is being treated on the same footing as all other foreign currencies. Nevertheless, thus far there has been only limited interest in the use of the Ecu.

12: European Currency Unification: Technical Lessons From Earlier Experiments

by Eirik Svindland, DIW, Berlin

12.1 Outline

The Single European Act (SEA) of 1986 declares all barriers to the movement of goods, services, labour and capital are to be removed within the EC as from the end of 1992. For this purpose it seeks to abolish administrative, legal and technical barriers to harmonizing standards; it seeks to end national preference in public procurement; and it seeks to reduce tax differences among member states. Surveys, 1988/89 (*Eurobarometer: 1988,* and *Ifo-Munchen: 1989*) revealed, however, that the Germans were sceptical about the attainment of this demanding goal. At that time a typical German manager did not expect achievement of the promised opening-up of the markets before the end of 1992. He thought tax harmonization and public procurement to be less important issues than the freedom from customs controls and from restrictions on capital and people's mobility. Also, he urged the benefits of currency unification – even if the new Ecu were to be a bit more inflation-prone than the Deutschmark. Recent political developments in Germany have probably made everybody even more sceptical about the achievement of the demanding goals of the SEA. It is therefore time, I suppose, to centre political efforts upon realizable, urgent objectives of the EC integration.

In this chapter, I develop the argument that a monetary strategy in line with this opinion is possible. This strategy is a minimal version of the monetary union approach. I term the goal a 'currency union' in order to distinguish it from a common monetary system, which includes joint legal regulation of banking and other sections of the credit market.

My starting point is the following proposition: it may be desirable, but it is not necessary, that the progress towards EC monetary union has to match the progress towards an EC economic union. Their relationship depends on the precise meaning attached to the notions 'monetary union' and 'economic union'. If the latter only means ensuring conditions of free movement of goods, services and factors of production, then it is neither a necessary nor a sufficient condition for a monetary union. Such a union may be formed by countries with currencies which float against each other. In this case, however, let us term it a 'free-trade area', not an 'economic union' because exchange rate uncertainty exists which impedes the unification. And if two or more countries issue the same currency (exchange rate 1:1), then they may introduce barriers to trade and capital movements in order to combine the 'monetary union' with autonomy in economic affairs.

It is neither essential to construct a complete economic union (with a uniform system of business, fiscal and labour market organization) in order to become a free-trade area, nor is the formation of a complete monetary union (with a uniform system of banking and capital markets) a necessary condition for a common currency. The EC thus has the opportunity to choose a combination of two half-way measures and thereby to shape a 'free-trade area with a common currency', which will require less than SEA with respect to the harmonization issue and will still serve the purpose which business people at least demand of an economic and monetary union. The politicians of the EC only have to stick to an agreement and to some simple rules of central banking, if they want to live in a currency union in lieu of a very similar EMS. The most important difference would be never to question the exchange rate (1:1) between the domestic and foreign versions of the new Ecu. Actual and former experience with currency unions is evidence of the harmonization requirements. I refer to the pre-World War I gold standard, the German currency unification, the Latin Monetary Union, the post-World War I gold standard and the Scandinavian Currency Union. They were good lessons on the techniques of operating a minimal currency union, which I summarize at the end of the chapter. My description at this point fits in with the ideas of Padoa-Schioppa and Thygesen[1], who also suggested that the step to a monetary union is not as big as is often thought, and who have both recommended institutionalizing the co-ordination of monetary policy before the adoption of full centralization.

12.2 Pre-World War I gold standard

The simplest model of the balance of payments between national currency areas goes like this: a country's balance of trade becomes unfavourable if prices rise unduly in this country. Then a deficit in its international earnings occurs which is paid for by means of international money transfers. This entails a reduction of the money base, and subsequently, of the money supply. The consequence is pressure on the country's price level sufficient to restore the old international price equilibrium. On the other hand, the country receiving money as a consequence of its balance of payments surplus will experience a rise in its prices, which counteracts its surplus and, hence, further money inflows. Thus the system promotes general stabilization by means of simultaneous price level adjustments and rational redistribution of the world's monetary base.

Today this model is known and discussed as the 'monetary approach to the balance of payments'. In earlier times it was termed the 'price-specie-flow mechanism', a term which is due to the monetary use of precious metals. Hume, Ricardo and others developed the model and it is complementary to the 'quantity theory'. The advocates of these ideas were known as the Currency School in the 19th century debates about banking legislation and their view was generally accepted – for instance by the British Bullion Committee. Subsequent banking legislation (like Peel's Bank Charter of 1844) strongly reflects their influence. Thus, the gold standard was introduced as machinery-like monetary system – it was expected to work automatically, without any political management, in sustaining international monetary equilibrium.

Actually, the gold standard system did not work according to plan. The central banks held gold reserves of a size which had little to do with the country's balance of trade, and they were inclined to accumulate gold reserves and to hold more than was strictly required. Exports and imports of monetary gold could thus take place without the expected effects on the domestic stock of money. Above all, everyone tried to avoid a loss of gold reserves. Most important, central banks learned to apply monetary policy by varying the rate of discount – they raised the rate of discount in cases of excess demand for foreign currency. From the very beginning of the gold standard system, businessmen settled their international obligations not by shipments of specie, but by mailing of a bill of exchange. For instance, someone in Hamburg, who had to pay a certain amount of sterling either sent a matching sterling bill of exchange, which he bought in the Hamburg discount market, or he delayed his effective payment by sending his own bill of exchange. In both cases, title to a bank balance in London was acquired and used for the payment.

Now, consider a rise of the domestic rate of discount. What happened? First of all, the price of bills sank in the domestic market. Domestic and foreign traders who wanted to purchase bills and use them as a means of payment therefore switched over to this market, whereas credit-demanding traders issued more bills abroad than before. The net result was a capital import used for payments. That is exactly the way inter-regional payments imbalances are settled. It is also the reason for my choice of a roundabout method of description – it makes the first lesson from the experiences with a gold standard evident: *the inter-regional payments mechanism works well because nobody doubts that settlements of debts will be just as free of political obstacles as in the case of an unrestricted, unconditional convertibility of the debtor's currency.*

The continental central banks used to protect their gold reserves by fixing their discount and lombard rates slightly above the same rates in London. In this way, they drew on British capital too; wealthy Britain provided the (net) credits which were necessary to maintain the international monetary system in spite of the central banks' hoarding or reserves. Sterling served as a generally accepted means for international payments. Therefore, the pre-war gold standard system may alternatively be characterized as a sterling bloc (or system) which was held together by the world-wide dominance of London as a financial clearing centre. This interpretation comes out very clearly in the quotations of exchange rates: London still measures the *foreign* currency equivalent of one pound sterling. Other banking communities measures the same quantity, but as the *domestic* currency equivalent of one pound sterling. From this experience with financial centralism we can draw the following, second lesson: *a currency bloc or union will work if it has a centre which supplies the rest with sufficient reserves and if the periphery competes for these reserves by varying short-term (money) interest rates slightly, but constantly above the same rates at the centre.*

12.3 Deutsches Reich: Growth of a central bank

In 1871, after the Franco-Prussian War, a proclamation of the German emperor completed formation of Deutsches Reich. At that time all the incorporated states had at least one bank of their own issuing bank notes. These issuing banks were neither closed down nor absorbed by the Prussian bank. *The government instead,* in correspondence with our two lessons, *chose a strategy of gradual integration and unification.*

A law of 14 March 1875 named the Prussian bank the Reichsbank. It did so without depriving the other 33 German issuing banks of their privilege – rather they were made subject to the same law. The Reichsbank, however, had the best location (in Berlin) and it was favoured by the government. It was the centre of the new German monetary system and it therefore (later) grew in relation to its competitors. By and by, the local banks renounced note issuing, but Bavaria, Saxony, Wurttemberg and Baden each had their own issuing bank and kept it until the time of the Reichsbank Mark became legal tender (as from 1 January 1910).

12.4 The Latin Monetary Union: Failures as a union

In the mid-19th century gold from the new fields in North America and Australia had a strong impact on the exchange rate between gold and silver. This appreciation of silver disturbed the money system in many countries because of their bimetallism – they used large gold coins and small silver ones. The silver coins disappeared into hoards in accordance with Gresham's Law. Instead of adopting a pure gold standard, Switzerland and some other European countries began to mint coins with a reduced silver content, and Italy even issued small bank notes and declared them to be legal tender. However, differences between old and new coins caused problems in cross border relations. The French government (Napoleon III) therefore initiated a conference at which delegations from Belgium, France, Italy and Switzerland negotiated the foundations of a monetary union. On 23 December 1865 a treaty was ratified, which formed the Latin Monetary Union with a bimetallic currency – i.e. an agreement on a rate of exchange between gold and silver (1.5:1) and on the size and weight of coins to be issued (100, 50, 20, 10 and 5 francs in gold, and 5 francs in silver). These coins were to circulate freely throughout the union and to be accepted as legal tender. In addition, the parties agreed upon minting up to 6 francs per inhabitant of small silver coins (2 and 1 francs, 50 and 20 centimes) with a limited acceptance as legal tender (up to 100 francs). And finally, the deadline for the withdrawal of the old coins was scheduled for 1 January 1869 (1 January 1878 for some small Swiss coins). In 1868 Greece joined the Union.

Shortly after the treaty (from 1867) the supply of silver increased. It effected a reappreciation of gold in relation to silver on the free market and Gresham's Law now worked the other way: gold coins were withdrawn from circulation (exported or hoarded) and silver coins came back. This eroded the bimetallic foundations of the Latin Monetary Union and impeded the withdrawal of older coins. In addition, the redemption of Italian coins was strongly complicated by the use of irredeemable paper money too.

On several occasions the members of the Latin Monetary Union met to repair its structure. In 1874 they limited the volume of silver coins and in 1878 they agreed to stop the coinage of silver. However, it didn't work out. In 1885 a new treaty was ratified which cancelled the legal tender acceptance of 5 franc silver coins outside the minting country. Hence the parties had to withdraw coins of this kind from circulation, exchange them and settle the net balances in gold.

This agreement was disadvantageous to Belgium. Its government had leased the minting privilege to private individuals. A large part of all Union-wide circulating 5 franc silver coins came from these mints, which did not cease operating in 1885. Consequently, the Belgian government tried to stop the export of coins. Rigorous customs controls, even of private luggage was the result.

Italy too did not participate as intended. Its government did not stop financing its own expenditure by issuing legal tender banknotes. Instead it tried to control international economic relations in order to stop the export of precious metals and to secure the repatriation of proceeds from exports.

And finally, in Switzerland there was no monetary policy, which ensured the consistency with the money market at the Union's financial centre, Paris. Swiss banks paid a higher price for bills than their French competitors, resulting in undesirable currency export levels. The foundation of the Swiss national bank (completed in 1905) was a measure designed to eliminate this problem.

The main deficiency of the Latin Monetary Union was the lack of regulation of the total money supply. After World War I France also took advantage of this deficiency in order to solve its public finance problems. Banknotes were issued, even at the level of municipalities, during this period of inflation.

Officially, but not in practice, the Latin Monetary Union lasted until 1927. The lesson from this attempt to combine a currency union with national monetary autonomy is: *apply a single, simple definition of money, keep a centralized control of the issue of legal tender and prevent central banking from being mixed up with public finances, if you want to have both a currency union and no controls of capital movements within the union.*

12.5 Post-World War I gold standard

The post-war restoration of the gold standard also allows us to draw a lesson from a malfunctioning currency system. This time, however, political mistakes and failures to adhere to the appropriate rules of the assumed policy game were the cause of the problems.

Firstly, gold was remonetized with an inexpedient low relative price in terms of consumption goods or labour. At this parity, there were insufficient monetary gold reserves. A money shortage occurred. France, however, joined the system with a probably undervalued franc and certainly with the desire to build up a large gold reserve corresponding to the extraordinary liquidity preference (and money hoarding) in this country. Its one-sided accumulation of gold on a large scale jeopardized economic life in neighbouring countries and contributed significantly to the occurrence of other policies working against the rules of the monetary system.

Secondly, in their attempts to keep and accumulate the urgently needed gold reserves, countries fell back into the trap of mercantile policies: dumping, import restrictions and information regulations of foreign access to the domestic credit market. Responsible people spoke about the restoration of a monetary system which worked in accordance with its ideology – in other words, about operating the price-specie-flow mechanism, but their monetary policy *de facto* aimed at national autonomy. Therefore, if a central bank had the opportunity to acquire more gold, which for instance was attracted by the interest policy, then it increased its excess reserves – it sterilized the inflow by reducing another component of the money stock. And in case of an outflow the same bank tried to neutralize the domestic monetary effects by limiting the reserve loss to the extent of a variation of these excess reserves.

Thirdly, however, this satellite policy could not work systematically so well as it did before World War I because the post-war system had at least three competing financial centres: London, New York and Paris. The United States at the time experienced a rapid growth which had transformed her from a debtor country to be the world's largest annual capital exporter and the owner of a large proportion of all gold reserves. In France there was a similar growth of gold reserves and of foreign exchange assets. Due to the level of old stock-in-hand, however, London still was at least as influential as New York. It is not the existence of three separate centres that caused trouble, but the lack of monetary policy co-operation and co-ordination. Funds were, like today, liable to move from one centre to another in response to interest rate changes and other information. There was competition for funds in which the satellites could not act according to a simple rule. They were caught in a policy game without a stable interest rate solution.

The efforts of the US Federal Reserve to use a 'tight money' policy as a brake to the 1928/29 stock market boom tightened money in many other countries too. And the stock market crash – at least hastened by this policy – gave rise to a demand for liquidity which forced US banks to recall capital. The devastating economic consequences of the crash were exported by the chain reactions of banks in Europe and elsewhere. In the following period, confidence in the monetary system dwindled. Attempts to liquidate foreign exchange holdings and sharp interest rate increases contributed to the system's collapse in September 1931.

From this experiment with a world-wide monetary order, which essentially resembled a currency union, we can draw at least the following lesson: *central banks must co-operate, pool reserves and co-ordinate policy actions if they belong to a multi-polar currency bloc or union – in principle they must form a 'reserve system'. Otherwise the union will not be stable nor work well in combination with internal free trade and capital mobility.*

12.6 The Scandinavian Currency Union

We now turn back to pre-World War I gold standard experiences. In connection with the discontinuation of their silver standard, Denmark, Norway and Sweden in a treaty of 18 December 1872 formed a complete gold standard currency union – i.e. they agreed on rules for issuing money and on the use of their coins as legal tender throughout the union.

The co-operation of these three central banks, was, at that time, rather modern. They opened credit lines for each other – up to Kr2m, later Kr3m was available on demand. They balanced their mutual drawings regularly. The net debtor would then pay his debt in gold within the next three months. However, he escaped this obligation if during this time he accrued a positive balance. Therefore, the arrangement was first and foremost a measure of economic reserve holdings – in effect, a pooling of reserves.

On the whole, the co-operation of the three authorities worked well; it worked as intended and in accordance with the prescribed rules. Together they operated a satellite of the financial centre, London. The destruction of the union was effected by another kind of political problem. In 1905, Sweden cancelled its membership after the political segregation of Norway from Sweden, but it resumed almost exactly the same form of co-operation with Denmark. Different degrees of involvement in World War I finally made this co-operation impracticable.

12.7 Conclusion on an EC currency union

Shortly before the end of the gold standard, Keynes urged the foundation of the multinational central bank. He thought a real possibility existed to save the gold standard. Many of his ideas have been incorporated in the IMF and EMS. A further development of the EMS into a European Currency Union can to some extent follow the original Keynes proposal. I would, however, prefer to emphasize the federal character of such an arrangement, in order to encourage early acceptance by the national governments.

The EC central banks would thus constitute a reserve system. The board of this system issues a new currency – the new Ecu; it does not need any initial capital of its own, but its liabilities to non-members have to be guaranteed by the central banks involved; it does not do business except with central banks; its liabilities thus consist of the new Ecu reserve of its member banks and of liabilities to non-member central banks; its assets consist of securities which it receives from its members in exchange for new Ecu, and of international reserve assets; it therefore has much the same relation to the member banks as these central banks have to their domestic banks.

The board of the system decides on (i) the total volume of its Ecu liabilities; (ii) a quota for member banks in case of the planned growth of this volume; (iii) the standard of securities which its members and itself will accept in exchange for new-Ecu; and (iv) its own central Ecu reserve requirements.

I do not recommend a quantitative Friedmanian Rule for the balance sheet expansion of the reserve board, because such a rule cannot replace an independent management which has a high degree of authority and discretion. A well-qualified, serious management gives the bank its needed credibility, because every rule has its exceptions and it is silly to stick to rules in exceptional cases.

The member banks issue their national version of the new Ecu – the Queen might therefore appear on the British Ecu notes – but it is only a regional issue of a common legal tender, which takes place in accordance with common rules. The lessons from previous experiments with currency unions must be learnt in the business with local banks and with members banks. Above all, members must stick to the currency union agreement (1:1 exchange rate of member monies) and forget that they have the opportunity to carry on their own monetary policy and – eventually – to contribute to the national fiscal policy. It is probably helpful to remember that the opportunities within the EMS of today are very much the same as in earlier situations. One of the members alone should take care of the foreign exchange market business.

Market developments and growing familiarity with the Ecu reserve systems will determine the path and pace of harmonization of the rest of the money and credit system (banking laws etc). Of special importance is that community member states do not begin by transferring all their monetary authority to a common European central bank. Instead, gradual steps need to be taken in the direction of co-ordination of, and co-operation in, a fixed exchange rate monetary system.

It is important to recognise that there would be a quite simple transition from the present EMS-system to the outlined new-Ecu-system. None of the nations involved would experience a currency reform like that of the 1948 replacement of the Reichsmark by the Deutschmark, which changed the composition as well as the distribution of personal income and wealth. There is no need for such a currency reform, because there is no actual demonetization of currencies prior to the introduction of the new-Ecu. And there would be no problems on incongruent price and asset structures for discussion as in the case of the ongoing adoption of the Deutschmark-currency in the GDR. Contrary to the changes in the GDR, the introduction of a new-Ecu will not intermingle with any other changes to the economic system. Every debt and other contractual payment obligations will remain unchanged in terms of their real value. They will simply be multiplied by the uniform rate of conversion from the national currency to the new-Ecu.

Such a simple currency change can be announced in advance. A credible announcement of the date and the rate of conversion will have rational expectation effects; national authorities should adopt matching policies and private business make appropriate arrangements for the 'big bang'. Consequently, the outcome will not really be a 'big bang', but a gradual transition into the currency union. The longer the period of transition, the smoother and more complete the adoption of the rules of currency union. However, the longer the period, the greater the chance of unforeseen developments which may affect the completion of the currency union. Also, the less likely it is that decisions and the credibility of the proposal will be affected. Taking the widespread existence of long term contracts into consideration, my own guess, therefore, is that the transition period should last at least two years.

[1] Padoa-Schioppa, T.: 'The European monetary system: A long-term view', in Giavazzi, F. Micossi, S. and Milker, M. (eds.): *The European monetary system*, Cambridge 1988. Thygesen, N.: 'Decentralization and accountability within the central bank: Any lessons from the US experience for the potential organization of a European central banking institution?, in De Grauwe, P. and Peeters, T. (eds.): *The Ecu and European monetary integration*, London 1989.

13: The Economic Consequences of a Single European Currency on Centre-Periphery Relations within the Community*

By Stefan Collignon
Director, Research and Communication, the Association for the Monetary Union of Europe[1]

Two fundamental variables will determine the failure or success of the creation of economic and monetary union (EMU). One is the political will to do so. The other is linked to the structural differences between European countries which will determine the feasability and sustainability of economic and monetary integration and which will give rise to the formation of national interests. The willingness to surrender national authority for monetary policy to a European Central Bank, and to accept the Ecu as the single currency, will only exist if all member states clearly perceive a net benefit of EMU over the present monetary system, or its eventual alternatives. Contrary to other historical precedents, of which the recent monetary union of the two German states is only the most recent example, EMU is not a necessity related to the rejection by the people of bad currency and who wish to substitute it for a better one. It is a model for consensus building.

European businessmen clearly perceive benefits from EMU, they anticipate greater stability and security in their investment decisions and greater transparency for their operations in the single European market after 1992.[2] They are, however, sometimes less evident to macroeconomic decision makers whose attitudes are coloured by a mix of some defunct economic doctrine[3] and perceived national interests. This chapter is an attempt to reconcile microeconomic perception with macroeconomic theory. First, the main positions in the present debate about EMU will be outlined. Then an alternative approach will be proposed – one which takes into account the hierarchy and competition in a multicurrency system. Based on this analysis we will be able to evaluate the effects of the Ecu as a single currency in phase III of the Delors Report and its prior role as a common basket currency in phases I and II.

13.1 Perceived interests in the debate on EMU

It is generally accepted that the establishment of monetary union requires an increasing convergence of economic and monetary policies and performances.[4] However, a certain number of ambiguities persist as to the precise nature of this convergence. While public debate has long been dominated by the so-called 'crowning theory' whereby monetary integration is to occur at the end of a long process of economic convergence, the Delors Report has clearly established a parallel between economic and monetary convergence.

This poses a question of priority: is it more important to remove structural disparities between national economies, or to reduce differentials in national rates of inflation, thereby achieving monetary convergence? The original idea of the Delors Report is to establish convergence of economic performance as the aim[5] and monetary convergence as the tool.[6] But this does not solve the problem of an appropriate standard against which convergence is measured. If inflation rates are used, economic performance has to be adjusted and the question remains: what are the implications for regional growth rates and disparities?[7] If national income creation is used as a standard,[8] inflation rates have to be adjusted to growth requirements and this may be incompatible with price stability. In monetary terms this contradiction is often expressed as the choice between convergence towards the standard of the strongest currency or towards an average mean.

This is where the political obstacle appears. For it is unthinkable that Germany, or some of the other northern European countries linked to the Deutschmark bloc, would accept such a weakening of their money standard.[9] On the other hand, 'there are some in France and Spain, and doubtless in other countries, who wish to work within the European System of Central Banks to achieve a European monetary policy that attaches a higher priority to rising growth and employment in the short term, and lower priority to immediate price stability than the policies of the Bundesbank which have dominated the present European Monetary System'.[10] Put like this, the project of monetary union appears as if either southern Europe has to submit itself to the 'Europeanization of the

Deutschmark philosophy'[11] against its own interest, or as if Germans can be cheated into it.[12]

However, the problem of perception is linked to the lack of a common standard against which economic and monetary convergence is measured. If the ultimate purpose of EMU is greater convergence and better performance of income and wealth creation, and monetary union is a tool to achieve it, then it has to be shown how monetary policy can reduce regional imbalances. More specifically, European consensus requires that economic convergence (ie the interest of the periphery) is compatible with monetary convergence to the standard of the strongest currency, as this is the *conditio sine qua non* of German participation.

Economic convergence implies, by definition, that the structural disparities between regions are progressively reduced.[13] These disparities are expressed by the differential of per capita GDP in purchasing power parity, which amounts to a relation of 1:5 between Thrace in Greece and Hamburg in Germany,[14] or by the international competitiveness of individual countries which cause the structural surplus/deficit in the balance of trade between the centre and the periphery. Sometimes they are also attributed to different population growth. But regardless of what indicator one may use, one thing is clear: economic convergence necessitates that peripheral economies grow faster than centre economies.[15] Hence, the fundamental problem is to explain if, and under what conditions, price stability-oriented monetary policies will contribute to more accelerated growth in the periphery.

The answer is not obvious. Economic doctrine in the 1960s and early 1970s assumed the contrary: it was considered that economic growth was stimulated by fiscal and monetary policies, expanding effective demand at the 'price' of some inflation. In the 1980s this view was replaced by the 'neutrality of money' approach, according to which monetary expansions lead – in the long term – only to changes in the price level, and not to real variables like output, employment and interest rates.[16] Growth was to be fostered by increasing the economy's elasticity and more efficient productive capacity, ie by 'supply side economics'.[17] But this required not only tax cuts, but also structural interventions whose effects were only felt in the long run. Short-term demand managment returned through the back door in the form of fiscal or external deficits.[18] Thus, contrary to common belief, the true supply side policy was not conducted in the USA or the UK but in the Federal Republic of Germany.[19] Here the combination of tight monetary policy by the Bundesbank, and proper supply side policies with respect to wage bargaining technology, vocational training etc., created the conditions for minimal inflation and, simultaneously, some economic growth.

But what could be done to accelerate growth in the periphery? Simple alignment to a German-type economic and monetary policy would at best create convergence of growth rates, but not of standards of living, as these require *higher* growth rates in the periphery.[20] If German financial orthodoxy is considered to 'sacrifice the prosperity of the whole of Europe'[21] then it is not such a big step to suggest more accommodating monetary policies in order to foster growth.

According to conventional Keynesian theory, rapid growth may be stimulated internally – by expanding aggregate demand which would raise the rate of investment. In a closed economy this is achieved by a policy of easy money, leading to lower interest rates which – given the rate of expected profitability of capital investment – will raise the demand for real investment. Productive capacity and employment would increase, even if structural inelasticities caused a moderate permanent inflation. However, this argument is untenable in an open economy, where low interest rates would cause capital funds to flow to countries with tighter monetary policies and higher interest rates, thereby reducing local investment. Consequently, either capital controls would have to be introduced or higher interest rates would have to prevent the outflow of funds. In a liberalized, open economy a national growth policy is limited by the monetary policy of the major trading partners.

Thus, in an area with highly interdependent economies, as in Europe, it has become impossible for the periphery to accelerate the growth of demand beyond the constraints set by restrictive monetary (and fiscal) policies in the centre. But even the alternative solution of stimulating demand in the centre, so that the periphery's exports benefit from the centre's increased imports,[22] does not help economic convergence: the whole of the community may grow faster, but the centre-periphery disparities are not overcome.

A second option to stimulate growth at the periphery is that of raising its international competitiveness, thereby increasing exports which, in turn, affect investment. A measure for the competitiveness is the real exchange rate which measures the domestic price level against the international price level.[23] If, at a given nominal exchange rate, the domestic price level is higher than abroad, a currency is overvalued and the country's competitiveness is hampered. Consequently, an undervalued currency will be an incentive for the export industry. However, in case the peripheral country conducts an inflationary monetary policy, (either in order to encourage private investment or by running high budget deficits financed by seigniorage) domestic prices will rise faster at home than abroad. The currency will be increasingly overvalued unless a devaluation of the nominal exchange rate re-establishes competitiveness. Yet, given the policy of easy money, a devaluation does not solve the problem, as it induces an increase in the domestic price level through import prices which, in turn, may be amplified by wage bargaining that aims to compensate for the loss of purchasing power.[24]

Therefore, renewed devaluations are necessary, which can only be stopped by either following a tight, ie non-accommodating monetary policy at home, or by greater inflation abroad. Given this method of reasoning it is hardly surprising that countries with traditionally soft currencies favour a monetary union from which they expect an easing of the restrictive effects of the present Bundesbank policies[25]. Yet, even if the accommodating policies of such a monetary union may reduce the inflation differential between centre and periphery, and thereby balance competitive advantages *within* the union, it would reduce competitiveness with regard to the outside world. The consequence would be a potential pressure for greater protectionism (fortress Europe). Besides the evident efficiency losses, this would also be particularly harmful for the rapidly transforming economies in Eastern Europe, who need the European Community market for their development.

This perspective places the periphery in direct opposition to the interests of the hard currency bloc around the Deutschmark; for these countries have obtained their status as centre economies precisely *from* the competitive advantage of an undervalued currency which results from their restrictive monetary policies. As long as a country's rate of inflation remains below the level of its major trading partners, its real exchange rate will depreciate, thereby increasing competitiveness. Exports will boom and the balance of trade will achieve a structural surplus. Repeated modest revaluations will not jeopardize this development, as revaluations lower import prices and contain wage pressures, thereby further improving the competitive advantage. Even if centre economies were willing to give up their competitive advantage with regard to their partners in the economic and monetary union, they would still wish to maintain minimal rates of inflation in order to keep their competitive position on the world market.

Thus, centre economies have a lot to lose from a monetary union which converges towards an average, rather than towards the strongest currency. Not surprisingly, Germany's precondition for joining EMU is a

Bundesbank-like European Central Bank.

In the present European monetary system (EMS) a compromise between these two (somewhat simplified) positions is made by allowing occasional exchange rate re-adjustments provided they do not fully compensate for inflation differentials, thereby maintaining the pressure on the periphery to improve its competitiveness by reducing inflation and improving productivity. It introduces, however, an asymmetry into the system owing to the fact that the periphery has to determine exchange rates in relation to European trading partners, while the exchange rate policy of the centre currency, ie the Deutschmark, is also determined by competitive considerations *vis-à-vis* to the US dollar and the yen.

Thus, we must conclude that the conventional approaches towards stimulating growth in the periphery through accommodating monetary policies are not conducive to economic convergence. But they may also block the political consensus necessary for the rapid advancement of EMU.

13.2 The importance of sound money in a multicurrency system

The soundness of the conventional arguments for more accommodating monetary policies may be questioned on empirical as well as on theoretical grounds. If the logic developed in the last section would hold, inflation and growth in the European periphery would have to be higher than in the northern countries, thereby reducing the per capita income differentials. This is not supported by statistical evidence.

Two studies by the European Commission[26] show that inequalities in GDP between member states of the European Community, fell from 1960 until the early 1970s – that is to say, during a period with high growth rates and low rates of inflation. This development came to a halt after 1974, when inflation was high and growth was slow. Further evidence is obtained from a study on the impact of the EMS on inflation and output of some selected countries.[27] While inflation came down in Denmark, France and Italy, after creation of the EMS, their output performance improved (with the exception of France in 1980-84). In contrast, Germany experienced higher than predicted inflation and a substantial loss in output. Thus, empirical facts teach us the opposite of conventional theory.

An alternative explanation, consistent with observed reality, can be derived from the analytical tools of monetary Keynesianism[28]. The opposition of conventional Keynesian theory to tight monetary policy for peripheral countries is linked to the argument that their economic capacity and productivity is too low to compete effectively with the centre economies, so that deflationary policies place a greater burden on the periphery than on the centre. The alternative approach claims that regardless of the structure of the 'real economy', monetary policy has to follow the fundamental rules according to which a monetary economy functions. Thus, there is only *one* set of monetary policies for a market economy and not one for the centre and one for the periphery.[29]

The difficulty with monetary theory is that money serves both as a stock and as a flow category. As a means of payment, money has to be a unit of account, a medium of exchange and a store of value. The first two functions are related to the circulation of commodities, the third is 'a subtle device for linking the present to the future'.[30] As a flow category money is used to appropriate resources, thereby realizing its purchasing power; as a stock category it is an asset, securing wealth. Being the latter, money functions as liquidity reserve, ie as a store of general purchasing power. Its transfer discharges debt contracts and price contracts.[31] Therefore, in a modern system money in its proper sense is 'high-powered money' or monetary base; it is 'a sort of "ultimate money" without regress to other types of money'.[32] As we will see, this implies that money does not carry an interest rate but that interest is paid in order to obtain money.[33] Only the State as legislator decides 'what it is that must be delivered as a lawful or customary discharge of a contract'.[34] This assignment of the legal tender function makes money a public good and constitutes its low elasticity of substitution.[35] In fact, money has to fulfil two conditions in order to function as a standard of value.

First, it must have a very low elasticity of substitution, which means that as its purchasing power falls 'there is no tendency to substitute some other factor for it'.[36] This is the prerequisite for money to serve as liquidity, ie to be a protection against uncertainty. Classical theory ignored the security motive in the demand for money.[37] Yet, it is of particular relevance when discussing international currency competition in open economies. For, if free convertibility is granted, the national currency with the lowest elasticity of substitution provides the highest liquidity service and can therefore substitute for monies with higher elasticity. Therefore, one should clarify that low *domestic* elasticity of substitution leads to a high foreign currency substitution effect.

Second, it must have a very low elasticity of production, ie money can not be readily produced. This condition requires that the supply of money be reserved for the Central Bank who 'contrives its scarcity' and thereby maintains its low elasticity of substitution.[38] Thus, the essential role of the Central Bank is to maintain the viability of the monetary system by preventing the erosion of the store of value function of money, by keeping it scarce.[39]

This analysis immediately reveals the difficulty for the Ecu to function as money: although its scarcity is collectively contrived by the scarcity of its individual component currencies, its elasticity of substitution is higher than the elasticity of the 'hardest' component currency and lower than the 'weaker' currencies. This results, in part, from the fact that Ecu is not legal tender. Therefore, the basket Ecu does not fulfil the function of liquidity, although its individual component currencies do.

The fact that money discharges debt contracts implies that it is liquidity. As such it is distinct from a promise to transfer means of payment which is debt (deferred payment). Consequently, it is also distinct from the claim over the debt which is a financial asset.[40] The reasons for holding money as liquidity are therefore distinct from the reasons for holding financial assets. The owner of a financial asset has surrendered liquidity in return for (financial) interest payments. He seeks a monetary return which extends his control over resources. The holder of liquidity, however, does not benefit from interest payments on her cash balance but from the 'sense of comfort and confidence'[41] which is the utility of holding money.[42] The price at which she is willing to surrender the convenience of liquidity is called the *liquidity premium*[43] and is dependent on the liquidity-holder's fear of loss of wealth. Thus, her motivation for holding money is to secure her wealth. The greater the perceived insecurity, the higher the liquidity premium, provided money fulfils its function as a store of value. The owners of wealth always have a choice between holding money (cash balances) in order to *secure* their wealth and relinquishing money in return for interest yielding financial assets which *increase* their wealth.

However, not all financial assets are alike. For some there exist deeper markets and lower volatility than for others. This is represented by the different 'degrees of liquidity' for financial assets,[44] or rather by the premium for not running a loss upon realizing the asset's value. In this context one should also consider transaction costs, which are related to the asset's transfer of ownership, as they constitute an 'institutional loss' upon realizing the asset's value. The different degrees of liquidity represent a non-monetary utility to their owners and add to the attractiveness of financial assets. The lower the asset's price volatility and transaction costs, and the greater its market depth, the higher the safety premium.[45]

This establishes the private basket Ecu as a financial asset, for it is created by surrendering liquidity in the form of different national monies. With respect to some foreign currencies, its degree of liquidity may be high, but it is never liquidity *per se*. Not being legal tender, its utilization is always linked to financial intermediation (hence its 'private' character) and subject to transaction costs. This fact explains the Ecu's spectacular success in the financial markets, but also its difficulty in becoming a widely used means of payment. Given the Ecu's transaction costs, its safety premium will be higher, the greater the monetary uncertainty is between its component currencies.[46] Furthermore this explains also why European Central Banks allow the development of the Ecu through private asset markets, but object to it becoming 'money' in the form of a parallel currency, in order to maintain stability.[47]

In order to create a financial asset the holder of liquidity must be willing to part with it. She will only do so if the borrower of her money offers her, in return, a financial asset that yields a monetary interest rate plus a safety premium at least equivalent to the utility of holding money which is expressed in the liquidity premium.[48] In a closed economy, the level of interest rates in financial markets is governed by the liquidity premium which expresses the subjective evaluation of the convenience and security of disposal over liquidity. This is the reason why price stability is a necessary condition of a well functioning monetary economy.

Inflation undermines the purchasing power of money. Although price variations do not affect the function of unit of account, they create disturbances for the means of exchange if the variations are not correctly anticipated. They thereby undermine the confidence in the store of value function of money. The utility of holding money as a protection against uncertainty decreases, (the liquidity premium falls) and the elasticity of substitution increases. Wealth owners exchange their liquidity for 'real assets' such as gold and property. It could be argued that the holding of liquidity is not a very important part of asset portfolios and, consequently, nominal interest rates on financial assets can compensate for the loss of purchasing power. This overlooks the fact that, in inflationary societies, the interests of debtors always have priority over the interests of creditors and savers.[49] If inflation could be compensated for by a perfect index – which is far from being a realistic assumption[50] – why would it persist? Inflation necessarily undermines the confidence in the store of value function of money.

In an open economy wealth owners substitute eroding money for foreign, more stable currencies.[51] Therefore, internal instability becomes the cause of external instability leading to far-reaching consequences in the balance of payments and the exchange rate. A multicurrency system, defined by autonomous national monetary authorities, is necessarily denoted by the existence of a potential instability and currency hierarchy.[52]

We express the open economy impact on the formation of rates of interest by adding an *external value premium* to the liquidity and the safety premiums.[53] It expresses the utility of either holding liquidity or financial assets in the form and denomination of a specific currency. It is, therefore, at the cause of the above mentioned foreign currency substitution effect, and estimates the open economy impact on the wealth preservation function of money. In a closed economy it is zero. It is very close to zero in the case of non-convertible currencies, and high for international reserve currencies. It is also influenced by the economic size and structure of foreign trade and financial markets. Further to these structural qualities, variations of the external value premium are also dependent on monetary policy.

A hierarchy of currencies implies that the utilities of soft currencies in the periphery are less than those of hard currencies in the centre: in the international context the quality of money is determined by its scarcity and price stability, but also by the confidence in the political environment of a country and by the expectations about the currency's future external value, ie the development of the exchange rate. Thus, a policy of easy money, which is gradually eroding internal price stability and inevitably leading to a fall of the internal liquidity premium, simultaneously reduces the external value premium. Likewise, if the government finances a significant part of its budget deficit by seigniorage,[54] it undermines the confidence in the currency, thereby causing the external value premium to fall. Furthermore, as the monetization of government debt is equivalent to defaulting on part of the debt,[55] it implies that an unsound fiscal authority is able to dominate the monetary authority. Hence, the utility of holding or investing in such currency is lower than for sound money. We can therefore define centre and periphery by the relative level of their respective external value premiums. We say that the centre's external value premium is higher than the periphery's.

While the external value premium depends on fundamentals of economic policy, the safety premium was of a structural character, being a function of the size of respective economies, but also of the volatility and institutional and technical development of financial markets and related transaction costs. As a general rule, it is reasonable to assume that these structures are more developed in the centre. A high liquidity premium concentrates the liquidity function on the currency of the centre economy, and, thereby, creates some kind of external economy of scale for the development of such a currency.[57] Consequently, the safety premium in the centre is superior to the periphery.[58]

Considering the choice between two assets denominated in different currencies, say of the centre and of the periphery, the holder of liquidity evaluates the monetary return of a financial asset *plus* the international utilities of the currency in which it is expressed. The relative utility of the higher safety premiums in the centre can be called the *risk premium*, and the relative advantage of a higher external value premium is called the *hierarchy premium*.[59]

The interest rate in the periphery exceeds the nominal rate of interest in the centre by the risk premium and the hierarchy premium.[60] Thus, the observable differential of nominal interest rates is due to fundamental factors relating to the internal and external management of currencies. But the structural determinants of the currency hierarchy may persist even with sound economic policy for a long period, as it takes time to build up trust and confidence in a specific currency. This explains why three-month interest rates in French francs are, even after seven years of effort, still two percentage points higher than in Deutschmarks. Herein lies an important argument for a single European currency.

Sound monetary policy produces low nominal interest rates, easy money leads, in the medium to long term, to high nominal interest rates.[61] The conventional Keynesian doctrine – whereby easy money reduces interest rates and stimulates aggregate demand – only holds true for the closed economy. In the open economy the interest rate becomes a tool for maintaining external stability.[62]

This has important implications for economic growth in the periphery, as investment in productive capacities depends on the difference between expected profitability of the investment (Keynes' marginal efficiency of capital) and the nominal interest rate in financial markets.[63] It is clear that the volume of investment in the periphery is suboptimal, when compared with the nominal interest rate in the centre. Furthermore, the expected profitability of investment is itself a function of the nominal rate of interest, as interest payments on borrowed funds are a cost element.[64] Thus, the higher the interest rate, the lower the expected profit rate, particularly on capital-intensive projects which are likely to make the greatest contribution to productivity growth. In other words the risk premium and the hierarchy premium prevent a higher level of productive investment in the periphery, and thereby act as an obstacle to higher growth. Thus, contrary to the conventional doctrine, it is not the tight monetary policy of the northern European countries which prevents the periphery from 'catching up' with the centre, but the laxities in monetary and fiscal matters in the south, which are the cause for the periphery's high hierarchy premium.

Of course, it could be argued that a more relaxed monetary policy in the centre would also reduce the hierarchy premium between soft and hard currencies, thereby having a stimulating effect. But this would require that all hard currency areas soften simultaneously, although an individual country would obtain a competitive advantage by *not* doing so (Prisoner's Dilemma). Furthermore, the world would collectively erode the workability of the monetary system with the consequence that money would be substituted by real assets.[65]

Therefore, we must draw the conclusion that only sound fiscal and tight monetary policy will provide the necessary conditions for long-term growth in the periphery. The implication for economic convergence in the European Community is that the standard for monetary policy must be set by the Deutschmark which is, qualitatively, the best currency, and not by some average. However, monetary policy will also need to be assisted by suitable supply side policies, and this will be discussed briefly in the next section.

13.3 The economic consequences of common and single European currencies

On the basis of this analysis we can now evaluate the role of the Ecu as a basket currency before, and as a single currency after the completion of full EMU.

The Ecu as a basket of weighted national currencies functions as a common unit of account. As such it is particularly useful to those who operate in many different European currencies and have circular financial flows requiring financial netting. Many companies who have such an organizational structure already use the Ecu in this function. However, for companies with either no, or mainly bilateral transactions, the utility of such a common unit is less obvious. Custom, habit and the related transaction costs will then give, with all likelihood, a slight comparative advantage to national currencies.

By contrast, the basket nature of the Ecu has been a strong incentive for its rapid development as a financial instrument. The risk-reducing character of a portfolio of currencies strengthens the wealth preserving function of an international store of value. This makes it superior to monies whose internal liquidity function is rapidly undermined by inflation. On the other hand it is never liquidity in the (proper) sense that it could legally extinguish debt contracts.[66] However, due to its high degree of liquidity as a financial asset, the Ecu has started to develop a kind of 'international liquidity' of its own. This means it has the appearance of liquidity which is derived from its component currencies and may be accepted by the public as if it were legally enforceable. Consequently, the Ecu has the strange particularity that its external value premium is high, while its internal liquidity premium is very low. For a national currency, the liquidity premium governs the external value premium and both together determine (after allowance for the safety premium) the financial asset's interest rate. In the case of the Ecu it is the opposite: the extremely low utility of Ecu liquidity (lacking legal tender status, it cannot be used in final consumption) implies that the external value premium is governed by the composite interest rate of the financial markets, while each component interest rate is dependent on national monetary policy.[67]

Consequently, these characteristics make the Ecu a medial European currency. This is also true for the position of the safety premium: market depth for Ecu-denominated assets is less than for major currencies like Deutschmarks or sterling (whose liquidity premium is significantly lower), but it is greater than for some of the smaller European currencies – such as the drachma, the escudo and the peseta.

Even though the Ecu's attractiveness is largely due to its high safety premium in an uncertain monetary environment, it would still be handicapped if currency competition would select a 'winner' rather than create chaos; the greater attractiveness of strong currencies for wealth owners reinforces their competitive advantage and thereby has the negative effect of reduced scale on the safety premium of the other currencies. This disadvantage could largely be compensated for by a credible announcement that the Ecu will become the single European currency within a reasonably short time span. This announcement would therefore raise the external value premium and subsequently the liquidity premium of the Ecu.

The question is of course: what is a 'credible announcement'? It can hardly be the public declaration of some politicians or statesmen alone, as these are liable to political pressures or democratic votes which could quickly overturn a decision. What is needed is the proof that the rules of the game are to be changed. It would therefore appear that only the linking of the creation of a European Central Bank in phase II of the Delors Report along with the declaration that the Ecu will replace all national currencies in due course, will constitute a 'credible announcement'.

Given appropriate management by the European Central Bank in cooperation with the national Central Banks, the Ecu's liquidity premium could then rise in the run-up to 'big bang' and reach, shortly beforehand, a level compatible with the subsequent liquidity and external value premiums of the single currency.

It is likely that after 'big bang', ie in phase III of the Delors plan, that the monetary policy of the European Central Bank would, at first, have to be very tight in order to create the necessary trust and confidence in the newly created, full-blown money called the Ecu.[68] The development of the basket Ecu in phase II would, however, help to soften this requirement, as greater private use of the Ecu before 'big bang' does already build up some trust and confidence in the Ecu. This is one of the most important arguments why the private Ecu should already be developed as a common currency *before* its introduction as a single currency.

The major difficulty of the Ecu to develop the means of exchange function lies in the fact that, lacking legal tender status, it nearly always has to pass into the form of a national currency in order to appropriate resources and transfer general purchasing power. Because this transformation causes transfer costs that have to be paid to financial intermediaries or to internal currency operators of the firm, the appropriation of goods and services by means of the private Ecu is not free, and the Ecu is – contrary to money – not a public good in the strict sense. Therefore, the Ecu is able to serve its function as a stock category, but finds it difficult to be transformed into a flow category. Even a credible announcement about its future will not change this structural disadvantage of a common currency. Therefore, the basket Ecu is unlikely ever to become a serious competitor against the national currencies in terms of means of exchange.

All this will change dramatically when the Ecu becomes the single currency, replacing national monies that were the components of its basket. The newly created European Central Bank would now have to keep the Ecu scarce, thereby securing its value and preserving high liquidity and external value premiums.

What will be the consequence of such a change in the monetary regime for economic convergence?

If the management of the single currency Ecu is at least as sound as it was previously for the Deutschmark, not much would change in the economic environment of the centre economies. However, significant benefits would be reaped by the periphery: in relation to the previous national currencies the new Ecu would dismiss the safety premium and the hierarchy premium – all European countries would now use the same hard currency which would be the new Ecu. Hence, interest rates in the periphery would fall from the previously high levels to a new level close to the one prevailing in the centre. This reduction simultaneously increases the expected profitability of capital in the periphery and produces a 'big push' of new investment.

In order for this investment to produce growth effects that lead to economic convergence, certain supply side conditions have to be fulfilled. Most importantly, wage increases must be restrained and productivity increased. Yet, given the tight monetary regime of the new European currency, the conditions for moderate wage policies are automatically strengthened. As for increases in productivity, they have a discretionary and an endogenous dimension. Discretionary regional policies and structural interventions have to correct market failures and imbalances in the infrastructure between centre and periphery.[69] More important are the endogenous dynamic effects.

If production is subject to economies of scale, the change in monetary regime will induce an endogenous process of circular and cumulative causation in the periphery.[70] The growth process caused by higher investment and booming demand, under conditions of relative price stability, will increase productivity (Verdoorn's Law) by lowering unit costs in the firm, and external economies in the region.[71] Competitiveness will increase in the region. The resulting 'exports' into the centre, as well as into the rest of the world will require further investment and reinforce the growth process.

Consequently, it is not so much the *relative level* of economic capacity and productivity in the centre and the periphery which determine the competitive position, but the *relative growth rates* of productivity. However, the dynamic process of transformation in the real economy is caused by and dependent on the monetary regime.

The degree to which a peripheral country would benefit from monetary integration will of course also depend on its productive structure. Productivity gains are more likely in industry than in agriculture or services. Consequently, less industrialized regions within one country would benefit less. They would still require structural support from regional funds. But the fact that there are, necessarily, *some* regions within a peripheral country that would gain from monetary union, increases overall welfare and helps to conduct regional policies on a national rather than a European level. Monetary union with a strong, centrally administered currency is therefore conducive to decentralized regional policies, as requested in the Delors plan.[72]

We have assumed so far that no major growth impulse will result from the single currency for the centre economies. This is unlikely, as the existence of a large world currency, covering a quarter of world trade transactions, would most probably increase the safety and liquidity premiums for Ecu operators with respect to other international currencies such as the US dollar or the yen. Consequently, there would also be a positive growth effect in the centre.

13.4 Summary

Research by the Association for the Monetary Union of Europe has proven[73] that European businessmen clearly perceive the benefits from a single European currency for their respective businesses. This paper has shown how these microeconomic expectations fit into a macroeconomic model which is based on the analysis of the ground rules of monetary systems and the choice of wealth owners between liquidity preference and accumulation.

The results are that EMU would lead to the acceleration of economic growth in the periphery without sacrifice in the centre. The perceptions of these benefits should facilitate the political will to make a success of European Monetary Union.

* This chapter was not prepared in time for the incorporation of its results into Part I of this book.

1 The views expressed in this chapter are those of the author and do not necessarily correspond to those of the institution to which he belongs.

2 See several opinion surveys by the Association for the Monetary Union of Europe.

3 Keynes (1936), p. 383.

4 See for example Delors Report (1989).

5 See §11 Delors Report (1989).

6 See §12.

7 See: J. Delors, 'Regional implications of economic and monetary integration'; in Delors Report (1989).

8 See Maurice F. Doyle, 'Regional policy and European economic integration'; in Delors Report (1989), p. 74-75.

9 'But even insofar as high esteem for stable money is an expression of a special national preference, it must not be disposed of. Even disregarding the specific negative consequences, a change from the D-Mark to an inferior

European currency would be equivalent to the negation of fundamental economic attitudes and expectations of [German] people and of the resulting coordination mechanisms and asset positions. The protection of price stability is not even in the Federal Republic a constitutional right. But it is very close to it.' Wissenschaftlicher Beirat beim Bundesministerium für Wirtschaft; January 1989.

10 Walter Eltis (1989), p. 272.

11 Wilhelm Hankel (1989), p. 352.

12 Eltis (1989) seems to suggest this.

13 Being concerned with monetary integration we will, unless otherwise stated, identify a 'region' with a 'currency area', ie in our case with European 'countries'.

14 See T. Padoa-Schioppa (1987), p. 162.

15 See also G. Amato (1989), p. 61.

16 R. Dornbusch and S. Fischer (1988), p. 240.

17 James Tobin (1989) and the contribution by Mario Arcelli in Baldassarri (1989), p. 83.

18 Tobin (1989), p. 17.

19 Marcello DeCecco, Debate in Baldassarri (1989), p. 96.

20 Amato (1989), p. 61.

21 Tobin (1989), p. 16.

22 See eg the proposals of Miguel Boyer quoted in Eltis (1989), p. 270.

23 The real exchange rate can be written as: $R = P/e\,P^*$, where P is the domestic and P^* the international price level, while e expresses the nominal exchange rate e=Domestic currency/Foreign currency. We call a currency overvalued, if $R > 1$ and undervalued if $R < 1$. For $R = 1$ purchasing power parity applies.

24 Hansjörg Herr (1988), p. 74.

25 See H. Riese (1989).

26 T. Padoa-Schioppa (1987), p. 163 and G. Magnifico (1985), p. 35-39.

27 F. Giavazzi and A. Giovannini (1988).

28 This approach has specifically been developed by the Berlin School around Prof Hajo Riese.

29 The Spanish prime minister Felipe Gonzales has expressed this fact by saying: 'Our only freedom is the freedom to make mistakes ... but we have to pay for them!'

30 Keynes (1936), p. 294.

31 Keynes (1930), p. 4.

32 cf. K. Brunner (1989), p. 175 and Riese (1989 b), p. 2.

33 Riese (1986), p. 61.

34 Keynes (1930), p. 4.

35 Riese (1989 b), p. 33.

36 Keynes (1936), p. 231.

37 A. Meltzer (1988), p. 286.

38 Riese (1986), p. 62-65.

39 This is expressed in the article 3 of the law regulating the Deutsche Bundesbank: 'Die Deutsche Bundesbank regelt (...) den Geldumlauf und die Kreditversorgung der Wirtschaft mit dem Ziel, die Währung zu sichern und sorgt für die bankmäßige Abwicklung des Zahlungsverkehrs im Inland und

mit dem Ausland.'

40 Riese (1989 b), p. 1-2.

41 Meltzer (1988), p. 286.

42 'Casual empiricism suggests that the benefits from using money might be quite large; the opportunity cost of holding cash is large and yet banknotes are a major means of payments in all industrial countries.' Marcello deCecco and Alberto Giovannini (1989), p. 6.

43 Riese (1986), p. 23.

44 Riese (1989 b) has demonstrated that financial assets can be said to have 'degrees of liquidity' but not money, as money is liquidity.

45 cf: Padoa-Schioppa and S. Papadia (1984).

46 For details see Stefan Collignon (1989 b).

47 See Karl Otto Pöhl, The further development of the European Monetary System; and W.F. Duisenberg, The Ecu as a parallel currency in: Delors Report (1989).

48 Thus, in equilibrium: (1) $\mathbf{i} + \mathbf{z} = \mathbf{l}$, where **i** stands for the monetary interest rate, **z** for the safety premium and **l** for the liquidity premium.

49 Hankel (1989), p. 353.

50 See W. Eltis, Debate in: M. Baldassarri (1989).

51 Herr (1986), p. 9.

52 Herr und Westphal (1988).

53 If the *external value premium* is s, equation (1) becomes: (1a) $\mathbf{i} + \mathbf{z} + \mathbf{s} = \mathbf{l} + \mathbf{s}$.

54 Allan Drazen (1989) shows that seigniorage as a % of tax revenues is significantly higher in Southern Europe than in Northern Europe.

55 We assume that government debt is always nominal, ie not perfectly indexed. See Th. Sargent (1986), p. 32.

56 Hence $\mathbf{s}_c > \mathbf{s}_p$ where **c** for centre and **p** for periphery.

57 Herr (1986), p. 78.

58 $\mathbf{z}_c > \mathbf{z}_p$

59 The portfolio is in equilibrium, if: (2) $\mathbf{i}_c + \mathbf{z}_c + \mathbf{s}_c = \mathbf{i}_p + \mathbf{z}_p + \mathbf{s}_p$
Thus, the relation between monetary interest rates in the periphery and the centre is: (3) $\mathbf{i}_p = \mathbf{i}_c + (\mathbf{z}_c - \mathbf{z}_p) + (\mathbf{s}_c - \mathbf{s}_p)$, where $(\mathbf{z}_c - \mathbf{z}_p)$ is the *risk premium*, and $(\mathbf{s}_c - \mathbf{s}_p)$ is the *hierarchy premium*.

60 This is in accordance with portfolio theory according to which low yield assets may be kept in order to diversify the portfolio and thereby reduce its risk. See Schelkle (1990).

61 Note that this result has been obtained without recourse to specific rates of inflation or real interest rates, thereby avoiding the problem of indexation.

62 Riese (1986), p. 248.

63 This statement implies that the expected profitability anticipates price increases. It therefore does not contradict the neoclassical axiom according to which investment depends on real interest rates.

64 Riese (1986), p. 94 argues that the cost of holding money is the cause for the non-neutrality of inflation.

65 The outcome of such a development can presently be studied in Eastern Europe.

66 With the exception of 'official' Ecu transaction between Central Banks.

[67] Thus, for national monies equation (1) reads from right to left, while it reads from left to right for the Ecu.
[68] I thank Hansjörg Herr for pointing this out to me.
[69] See M. Doyle, Regional policy and European economic integration: in Delors Report (1989).
[70] For a discussion of this concept first developed by G. Myrdal and its qualification see S. Collignon (1989).
[71] For further development of this argument see N. Kaldor (1985), p. 69 and G. Magnifico (1985), p. 33.
[72] See J. Delors, Regional implications of economic and monetary integration; in: Delors Report (1989).
[73] See opinion poll in 1988 and 1989 as well the microeconomic study by Ernst & Young in this report.

Bibliographical references

Amato, Giuliano (1989): Sulla moneta unica europea gravano problemi strutturali; in: *Revista di Politica Economica*, March 1989.

Baldassarri, Mario (1989): *Keynes e le politiche economiche negli anni '80*, Rome 1989.

Brunner, Karl (1989): High-powered money and the monetary base in: Eatwell, John, Milgate, M and Newman, P. (ed.), *The New Palgrave: Money*, London (1989).

Collignon, Stefan (1989b): Regionale Integration und Entwicklung. Das Beispiel Ostafrika. Dissertation: Berlin.

Collignon, Stefan (1989): The commercial use of the Ecu: a victim of EMS success or an infant industry? in: *Ecu Banking Association Newsletter*, October 1989.

Delors Report (1989): Committee for the Study of Economic and Monetary Union, *Report on economic and monetary union in the European Community*; Luxembourg.

Dornbusch, R. and Fischer, S. (1988): *Macroeconomics*: Singapore.

Drazen, Allan (1989): Monetary policy, capital controls and seigniorage in an open economy, in: Marcello de Cecco and Alberto Giovannini (eds.), *A European Central Bank? Perspectives on monetary unification after ten years of the EMS*: Cambridge.

Eltis, Walter (1989): The obstacles to European Monetary Union, in: *De Pecunia*, vol. I, Nov., October 1989.

Giavazzi, Francesco and Giovannini, Alberto (1988): The role of the exchange-rate regime in a disinflation: Empirical evidence on the European Monetary System, in: F. Giavazzi, S. Micossi, M. Miller (eds.), *The European Monetary System*: Cambridge (UK).

Hankel, Wilhelm (1989): Europäische Währungsperspektiven; in: *Europa Archiv*, Folge 11.

Herr, Hansjörg (1986): *Geld, Kredit und Ökonomische Dynamik in marktvermittelten Ökonomien – die Vision einer Geldwirtschaft*: Munich.

Herr, Hansjörg und Andreas Westphal (1988): Zum Verhältnis von realwirtschaftlicher und monetärer Integration Westeuropas; *Prokla No. 75*.

Kaldor, Nicolas (1985): *Economics without equilibrium*: New York/ Cardiff.

Keynes, John Maynard (1930): *A treatise of money: collected writings, vol. V*; Cambridge/London. 1971.

Keynes, John Maynard (1936): *The general theory of employment, interest and money: collected writings, vol. VII*: Cambridge/London ed. 1971.

Magnifico, Giovanni (1983): *Regional imbalances and national economic performance*. Report prepared by a Study Group for the Commission of the European Communities; Luxembourg.

Meltzer, Allan (1988): *Keynes's monetary theory. A different interpretation*: Cambridge.

Padoa-Schioppa, Tommaso (1987): *Efficiency, stability and equity. A strategy for the evolution of the economic system of the European Community*: Oxford.

Padoa-Schioppa, Tommaso and Papadia, S. (1984): Competing currencies and monetary stability; in: Masera, R.S. and Triffin, R. (eds.), *Europe's Money*: Oxford.

Riese, Hajo (1989): Thesen zum Referat 'Das Project "EG 1992"' Freie Universität Berlin: Manuskript, November 1989.

Riese, Hajo (1989b): Geld, Kredit und Vermögen Begriffliche Grundlagen und preistheoretische Implikationen der monetären keynesianischen Ökonomie; in: H. Riese und H.-P. Spahn, (Hg): *Internationale Geldwirtschaft*: Regensburg 1989.

Riese, Hajo (1986): *Theorie der Inflation*; Tübingen.

Sargent, Thomas I. (1986): *Rational expectations and inflation*: New York.

Schelkle, Waltraut (1990): Peripherisierung in Binnen und Weltmarkt; in: H. Riese, H.-P. Spahn (Hg): *Studien zur monetären Ökonomie Bd. 6*: Regensburg (forthcoming).

Tobin, James (1989): La teoria Keynesiana: è uno strumento ancora utile nella realtà economica odierna? in: Baldassarri (1989).

Wissenschaftlicher Beirat beim Bundesministerium für Wirtschaft (1989): Gutachten zur Europäischen Währungsordnung; Studienreihe 61 des BMW, February 1989.

Appendix 1: Historical Background

Context in European history

The idea of EMU is not new. The Werner Report of 1970 presented such a plan. However, the concept has now gained considerable impetus from the steady progress of the 1992 programme and from the EMS results. Irreversible steps towards the creation of an economic union in which goods, services, people, and capital can move freely have been taken since the White Paper of 1985 detailing the plan, and the Single European Act, in force in 1987 ensuring its feasibility. Awareness of the programme among European consumers and producers has engendered a new dynamism to the debate and concern that its full potential should be realized.

It is in this context that, at the Hanover summit in June 1988, the Heads of State and government decided to set up a committee to explore the implications of an economic and monetary union (EMU) and the ways and means of achieving it, should it be deemed desirable.

In its report to the 1989 Madrid summit the Delors Committee began by surveying the advantages and difficulties linked to the creation of EMU and then went on to suggest a loose, three-stage framework (included in sections 45-9 of the Delors Report reproduced below) to achieve this result.

S45 The Committee investigated various aspects of the role that the Ecu might play in the process of economic and monetary integration in Europe.

S46 Firstly, the Committee examined the role of the Ecu in connection with an eventual move to a single currency. Although a monetary union does not necessarily require a single currency, it would be a desirable feature. The Committee was of the opinion that the Ecu has the potential to be developed into such a common currency. This would imply that the Ecu would be transformed from a basket of currencies into a genuine currency. The irrevocable fixing of exchange rates would imply that there would be no discontinuity between the Ecu and the single currency of the union and that Ecu obligations would be payable at face value in Ecus if the transition to the single currency had been made by the time the contract matured.

S47 Secondly, the Committee considered the possibility of adopting a parallel currency strategy as a means of accelerating the pace of the monetary union process. Under this approach the definition of the Ecu as a basket of currencies would be abandoned at an early stage and the new fully-fledged currency, called the Ecu, would be created autonomously and issued in addition to the existing Community currencies, competing with them. The proponents of this strategy expect that the gradual crowding-out of national currencies by the Ecu would make it possible to circumvent the institutional and economic difficulties of establishing a monetary union. The Committee felt that this strategy was not to be recommended for two main reasons. Firstly, an additional source of money creation without a precise linkage to economic activity could jeopardize price stability. Secondly, the addition of a new currency, with its own independent monetary implications, would further complicate the already difficult endeavour of co-ordinating differing national monetary policies.

S48 Thirdly, the Committee examined the possibility of using the official Ecu as an instrument in the conduct of a common monetary policy. The main features of possible schemes are described in the collection of papers submitted to the Committee, which represent personal contributions.

S49 Fourthly, the Committee agreed that there should be no discrimination against the private use of the Ecu and that existing administrative obstacles should be removed.

The Delors Report did not suggest a timetable except for the beginning of Stage one, and did not specify the precise route and practical steps on the path to monetary union.

Many of the questions left unanswered by the Delors Report are essentially political, and as such have provoked intense debate across Europe in the run up to the Dublin Summit of June 1990 when the Heads of State and Government meet to discuss MU.

Current uses and users of the private Ecu

Official uses

The Ecu was created in 1975 (*Decision du Conseil, 21/04/1975*). It is a synthetic or 'basket currency' composed of the national currencies of the 12 member states of the European Community. The weighting of these currencies within the basket reflects the relative importance of the economies and currencies of the member nations as determined by each member's GDP, its share of intra-European trade, etc. The basket is described as an 'open' one because of the provision that exists to review these weightings every five years.

The Ecu was chosen by the European Council to be the central element of the EMS, where it serves as numeraire and to denominate operations in both the intervention and credit mechanisms. It is a reserve asset and a means of settlement for EMS central banks. This use conforms to what is called the official Ecu.

But, since 1975 for the ECSC and 1977 for the EC, the Ecu has been the unit of account of Community institutions and increasingly used as a unit of payment; in 1989 a quarter of Commission borrowings were in Ecus; the EIB has made loans of Ecu 6·5 billion; ECSC has assets of over Ecu1 billion.

If use of the Ecu by private operators was very limited during the 1970s, in the decade following its adoption as the central element of the EMS, the official definition of the Ecu was taken up spontaneously by the financial markets, and the resultant financial instruments and transactions came to be known as those of the 'private Ecu'. The private Ecu results from a private contractual agreement to adopt the definition of the official Ecu.

Although the private Ecu has not, at present, all the qualities for it to be considered a fully operational currency, it is in fact used by certain institutions, organizations and firms for quasi-currency purposes. There are three main ways in which the private Ecu is used by private and public organizations.

Financial markets

The most common use for the Ecu is in financial markets. Since the first Ecu bond issue floated by SOFTE (a Luxembourg company) in March 1981, the development of Ecu issues has been very rapid, to the point where it is now the fifth or sixth most used currency for international bond issues.

At first, most of the issues were for nationalized firms, and national and EEC institutions (particularly French, Italian and Belgian). However, by the 1980s an increasing number of corporate players were issuing in Ecus. More encouragingly, a number of Canadian, American, Japanese and other non-European companies and governments were turning to the Ecu for part of their financing needs.

The growth in the primary market would not have been possible without an active secondary market to back it. The secondary market in Ecu bonds has taken the form of an increasing number of market-makers in Luxembourg, London, Paris and other financial centres. The most important aspect of the secondary market is that it allows a specific Ecu interest rate to be determined through market conditions, rather than relying on an average of the rates of the component currencies which an issuer could obtain on the national markets.

Money markets

The Ecu has also managed to carve out a place for itself in the money markets, in spite of the costs linked to bundling and unbundling. Although the market started as a deposit market, it soon developed fully as banks looked for borrowers to avoid having to unbundle their Ecu deposits. This was made much easier with the creation of an effective clearing system through the Bank for International Settlements in Basle.

The money market for the Ecu is mainly centred on inter-bank operations in the principal Ecu-orientated countries (e.g. Belgium, Luxembourg, France, Italy and the UK). It is used as a reserve by central banks (approximately Ecu18 billion) and in exchange rate intervention.

Aside from inter-bank operations, a large market in government treasury bills and corporate certificates of deposit has emerged. The main attractions of the Ecu in these cases has been the relatively high and stable cost yield it offers against the variations of other European currencies.

It is also interesting to note that a number of countries had their own reasons for putting forward the Ecu as a possible alternative. For example, it appears that several countries felt that, since their currencies were not serious contenders, the Ecu should be officially encouraged as preferable to a *de facto* Deutschmark zone.

Commercial transactions

The Ecu is still very little used as a means of settling commercial transactions. It represents less than one per cent of total Community trade. The situation is, however, quite different in each member state. Thus, around 12 per cent of Italy's foreign trade is invoiced in Ecus, while in Germany and the UK on the other hand, use of the Ecu for invoicing purposes is negligible if not non-existent.

The Ecu is also used to a limited extent for internal use by large firms. This aspect of the Ecu was pioneered by the French company St. Gobain which used the Ecu for its internal accounting as early as 1980. For companies with operations in more than one member state of the

European Community, there is a definite advantage to being able to use a single currency for internal pricing, putting together an efficient transfer price co-ordination system and publishing consistent consolidated accounts. Currently, Ecu accounting can be used mainly for internal management purposes, since in all member states (with the exception of Luxembourg and The Netherlands) accounts have to be published in the national currency or the currency in which the company's main cash flows occur.

Individual users

Individual payments are the least used aspect of the Ecu. Although there have been a number of developments, particularly in Belgium and in Luxembourg, on providing cheques, current and deposit accounts, credit cards, travellers cheques and mortgages in Ecu, none of these have had any real success except as symbols of European unity.

Appendix 2: Purpose and Methodology of the Project

Introduction

Underlying the recommendations of this report was a detailed and thorough microeconomic and macroeconomic study.

The microeconomic study was conducted by Ernst & Young Management Consultants (Europe) using over 14 offices throughout the Community. Some 257 companies and banks completed a detailed questionnaire and 70 were followed up with an interview. The questionnaire was designed to explore the attitudes and current policy towards the Ecu, as well as testing which events would most likely change behaviour. In addition, the costs of change for using the Ecu were studied.

The macroeconomic study was completed by the National Institute of Economic and Social Research (NIESR) in the UK. NIESR worked in co-operation with the OFCE in Paris, the DIW in Berlin and Bocconi University in Milan. The NIESR also held discussions with, and obtained contributions from, the central banks of the UK, Germany, Italy and The Netherlands.

Three other key groups provided invaluable support and contributions: the European Commission Services, the AUME and a specially formed advisory group, all contributing in their personal capacities. Responsibility for this report rests with Ernst & Young and NIESR, given the questions we were asked to address.

From these various sources, a large amount of information and analysis was obtained. The methodological relationship between the sources is summarized in Figure 14.

The background to the study contains two key elements:

- The Delors Report recommended that obstacles to the private use of the Ecu should be removed – a better understanding of those obstacles is needed;

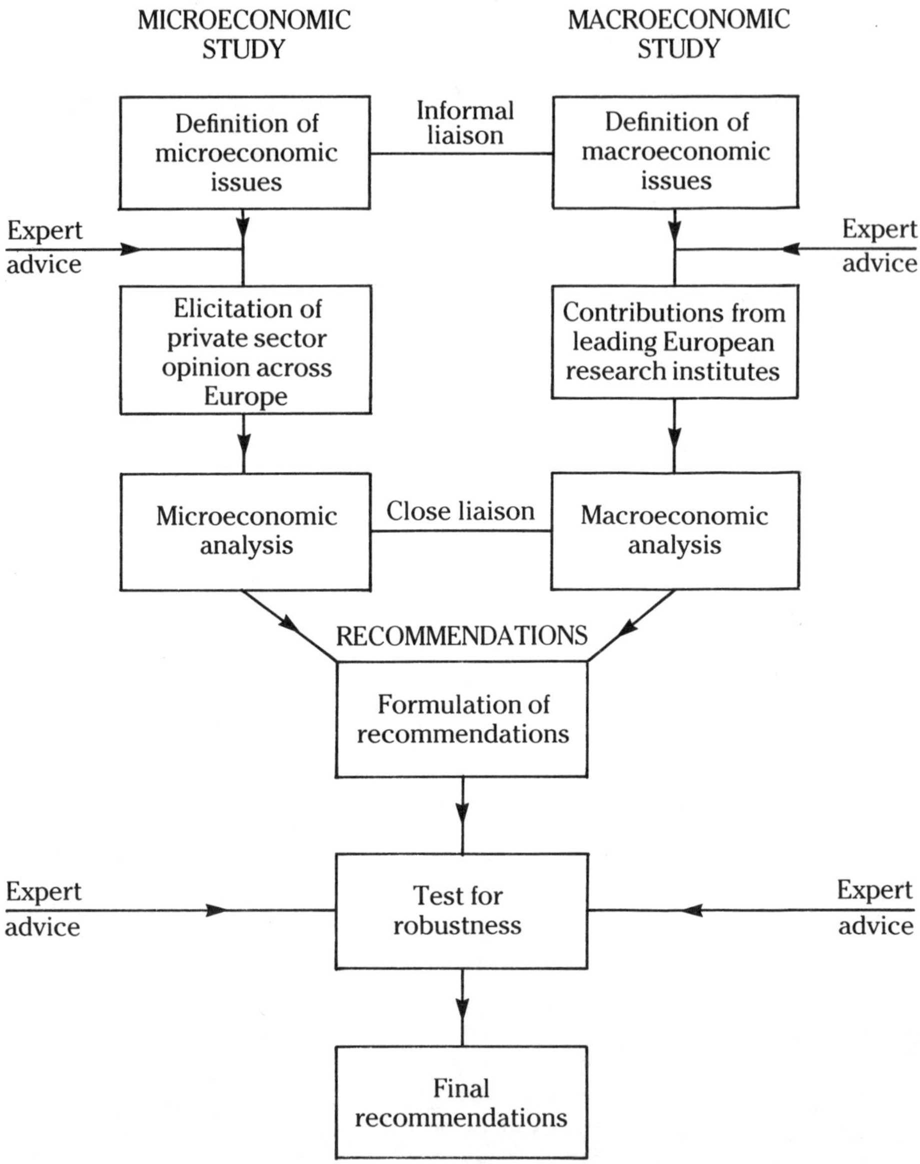

Figure 14: Methodological relationships between study sources.

- The result of a study conducted for the Association for Monetary Union in Europe (AUME), published in "Faits et Opinions", July 1989, showed that whereas 83 per cent of European business leaders favoured a common currency, only 11 per cent had taken practical steps to use the Ecu. Therefore it is necessary to identify what will alter firms' behaviour towards the Ecu.

Microeconomic study

Definition of microeconomic issues

Desk research was conducted in all countries of the European Community as to the current use and obstacles to the use of the Ecu by the private sector. This focused on legal, institutional and banking obstacles. It was supplemented by issues arising from Ernst & Young's knowledge of the operations of European companies, and the business environment.

An agenda for interviews and common questionnaires were designed for use across Europe. The objective was to assess the perceived importance of the obstacles, explore and amplify the issues and test interesting hypotheses. The obstacles are described in chapter six.

Country	*Companies*	*Banks*	*Total*
Belgium	22	6	28
Denmark	19	2	21
Netherlands	14	2	16
Luxembourg	2	1	3
UK	17	4	21
Portugal	13	3	16
Spain	14	8	22
Ireland	17	2	19
France	15	4	19
W Germany	36	6	42
Italy	22	5	27
Greece	19	4	23
Total	209	47	257

Expert advice
Views were sought from an advisory panel of distinguished experts as to how the microeconomic relevance of the above approach in assessing private sector opinion across Europe could be maximized.

Eliciting of private sector opinion across Europe
In each country the national office of Ernst & Young sought qualitative and quantitative information from the private sector. This was achieved by a combination of high-level structured interviews, postal questionnaires, desk research and considered professional judgement. The sample is set out in the table on the previous page.

Macroeconomic study

Questions
NIESR prepared a short paper setting out the questions which need to be addressed in the course of the study (see Appendix 4). NIESR discussed these with economists in four institutes in other European countries and seven central banks. The main responses are shown in Chapters Eight to Twelve.

Convergence
An examination of the outlook for economic convergence was undertaken, using NIESR's forecasts (see Chapter Seven).

Policy implications
Chapter five was prepared by NIESR analyzing the macroeconomic aspects of the removal of obstacles to the use of the Ecu, taking into account the NIESR study of convergence and the calculations of other experts and institutes.

Appendix 3: Attributions

Although the responsibility for the findings and conclusions rest with Ernst & Young and the NIESR, the methodology outlined in Appendix 2 and the project itself would not have been possible without far-reaching co-operation. We record here the key people involved in the report.

Private sector companies
We formally record our thanks to the companies and banks who assisted us in our survey. Many completed the questionnaires using a team of managers from various functions. For reasons of confidentiality their names are not detailed.

Advisory group
A special group was formed to act as advisors to the authors of the report:

M. Mentre	Crédit Nationale, Paris
M. Pons	European Commission, Brussels
M. Mingasson	European Commission, Brussels
Prof Thygesen	Copenhagen
Dr Walter	Deutsche Bank, Germany
M. Prate	European Investment Bank, Luxembourg
Mr Johnson	Lloyds Bank, London
Mr Freeman	ICI, London
Mr Gagalis	National Bank of Greece

European Commission Services
Thierry Vissol and Mark Vanhuekelen.

AUME
Bertrand de Maigret and Dr Stefan Collignon.

NIESR
Andrew Britton and Prof David Mayes.

Ernst & Young

UK Central Team
Malcolm Levitt
Michael Gardiner
Alfred Latham-Koenig
Michael Deakin
Nicholas Obolensky
Nicolette Boater
Fabien Jurdant
Beverley Drumm-Schäl
Elizabeth Alden
Dana Roberts

European Community Office
Patrick Flochel

Belgium
Ludo Swolfs
Marc van Steenvoort

Netherlands
Monique Brummans
Jan Balema
Rob Basart
Hans van Es
Lucas van Waveren

Denmark
Mogens Lundin
Sigfred Foighel

Spain
Javier Alvarez

France
Antoine Antoune
Lionel Lavigne
François Gonon

Italy
Massimiliano Dragoni

Greece
Cristos Glavanis
Sophia Mihalaki

Ireland
Michael McNulty
Martin Keane
Sarah Loftus

Luxembourg
Stephan Glancey

Portugal
Jose Pina
Claudia Balo

Germany
Manfred Niehaus
Ann Seidensticker
Juliane von Clausbruch
Astrid Filemon
Barbara Landers
Bernd Widmann

Appendix 4: Eight Questions Identified by NIESR

1. What are the advantages of a common currency?
2. What is the plausible anti-monde against which to assess the use of common currency?
3. What is the impact of 'announcing' that the Ecu will become the common currency?
4. Does it matter whether the Ecu is a basket or an independent currency in its own right?
5. What are the implications for monetary control?
6. Would early development of a private market in Ecu ease the process of convergence among the European economies?
7. Would the use of the Ecu strengthen the influence of Europe world-wide?
8. What should the timetable be for the transition to a common currency?